J:So
2
h

THE BATTLE TO
DO GOOD

Praise for *The Battle To Do Good*:

Bob Langert is a pioneer of the sustainability field and an artful storyteller. *The Battle To Do Good* is a compelling narrative about an iconic company's journey to be the best it can be for society and its shareowners. It is a new type of business book for leaders in the twenty-first century marketplace. The book is overflowing with great stories from the frontlines in sustainability and activism, as well as the back rooms of one of the most influential companies on the planet. A fun and informative read!

Dave Stangis, VP, Corporate Responsibility and Chief Sustainability Officer, Campbell Soup Company

The collaboration between McDonald's and EDF 30 years ago changed the corporate sustainability landscape. Bob was there, and he stayed with the company for another quarter century, leading them through many sustainability initiatives. In *The Battle To Do Good*, he provides a first-hand account of the most interesting and impactful of those episodes in what amounts to a series of well-told stories interspersed with pithy take-aways and principles. Bob's insights into the complex interactions with internal and external stakeholders are especially compelling. Anyone curious about the messy reality of leading meaningful change in corporations will find this fascinating, and because the stories amount to a series of real-world case studies, it is also ideal for college classes in sustainability.

Jonathan Johnson, Walton College Professor of Sustainability, Sam M. Walton College of Business, University of Arkansas; Founder and Chairman of the Board, The Sustainability Consortium

Transforming the world's largest fast-food chain into a sustainability leader is not for the faint of heart, but Bob Langert embraced it wholeheartedly. His remarkable story is not just a great read about an enviable career, but a hero's journey through the history of sustainable business and what it takes to be a leader, sometimes against the greatest of odds. Business students and corporate leaders alike should study and heed the lessons contained in these pages.

Joel Makower, Chairman and Executive Editor, GreenBiz Group

The Battle To Do Good really deserves attention and recognition considering how important corporate social responsibility is for businesses today. Utilizing this book provides the processes to manage such a daunting task. Bob Langert details step by step the journey he took. I loved this book!

Jan Fields, former President of McDonald's USA

Having been a vegetarian since the 1970s, and having been sued (unsuccessfully) by McDonald's because of our 1988 book *The Green Consumer Guide*, I loved slogans like "McCruelty" and "McSpotlight." Plus, the high drama of the "McLibel" trial. But Bob Langert does us all a service by explaining the journey McDonald's has been on as a result. Hard-Knock Nuggets indeed!

John Elkington, called the "Godfather of Sustainability," co-founded SustainAbility in 1987, collided with McDonald's in 1989, and is now Chairman and Chief Pollinator at Volans

Bob Langert is a true sustainability pioneer. *The Battle To Do Good* is a must-read account of how Bob led many changes that helped McDonald's address big issues that leveraged its brand and market presence to achieve big results. Bob's story has much to teach any sustainable business leader looking to make real change on crucial and complex questions ranging from beef, to animal welfare, water, and global labor conditions.

Aron Cramer, President and CEO, Business for Social Responsibility

The Battle To Do Good is an informative and insightful behind-the-scenes look at McDonalds' incredible sustainability journey over the past several decades. Bob Langert provides us with a detailed and compelling narrative of how the company struggled and ultimately succeeded in partnering with NGOs and experts to dramatically improve environmental practices, animal welfare, and more. Langert weaves concrete lessons learned and helpful tips into each chapter, making this a perfect playbook for any student or corporate professional aspiring to help their company's sustainability efforts. I recommend this book highly.

Liz Maw, CEO, Net Impact

THE BATTLE TO DO GOOD

Inside McDonald's Sustainability Journey

BY

BOB LANGERT

United Kingdom – North America – Japan
India – Malaysia – China

Emerald Publishing Limited
Howard House, Wagon Lane, Bingley BD16 1WA, UK

First edition 2019

Reprints and permissions service
Contact: permissions@emeraldinsight.com

British Library Cataloguing in Publication Data
A catalogue record for this book is available from the British Library

ISBN: 978-1-78756-816-7 (Print)
ISBN: 978-1-78756-815-0 (Online)
ISBN: 978-1-78756-817-4 (Epub)

INVESTOR IN PEOPLE

This book is not endorsed by or affiliated with McDonald's.

Contents

List of Figures

About the Author

(Photo courtesy of Stan Cottle)

Bob Langert led McDonald's CSR and Sustainability efforts from the late 1980s until 2015, when he retired. Currently he is editor-at-large for the GreenBiz Group, the senior sustainability advisor for The Context Network, and president of Mainstream Sustainability, his consultancy practice.

Acknowledgments

I thank George Macko who plucked me from supervising truck drivers and gave me the career I have since cherished. I am forever grateful to Shelby Yastrow, who saw enough in me to hire me into McDonald's in 1991 and mentor me. My adventures at McDonald's, and the thrill and extreme satisfaction of working on so many efforts that made the world a better place, is due to Shelby.

I thank McDonald's. I worked with an amazing array of good, ethical, caring, talented, creative people at McDonald's, including staff, owner–operators, and suppliers. In particular, I thank all the terrific people who worked on my direct team. Each one made major contributions to the McDonald's CSR Journey. Each one had a passion to make a difference: Joe Megacz, Juana Sanchez, Samantha Sturhahn, Heidi Glunz, Kathleen Bannan, Jeff Hogue, Jenny McColloch, Brian Kramer, Kyle Schott, Jessica Yagan, Sheila Young, Townsend Bailey, Nathan Lester, and Sarah Whitmore.

I thank the people featured and interviewed* for this book. Each one is proof that one person with passion, persistence, and patience can create packaging that is more environmentally sound, make animal welfare standard operating procedure for the entire meat industry, save the rainforest, preserve wild fish, and have the audacity to put a stake in the ground and proclaim McDonald's is going to buy sustainable beef.

I thank my editor Kelli Christiansen whose talent is superb. Her advice, insights, and outstanding editing expertise significantly improved my storytelling.

Thank you to Pete Baker, editorial director at Emerald Publishing, who believed that this story of *The Battle To Do Good* needed to be shared in order to help drive business leaders to what is the new norm of today

---

* I interviewed 51 people who are directly part of this book. I also interviewed others for context and background, including Cynthia Scott, Dean Danilson, Mike Siemens, Paul Shapiro, Heidi Glunz, Jason Saul, and Matt Sutton-Vermeulen.

and tomorrow: mainstreaming sustainability as fundamental to business success.

Most importantly, I am blessed with a great spouse, friend, and partner, Diane, who gave me the time and space to write this book, in addition to being a helpful first reviewer. To my daughters, Jenny and Laura, and their husbands, Greg and Michael, who give me such a fulfilling family life. And to my six grandchildren, who I hope live in a cleaner, brighter, safer, more sustainable society due in large part to corporate social responsibility and sustainability actions from companies large and small.

Introduction
From Defense to Offense

Taking on the Fuzziness of Sustainability

I was given a dream assignment in April 2010, a once-in-a-lifetime opportunity to shape the future of one of the most powerful brands in the world.

Don Thompson, the #2 leader then, but soon to ascend to McDonald's CEO, explained why he wanted to put corporate social responsibility (CSR) and sustainability on the agenda for his top management team. He put a twist on one of the catchy quotes from McDonald's founder Ray Kroc: "I don't know what we'll be selling in the year 2000, but whatever it is, it will be a lot of it." Thompson added that, "I don't know what people will be thinking about us, but I want them to be thinking better about McDonald's as a corporate citizen. A good citizen, better than any other company."[1]

Thompson described his vision of a McDonald's known as a force for good. That was a far cry from current perceptions, which included many who tended to consider McDonald's to be a parasitic drain on society. To combat that, he wanted us to develop a sustainability strategy for the company. Thompson asked that it be a bold, offensive strategy.

I was ready to burst with joy. Finally, after years of societal assault as one of the most visible and controversial global companies, muddied and maligned by external stakeholders as a poster child for countless issues—the obesity epidemic, deforestation, underpaid workers, and animal welfare abuses, to name just a few—McDonald's was going to set a strategy from the top down, define what we stand for, and shed the defensive posture that had stigmatized our reputation for years. As far as I was concerned, it was about time.

For the previous two decades, I had led McDonald's CSR efforts. While we accomplished quite a bit more than most people realized, much of what we did was reactive, undertaken in the wake of various societal pressures. Our corporate citizen efforts were largely ad hoc, although they emanated from a company made of many good people with solid Midwestern values who wanted to be both responsive and responsible. But for all the good we did at McDonald's, we were mostly silent about it.

Now I was being given a dream assignment to convert the fuzziness of sustainability into a tangible, high-level corporate strategy. I could hardly wait. I had long been convinced that doing good could help the business grow and prosper. Now it was time to prove it.

Devising a company-wide plan related to social and environmental goals and metrics was daunting. First, it was a relatively new discipline, with leading companies such as Walmart, Unilever, Coca-Cola, and Procter & Gamble developing such plans. For example, Walmart announced in 2005 that it was initiating a sweeping "business sustainability strategy."[2] Walmart committed to three ambitious goals: "To be supplied 100 percent by renewable energy; to create zero waste; and to sell products that sustain our resources and the environment." Taking something considered soft or intangible like CSR, which was not considered to be directly related to the profit and loss (P&L), and converting it into a hard, measureable part of McDonald's strategy was not yet widely accepted in corporate America, including among the mindset of most within McDonald's.

The Origins of Societal Clashes

McDonald's first clashed with society in the late 1980s. At the time, the long-standing business wisdom was defined by renowned economist Milton Friedman, who stated in 1970 that "there is one and only one social responsibility of business—to use its resources and engage in activities designed to increase its profits so long as it stays within the rules of the game, which is to say, engages in open and free competition without deception or fraud."[3]

Since its beginnings in the mid-1950s, McDonald's had remained relatively untouched by societal demands, aside from light brushes with external concerns, such as issues regarding litter in the early 1960s. McDonald's golden age of societal freedom extended for more than thirty years since Ray Kroc first observed the genius of the McDonald's brothers in San Bernardino, California, in 1955.

Then, in the mid-1980s, Corporate America's freedom to operate oblivious to societal impacts began to dissipate, replaced by skirmishes among a rising citizenry that expected more from companies than simply providing products and services and making a profit. Loud voices from nonprofits and activist groups emerged, raising issues that McDonald's wasn't used to handling, such as solid waste, the rainforest in Brazil, and the hole in the ozone layer.

As societal issues surfaced and increased, McDonald's grew more and more unsettled about how to deal with them. The company simply wasn't used to getting wrapped up in controversial topics. Up until the late 1980s, McDonald's was considered a model organization. Its mascot, Ronald McDonald, was admired as a positive symbol of the company. McDonald's fundamental business model, that of a hamburger company providing quality, service, cleanliness, and value (QSC&V), fueled its dramatic growth. For decades, the company enjoyed a stellar reputation unsullied by societal issues.

But then McDonald's confronted its first societal crisis. McDonald's image suddenly warped from a symbol of happiness and fun to an icon of waste amid a disposable society. The culprit was a sandwich container. Opponents argued that the Big Mac polystyrene foam container contributed too much garbage into overflowing landfills. These same activists depicted Ronald McDonald as "Ronald McToxic."

Such was the opening shot across the bow that thrust McDonald's into what would become an ever-growing battle pitting activists against corporations. As we at McDonald's saw it, thus was launched the battle to do good. It would evolve and morph over the years, taking on many other issues beyond polystyrene foam.

With the cries of "Ronald McToxic," McDonald's battle to do good and its resulting journey into the realm of sustainability began in crisis. The journey was only beginning; from that point on, McDonald's would see a series of ups and downs, proud accomplishments, and humbling failures for the next quarter century.

Leading Change

Throughout the pages in this book, we'll look at how McDonald's has tackled various battles with activists fighting around various issues. Although CSR today is becoming more and more commonplace, it was not always thus. Many companies, like McDonald's, were pushed beyond the normal boundaries of their business to address big issues of our times, such as climate change, animal rights, obesity, sourcing practices, and deforestation.

Leading change in the face of such complex societal issues is challenging, to say the least. Those of us tasked with paving the way were asking such questions as "When do we tackle these issues?" and "How do we lead change on these issues?" and "Who should drive this conversation?" We'll tackle those questions and more throughout this book.

Business leadership today takes more than understanding how to manage the business within its own four walls. It takes knowledge and sensitivity to societal issues, too. The best leaders know how to integrate selective, strategic sustainability issues to make their business more efficient, less risky, and more attractive to employees and customers. Top leaders understand that doing well must also include doing good because there's more to a business than providing goods and services. The best leaders also see building their brand and reputation through the smart prioritization of societal issues as relevant to their business.

McDonald's experiences provide some unique insight into the origins, results, and benefits of building a corporate sustainability and responsibility program. As I sprinted through a thirty-three-year adventure with the Golden Arches and dealt with its powerful brand and its complex system of employees, suppliers, and owner–operators, my primary mission was to find leaders within and without McDonald's to do good for society—and to do well for our business. I connected with many unique and courageous people, most of whom bucked convention, were willing to take risks, and found innovative ways to make our world a better place.

As we look into McDonald's history of CSR, we will offer insight into what to do—and what not to do—in times of crisis. We'll tackle key questions, such as "How do you deal with outside pressures from all kinds of interest groups?" "When do you decide to engage with an NGO?" "How do you decide which issues not to tackle?" and "How do you shift from reactive societal management to anticipatory issues management?" Stories from inside the walls of McDonald's will explain key insights into these questions, explaining how to manage emerging issues ahead of a crisis.

We'll also look at how to deal with the various activists and advocates who push organizations to tackle various issues. We'll explore NGO leaders who have had the knack to move McDonald's to adopt sustainable fish and beef, to advocate for the better treatment of animals, and to produce less waste, among other things. We'll also look at the untold power and influence NGOs have, the reasons consumers believe them, and why so many consumers are skeptical of companies like McDonald's.

In sharing these behind-the-scenes stories from McDonald's, you will learn how you, too, can shape strategies for your own organization in order to better connect with activists, advocates, and consumers—and with society in general. At a time when so many organizations are still sitting on the sidelines or simply playing defense, these strategies will go far in helping companies of any size build successful CSR programs.

Hard Knock Nuggets

I still marvel that I was in the room, on the team, and an eyewitness to the CSR history for one of the biggest and most visible brands of my generation. The stories shared and lessons learned in this book are not esoteric but based on many real-life examples from the school of hard knocks.

With that, each chapter is dedicated to a battle we faced at McDonald's, with the objective to share what we did right and what we did wrong, so you can learn from our experience. Each chapter also ends with "Hard Knock Nuggets" derived from McDonald's as well as those from NGOs that partnered with the company. These, too, serve to help make you a better leader and your company a better corporate citizen.

I have supplemented my own direct involvement with nearly fifty interviews with contemporaries within McDonald's, its suppliers, and NGOs who interfaced with McDonald's. Each chapter of the book features their reactions and thoughts. I took the liberty to take current interviews and insert their insights into the major events that unfolded in the past. I did this because I want to place you inside each battle in real time, in the midst of all the problems, dilemmas, and trade-offs. You will experience past events, such as McDonald's decision to partner with Environmental Defense Fund, to not partner with People for the Ethical Treatment of Animals, and to collaborate with Greenpeace International to save the Amazon rainforest, as if you were there.

I loved my work at McDonald's. My conversion to CSR started in the late 1980s and eventually led me to become McDonald's first vice president of CSR and sustainability in 2006. I stood right in the middle of nearly all the campaigns against us, working through the chaos to find solutions and coordinating the efforts to collaborate with NGOs and academic partners. My role was part catalyst, part cheerleader, part coach, and part critic—and, of course, part change agent. During my years at McDonald's, we found a way to do some things that fundamentally changed not only the corporation but the fast food industry as well.

In today's environment, the need for companies to successfully manage societal issues in a smart, strategic way is more important than ever because both opportunities and risks loom large. The old model of hunkering down and avoiding the tough issues that confront a business will only slow business growth—and could well damage an organization's reputation to the point that the bottom line is adversely affected.

We are in the midst of a major conversion when it comes to companies' relationships with society. For the past twenty-five years, the primary approach was risk aversion, laying low. In short, staying out of trouble. CSR was but a do-good thing on the peripheral of the core business, important only when a crisis occurred.

That approach no longer works. From now on, successful companies must see CSR as central to its business. The best companies will successfully locate and navigate through the intersection of doing good for society while helping their business prosper.

Finding that intersection is not always easy. McDonald's evolution in this battle to do good provides key lessons for leaders at companies in any industry about how to succeed in turning this battle into a beacon for how businesses and capitalism need both profit and purpose, a good financial bottom line, and a healthy societal bottom line.

1

The Battle Against Waste
McDonald's First Societal Clash

Fig. 1.1: Environmental Defense Fund Staff, Richard Denison and Jackie Prince, Working in a McDonald's Restaurant, 1990. *Source:* Photo courtesy of the Environmental Defense Fund.

Trash and a Clamshell

It's Halloween 1990 and the fate of the McDonald's first foray into a major societal conflict is at hand. McDonald's crafty top executive, Shelby Yastrow, is restless as he ponders the closing argument he will make to stop using the polystyrene foam (PSF) clamshell to the president of McDonald's USA, Ed Rensi.

Yastrow's newfound and unlikely partner, Fred Krupp, the president of the Environmental Defense Fund (EDF) discussed their steady push to encourage McDonald's to dump PSF with his waste team in New York City. It was unusual because this type of corporate–NGO partnership was virtually unprecedented. Plus, their personalities are opposite, with Yastrow as the charmer and Krupp as the studious one. Both were focused and determined to do something big.

Little did I know then that Yastrow would soon become my future boss. At the time, he served as McDonald's general counsel. Although he knew that PSF was the perfect functional package, thanks to its properties for heat retention, protection, and portability, he also knew that it had become a public relations (PR) nightmare. Activists were relentlessly attacking the company and the package. Their claims that PSF was filling up landfills and was toxic in its production were resonating with the public.

Within McDonald's Oak Brook, Illinois, Frank Lloyd Wright-ish-looking home office oasis, Mike Roberts, vice president of environmental affairs, was finalizing a big public announcement that the in-restaurant polystyrene recycling test program in place at the time would expand to all McDonald's eight thousand five hundred U.S. restaurants. I had managed the launch and the ongoing evolution of this recycling pilot program since 1989. It was a wreck.

Roberts's bold plan had forced McDonald's to an eleventh-hour decision: Should McDonald's continue to try to save PSF by recycling it or should the company replace PSF with paper-based replacements advocated by EDF?

The center of attention was the infamous Big Mac PSF sandwich box. Though featherlight (at 98 percent air, it weighed just 1/100th of a pound), the package weighed heavily on McDonald's reputation because PSF had come to symbolize a societal war on waste.

It was ironic that as Yastrow observed the big PSF recycling expansion plan of Roberts, who reported to him, Yastrow was souring on the plan. Yastrow believed the three-year PR battle McDonald's had been waging was lost—and was getting even worse still. Because of the relentless public characterization of McDonald's as a symbol of waste, McDonald's reputation was getting more sullied every day. Yastrow had come to the conclusion that there were eco-friendly and functionally suitable paper-based alternatives that McDonald's could use instead.

But Rensi and Roberts were gung ho on PSF. They believed the PSF clamshell to be one of the best food service containers ever invented. Indeed, it has superior insulating qualities, it's rigid enough to protect the Big Mac and other large sandwiches, and it's cheap to boot. At the time, the clamshell cost just short of two pennies per unit.

From my perspective, I was confused. Yastrow versus Roberts: two leaders, same department, taking the company in different directions. I couldn't help but wonder how this was possible in a business known for consistency and conformity.

The PSF dilemma had started to develop about four years earlier. McDonald's had become a lightning rod for the growing garbage crisis because various environmental issues during the late 1980s converged to create fear across the United States—and around the globe—that the amount of solid waste generated by citizens and businesses was escalating at an alarming rate. Soon, according to experts, we would run out of space to bury our trash.

The triggering event was a garbage barge. *Motherboard* magazine[4] captured the beginning of the landfill crisis craze:

> It was the spring of 1987, and a barge called the *Mobro 4000* was carrying over 3,000 tons of it—a load that, for various reasons, North Carolina didn't want to take. Thus began one of the biggest garbage sagas in modern history, a picaresque journey of a small boat overflowing with stuff no one wanted, a flotilla of waste, a trashier version of the Flying Dutchman, that ghost ship doomed to never make port.

As the *Mobro* meandered, environmentalist Lois Gibbs rose to prominence again. Gibbs had gained some fame a decade earlier by fighting the toxic landfill leaking pollutants into her community near Niagara Falls, New York. Now she was launching a national grassroots "McToxics Campaign"[5] to end McDonald's use of PSF. Her organization, called Citizen's Clearinghouse on Hazardous Waste (CCHW), was gathering support, especially from teachers, school children, and the media.

As with any campaign, whether based on truth or rumor, people rallied against a target. Fast food packaging, and especially McDonald's PSF disposable packaging, became the lightning rod for this antiwaste campaign.

It was the active involvement of children in this campaign that most disturbed McDonald's executives. An organization called Kids Against Pollution dovetailed with the emergence of CCHW, and together they coordinated a letter-writing campaign among school children that inundated McDonald's home office with thousands of letters and actual PSF containers. Kids were demanding that McDonald's get rid of Styrofoam.

The government wasn't on McDonald's side either. The U.S. Environmental Protection Agency had declared "A Solid Waste Dilemma," with a report by the same name in early 1989. The report said "[e]ach of us is contributing 1300 pounds (annually) to the growing mountain of garbage." It reported that one-third of all landfills in the United States would reach capacity by 1991.[6]

By 1990, dozens of communities in the Northeast and West Coast—from Suffolk County, New York, to Portland, Oregon—had enacted or were considering PSF bans.

In my eyes, the defaming of the company I worked for and admired hit rock bottom when I saw the cover of a New York–based magazine twisting Ronald McDonald into Ronald McToxic. Indeed, the notion that McDonald's was a bad corporate citizen was new to all of us at McDonald's. Since the company's birth in 1955, McDonald's had always been viewed as a beloved local business. Neighborhoods welcomed and celebrated a new McDonald's. Through the first thirty years of McDonald's growth, McDonald's was golden, and the Golden Arches were an esteemed and unblemished icon. For millions of people, McDonald's had long been a simple oasis, a place that allowed families to have fun and eat good, quality food at an affordable price in clean restaurants. As the waste scandal captured headlines, no one at McDonald's was working on this emerging issue. It was hardly a blip on the radar.

I suddenly found myself at the forefront, a task that forced me to shift from dispatching truck drivers to journeying through the environmental field. But I was no environmentalist—not yet, anyway. I had had idealistic visions of changing the world in my youth. Most of my idealism had come from absorbing the values and causes of the socially conscious 1960s in my formative boyhood years: Kennedy, King, Kent State, the Vietnam War, peace and justice, Bob Dylan, Neil Young, and Simon and Garfunkel—all of that grabbed me through stinging social commentary and stirring protest songs.

But that kind of idealism didn't do much to help anyone find a job, especially considering that there weren't any jobs in corporate social responsibility (CSR) back then. So, when I graduated in 1983 from Northwestern University's Kellogg School of Management with an MBA, I joined a privately owned supplier, HAVI, whose business at the time was dedicated solely to McDonald's packaging procurement and logistical support. Nobody has really heard of HAVI, but it is the largest supplier to McDonald's—even more so than its sizable business with Coca-Cola and Cargill.

I managed the truck drivers who made deliveries to McDonald's Midwest restaurants. In 1988, my job was eliminated. Out of nowhere,

George Macko, the head of a division of HAVI called Perseco, called me and asked me to consider a "temporary environmental assignment." Perseco served as McDonald's de facto packaging department, working with suppliers to test, implement, and purchase cups, napkins, bags, and polystyrene for all McDonald's restaurants.

Macko didn't mince many words. Macko told me that my new, temporary job was to save the polystyrene clamshell. He said I could handle the unknown ahead. After meeting with him, I had to look up P-O-L-Y-S-T-Y-R-E-N-E, which was far outside my area of expertise. Although I was blind to what this all meant, I accepted the position, and so began my adventurous, fulfilling, and uncharted journey in CSR.

Saving the Polystyrene Foam Clamshell

McDonald's invested in new actions, policies, and communications to defend and preserve the PSF clamshell. The best message the company had come up with to date was that McDonald's and all fast food waste made up just a small part of the nation's solid waste stream: less than 0.3 percent. In my mind, this minimizing of the issue served as a denial and hurt us more, even though it was the truth. Denial makes people think you don't care and aren't doing your part. To make matters more confusing, McDonald's also argued that paper-based alternatives were no better for the environment than PSF containers.

The common belief was that paper is better than plastic. To bolster support of PSF, McDonald's had commissioned Franklin Associates, a leading life cycle assessment consulting company, to study the cradle-to-grave environmental impacts of PSF versus paper-based replacements. Because PSF is so lightweight, these studies favored PSF, arguing that PSF containers created less pollution in manufacturing and fewer impacts in transportation. Paper packaging is heavier, takes more materials to make and transport, and is derived from a dirty manufacturing process.

While all of this also was true, the message simply didn't resonate with activists or consumers. Nor did it seem intuitively true to the average consumer, who saw the visibly bulky PSF packages left on tables or in cars as excessive packaging.

McDonald's helped support the work of Dr William Rathje, a trash archeologist who had dug up waste from landfills and found newspapers that were still readable from decades ago. The resulting message was that no matter whatever material goes into a landfill—PSF or paper or plastic—it doesn't go away. I saw the truth of this firsthand when I went with Rathje and his crew to explore Staten Island's Fresh Kills Landfill, where we found all sorts of packaging, newspapers, and even food waste still intact. Amazing.

Ed Rensi recounted how McDonald's partially funded Rathje's work: "I wanted to get his research out in the public domain. Rathje was literally pulling out newspapers from the Fresh Kills landfill on Staten Island from 1910 and earlier. Hot dogs that were buried amidst newspapers were still intact from the 1950s."[7]

The garbologist's revelations helped shift the discussion to the reality of landfills, which essentially are tombs designed to prevent the degradation of solid waste. As a result, all waste, including food, paper, and plastic, takes up permanent space.

Even so, Rensi did not want to give up the fight to keep using PSF. Seeing that nothing degrades in a landfill, not plastic, paper, or even food products, he said, "My attitude was that ultimately science is going to prevail in this thing. McDonald's needs to hang tough and pretty soon the PR stuff would dissipate."

He acknowledged that "we were absolutely vilified in the news media and by activists groups." Rensi wondered if Roberts's vision of a national recycling program would fix the problem. "We had all kinds of recycling things going on," he recollected, "but the fact of the matter is that recycling didn't deal with the fundamental issue: These social and environmental activists hated McDonald's, and [they] were using PSF as the lever to get McDonald's to do things that they wanted done."

Although some argued that fast food companies were major contributors to landfills, McDonald's did take concrete actions to make a difference on environmental issues. At the end of 1989, for example, McDonald's announced its Rain Forest Policy, noting that it "never has, and never will buy beef from recently deforested rainforests." The policy was still in place as of 2018.

In addition, in 1987, McDonald's became the first restaurant company to phase out of CFCs (chlorofluorocarbons), which were used as a blowing agent for PSF to provide its useful airy insulation properties. Even so, this move did little to take the pressure off McDonald's regarding PSF. (Indeed, we would learn years later that the replacement blowing agents had unintended consequences that heavily affected global warming.) CFCs had been identified as a primary contributor to creating a hole in the ozone layer, as reported by scientists in the mid-1980s. As *National Geographic* described it, "[t]he ozone layer is a belt of the naturally occurring gas 'ozone.' It sits 9.3 to 18.6 miles (15 to 30 kilometers) above Earth, and serves as a shield from the harmful ultraviolet B (UVB) radiation emitted by the sun."[8]

Our earth-friendly initiatives continued despite these setbacks. Early in 1990, McDonald's announced McRecycle USA, a promise to purchase $100 million of recycled materials for the construction and equipment of its restaurants, one quarter of its annual construction budget. McRecycle USA was a huge commitment, and it became an effective program, actually stimulating recycling markets across various industries.

Unfortunately, actions and communication efforts like these were but feathers facing a fierce storm of criticism not only from activists but also from mothers, children, and politicians. All of this created a perfect storm of PSF bashing that seemed impossible to reverse, except for one remaining strategy.

With all these efforts failing to help McDonald's turn the corner on using PSF, the priority became the recycling of PSF. As the primary leader testing and expanding the recycling of PSF from our restaurants, this task fell into my hands.

It wasn't as easy as it might sound today. Recycling was not the norm back then. Residential recycling was only just emerging, and few companies within any industry had yet to dive feet first into recycling initiatives. McDonald's was no different, but we were certain we could make a difference in this area. The thinking was that if we could recycle the PSF used in our restaurants, consumers would accept this as a positive compromise, and we could continue using the perfect package.

We started to collaborate with leaders in the plastics industry who were investing in start-up ventures to recycle plastic packaging and bottles. In November 1988, Mobil Chemical (later to merge into Exxon-Mobil) and Genpak Corporation, a food service packaging company, set up a recycling operation in Leominster, Massachusetts, called Plastics Again, which was later absorbed by National Polystyrene Council, the trade association for the polystyrene manufacturers. Earlier that same year, the Amoco Foam Products Company established Polystyrene Recycling Inc. in Brooklyn, New York, in association with McDonald's.

I was knee deep with both the Amoco and Mobil–Genpak projects, and both were failing for different reasons. The Brooklyn recycling center brought in all of the trash from all of the McDonald's restaurants in all six of New York City's boroughs. It was a true Rube Goldberg setup. Only 5 percent of McDonald's waste is polystyrene. But far from transporting only polystyrene trash, garbage trucks ended up delivering all the smelly and rotten food and packaging waste, only to sort out the 5 percent of it that was polystyrene. This was a fool's errand, little more than an expensive, multimillion-dollar PR maneuver. I vowed then never to stoop to such greenwashing again.

Unlike the Greenpoint operation, however, Plastics Again was a legitimate effort to recycle polystyrene. McDonald's challenge was to get the customers to separate their trash.

I worked closely with our communication experts and PR agencies to figure out how to ask customers to help McDonald's recycling efforts by properly separating their trash. We developed point-of-purchase graphics showing customers how to do it. We retrofitted trash containers with holes to fit the PSF packaging. And we created educational materials that explained how to recycle.

Despite these efforts, the whole thing baffled customers. As customers finished their meal, they took the dizzying array of packaging left on their in-store tray to the trashcans and recycling bins. They looked at the instructional signage maybe for a split second, froze, and then just dumped all the trash into the garbage bin. We kept track of how many diners followed recycling instructions posted in our restaurants. At best, only one-third of the customers got it right. By my observations, mothers with one or two children at their side had the most patience and desire to do it right.

Somehow, and in ways inexplicable to me, McDonald's had essentially trained customers to put all their trash into the waste containers. Asking them now to separate it into "waste" and "recyclables" proved a step too far. McDonald's customers expect fast food and quick service. Asking them to slow down and separate their own trash conflicted with McDonald's business model of speedy service. What we learned from putting a thousand restaurants on this recycling test was that most of McDonald's customers were neither ready, willing, nor motivated to separate their packaging waste after eating a meal.

This reluctance jeopardized our recycling program. The Plastic Again trucks picked up our poorly separated PSF—with more garbage and food waste than PSF—and took it to their Leominster, Massachusetts, PSF recycling plant, bringing with it odor and vermin. The recycling plant did its best to separate, wash, and sanitize the PSF before it was reprocessed into polystyrene resin. The market for recycled PSF resin was in its infancy, so there was little demand. Some recycled PSF went into making some rulers, yo-yos, and other small items.

On Halloween 1990, as I assessed the McDonald's impending huge recycling announcement, I knew the entire initiative was crazy. PSF recycling was a dismal failure, and I could see no path forward for improvement.

Mike Roberts looked past these obstacles, however, and saw a unique opportunity to make a difference. Roberts had recently been named the first McDonald's vice president of environmental affairs reporting to Yastrow, established a year earlier to get Roberts some corporate experience before advancing further in the company. Roberts had a contagious charisma and strong vision of making a positive difference in society. I admired his magnetic energy and ability to rally others. These traits foreshadowed his rise to the top of McDonald's system. In fact, thirteen years later, he would become president and chief operating officer of global McDonald's, the #2 leader in McDonald's Corporation.

Besides his charisma, Roberts had loads of conviction. To my mind, he was too resolute. He was determined to expand a problem-plagued PSF recycling program to all McDonald's USA restaurants.

"I thought we could be a leader," Roberts recollects. "So I was all about trying to put together with Waste Management and other stakeholders a national plastics recycling program that would accommodate all plastic materials, including our foam clamshell."[9] Roberts knew our recycling program would take time, engagement with many partners, and a long learning curve for customers. Indeed, plastic recycling needed a big impetus because it lagged well behind the progress of paper recycling.

This tug-of-war within McDonald's fascinated me: One side was pulling to save PSF, while the other side was pulling to make it go away. How could a company have two opposing efforts going on at one time? Were we dysfunctional, or was this normal?

The Wolf in the Hen House

My next stop was to the company's Communications Department. There I saw a draft press release dated for the next day, announcing the national PSF recycling program. I was shocked. The program was in disarray and the various factions within McDonald's were still arguing over next steps.

I headed straight over to Shelby Yastrow's office. The fifty-six-year-old could not stop tapping his heel. He squirmed in his leather desk chair as I shared with him the woes of the recycling test.

Yastrow is not your stereotypical corporate executive. He wanted his direct reports to call him "Uncle Shelby" because he cared about others and knew his success depended upon our success. He always deflected any credit and often praised his team. Beyond his pinstripe suit and reading glasses, which always seemed nestled at the very end of his nose, was a man with Churchillian depth and breadth. How could such a busy executive be a scratch golfer? How did he find the time to write a *New York Times* bestseller, *Undue Influence*?

Yastrow had been trying to solve this escalating and emotionally wrenching PR nightmare for three years. But nothing yet had been able to slow McDonald's reputational free fall.

While we chatted over coffee, he recalled a time when he was preparing to go to trial on a case in Paris, France. Yastrow was surprised to learn that none of his McDonald's people would testify. It seemed that the architects of the French legal system had assumed that a litigant would readily lie to promote his cause; therefore a litigant had to find independent witnesses to present his or her version of the facts.

Using the same thinking for the U.S. waste crisis, Yastrow had realized that what McDonald's needed was an independent and well-respected witness to explain, or at least endorse, McDonald's waste-reduction efforts. "After all," Yastrow recalled:

> We were in the burger business and had not achieved any special reputation in ecological sciences. But could we do that? Could we persuade the most reputable people to embrace and underwrite our new, aggressive environmental initiatives? Better yet, could we persuade such people to help us identify and develop these initiatives?[10]

A year earlier, Yastrow had been asked to give a television interview on Financial News Network (the precursor to CNBC). As it turned out, it was one of those remote, split-screen interviews where the interviewer was in one city and the two interviewees in two separate cities. It was fortuitous that the other person being interviewed was Fred Krupp, president of the EDF.

Yastrow had known of Krupp and the good work he was doing, but hadn't met him before then. During the course of the program, Krupp had made some points that were music to Shelby's ears: that polystyrene was not a terrible enemy; that, indeed, it had many virtues; and that McDonald's was a responsible company in many ways. Yastrow recalled that:

> Fred said something else that night that was a revelation to me, something that became the hook on which I would hang my hat for the next few years. He said that good environment is good business. His point wasn't simply that being green was good public relations; his point was that the Three Rs of the environment—reduce, reuse, and recycle—save money.

Yastrow saw in Krupp a McDonald's solution. Here was a scientific and public-minded deep thinker who knew what few business people knew: that sound environmental practices increased the bottom line. Yastrow figured that Krupp realized he would have little sway over corporate America if he appealed only to societal benefits, but if "he could show environment and profits are the same color—green—then he could appeal to the one stimulus that motivated every entrepreneur in the world: profits."

Yastrow called Krupp the next morning and arranged a meeting.

Prior to the dual TV interview with Yastrow, Krupp, thirty-five years old at the time, was convinced that his vision of a third wave of environmentalism would create a sea change of positive environmentalism by partnering with corporations, and by doing so create bottom-line benefits for both the environment and for organizations. The first wave started with Teddy Roosevelt's actions that led to the conservation of wildlife and wildlands. The second wave was born with Rachel Carson's seminal book, *Silent Spring* (1962), in which she focused on stopping pesticide pollution and curbing the harm it was doing to human health and ecosystems.

As Krupp ate at a McDonald's with his young boys and saw the loads of packaging waste in front of them, it triggered in his mind a practical third-wave partnership project that could shift the motivations and future direction of EDF's work and challenge the norm within the NGO environmental community that corporations are the enemy. Krupp wondered what would happen if EDF helped McDonald's reduce waste.

At that time, the notion of EDF partnering with a company like McDonald's was extraordinarily unconventional. That's because big companies and NGOs cooperating together was simply not done back then. In fact, EDF's early history had been more confrontational, with "sue the bastards" as the founders' informal motto in the 1960s. But now, instead of hollering at polluters and companies with environmental problems, Krupp became inspired by Yale University undergraduate professor Charlie Walker, who taught him that "people could solve more problems if they could just lower their voices."[11]

According to Krupp, the first two environmental waves were good movements, but they "created a backlash against environmentalists." He wrote about this in a 1986 *Wall Street Journal* op-ed, and later reflected that, "as a group, we were viewed as reflexive opponents to industry and as hostile to growth, a privileged elite indifferent to job creation."[12]

The third wave that Krupp envisioned could launch a paradigm shift when it came to the relationships between NGOs like EDF and companies like McDonald's. The third wave would be constructive, he later wrote, "in the way Charlie Walker had imagined, with environmentalists shouldering the burden of helping to find flexible and effective solutions, rather than just blaming others for the problems." His op-ed ended with a reference to using "market-oriented incentives" to achieve "greater environmental and economic benefits at a lower social and economic cost."

With this in mind, Krupp had been inspired to send a letter to Ed Rensi, president of McDonald's USA. He never heard back. Then he met Yastrow on Financial News Network during that interview. He accepted Yastrow's invitation to McDonald's headquarters in Oak Brook, Illinois.

Krupp arrived at McDonald's feeling pensive and expecting a formal corporate environment, with closed doors made of heavy, dark wood and a maze of bureaucracy. Instead, Yastrow informally and casually welcomed him. "He put me at ease," Krupp recalled.

> I had no idea [Yastrow] was going to eventually become a novelist. In retrospect, I wasn't meeting a typical corporate operative. I was meeting this guy with a vivid imagination. From five minutes after I walked in the door, when I said we realized we wanted to come up with solutions that were workable for McDonald's, and we weren't going to ask them to use Wedgwood china, he dreamed a dream that it would be great for McDonald's to do something with EDF, which was the same dream that prompted me to write the letter to McDonald's.

The two men connected and trusted each other. Krupp also met Ed Rensi in Oak Brook that day, and they eventually agreed to form the joint Waste Reduction task force, which was dedicated to finding ways to reduce waste within the McDonald's system of owner–operators, suppliers, and company staff. It took nearly a year of dialogue to structure a formal written agreement that defined the issues the task force was to consider and to establish some ground rules. Designed to anticipate potential conflict, the agreement included an escape clause in case of disagreement, preserved the parties' rights to note publicly their differences, provided for the parties' financial independence, and permitted each organization to pursue its own PR and advocacy agendas regarding the environment during the six-month period of the task force. McDonald's, however, was barred from publicizing the task force in marketing materials without EDF's prior approval. Yastrow insisted on one further key provision of the agreement: EDF could not change the basic fast food business model and turn McDonald's into a fancy restaurant.

Another part of the mutual agreement showed how Yastrow was ahead of his time in terms of transparency. Today, through the Internet and social media, we take it for granted that information is instantly available via our smartphones with a couple of clicks. In 1990, there wasn't an active Internet system. Yastrow insisted that EDF have an open door to McDonald's and made it a big part of the announcement. Yastrow noted that:

> At the (August 1990) press conference announcing our part- nership, I presented Fred with a symbolic key to McDonald's, saying that there wasn't a door or a drawer it wouldn't open. I urged him and his people to open everything, pry, question, and challenge everything. Further, to keep our own feet in the fire, we promised the press that we would be open to all their queries, and that we would actually send out monthly reports of the task force's accomplishments.

Yastrow and McDonald's took a risky gamble as they started the breakthrough, formal partnership with the EDF. As *Forbes* wrote, McDonald's "invited the wolf into the hen house."

Krupp and EDF took an even bigger gamble by initiating the work with McDonald's. Many of his NGO peers, such as the adversarial Lois Gibbs, sneered at Krupp's collaborative method of working with McDonald's. Indeed, Krupp rattled the environmental orbit by agreeing to partner with McDonald's to reduce waste. Many of his NGO brethren were critical of EDF. *Rolling Stone* wrote that "Krupp's willingness to talk with the capitalist enemy causes some environmentalists to curse him (usually off the record) as a kind of green Benedict Arnold, brownnosing big business and the White House."[13] Krupp had a lot to prove in order to show that he was a not a traitor to the environmental movement.

Once the detailed agreement was finalized, Yastrow asked that I lead the McDonald's team in this partnership with EDF. What had started as a temporary job two years earlier had escalated to a permanent one for me, with a staff of two to boot. Best of all, I simply loved doing this type of work: My 1960s save-the-world mentality now had an outlet. My job gave me great energy and joy as I tried to figure out how McDonald's could address big societal issues (e.g., reduce waste; save the PSF container by recycling) and do so in a way that satisfied the environ- mentalists and McDonald's financial and reputational success.

The EDF partnership got underway in August 1990, and I believed it had the potential to achieve its lofty goal of significantly reducing waste within the McDonald's system. But I worried that the impending PSF decision would be bad either way: If we pulled the plug on the PSF clamshell, EDF might conclude "job done" and move on rather than seeing through our six-month plan to look at every way to reduce waste; or, if we chose the national recycling option, EDF might end the partnership in protest.

The Tree Huggers Arrive

The ramifications of the draft press release bewildered me. The PSF decision was not in my hands, but the Waste Reduction Action Plan we were developing with EDF was my responsibility. I needed to prepare for our next meeting with the EDF solid waste team, crossing my fingers that our joint task force would still exist postannouncement.

I sat in McDonald's bucolic Oak Brook campus headquarters, resplendent with ponds, streams, and hundreds of big oak trees. On any given day, I could look out and see an eagle, a hawk, a flock of geese, or a deer, and the blue shining ponds of Lake Fred and Lake Ed, named after Fred Turner, Ray Kroc's right-hand man, and Ed Schmitt, a former president of McDonald's.

When I first met the EDF team, I envisioned them as stereotypical, passionate tree huggers, void of any business acumen. When we met in August 1990 for our first joint meeting, as we introduced ourselves and started a dialogue, I wondered whether this could work. As I assessed the EDF team, it seemed to me that there were stark differences between us.

Jackie Prince (today Jackie Prince Roberts) was the overall project manager. She was intense. Her rapid-fire questions made our meeting feel like an inquisition. EDF's senior scientist Richard Denison (with a PhD in physics) seemed and acted smart—brilliant, actually. He wore a scraggly beard that he combed with his hands as he expounded way too long about waste issues. Their economic and waste analyst, John Ruston, seemed like TV's Columbo, the bumbling but wise detective played by Peter Falk. Behind his uncombed hair, wrinkled shirt, and wry humor, I sensed a *laissez-faire* craftiness.

On the McDonald's team was the gregarious Keith Magnuson, director of operations. I saw him as our lynchpin because McDonald's is an operations-centric company, with everything focused on speed of service. Our waste recommendations needed the blessing of operations if they were ever to see the light of day. Terri Capatosto, then senior director of media relations, was our messaging guru. She became notorious for her red-ink edits as we drafted and redrafted our report. Rounding out our team was Dan Sprehe, a manager in McDonald's government relations group, who brought humor to our group. He was training at Second City in Chicago as a stand-up comedian, and he lightened the tenor of our meetings.

When we started this intense task force in August 1990, my McDonald's team had a big fear. We thought EDF might be out to get us, looking to use public rhetoric to force us to change. After all, our experience had long been that that was the model of many NGOs used to create change in the corporate sector.

I worried about a worst-case scenario, where our work would end up clouded and skewed by the pure mathematics of McDonald's garbage: Each restaurant generated about three quarters of a ton of garbage and recyclables on its premises per week. That doesn't sound bad. But multiply three quarters of a ton by eight thousand five hundred McDonald's restaurants in the United States times fifty-two weeks a year, and it computes to a jarring amount that McDonald's U.S. restaurants are producing, more than one-half billion pounds of trash a year.

When put in the context of the average McDonald's serving about two thousand people per week per restaurant, producing less than a pound of waste per customer, our waste was not out of line. But McDonald's waste numbers weren't what had propelled the issue into the spotlight. It was the visibility of the waste, especially in litter, and the mighty symbolism of the PSF container that put McDonald's at the battlefront.

Before Jackie Prince arrived for the first meeting, her view of McDonald's was simple. She said, "This fast food business, McDonald's, may be not particularly innovative, may be not particularly detailed. How hard could this be? Just throw a bunch of burgers together. I had this sense that it was not nearly as complicated a business as our team quickly learned it is."[14]

Prince stayed on campus at Hamburger University. The seriousness and scope of McDonald's training facility "gave her an appreciation for the culture of the company, and how professional, detailed and thoughtful it was." She learned that McDonald's people take pride in having "ketchup in their veins." She also learned firsthand the complexity and depth of operating a McDonald's restaurant when she and Richard Denison worked in one. As Ray Kroc once said, "No one takes the hamburger business more seriously than McDonald's."

"We got there at 9.30 in the morning," Prince said. "They set us up with a training video. The only thing they would let us do was the task where you dress the buns, which we thought was hilarious." She went on to describe her experience:

> You had your Big Mac, and it had two squeezes of ketchup and one squeeze of mustard. It was precise, like two squeezes and one squeeze, and three pickles, and one slice of onion. You had to know that set of condiments. Sixty seconds later, another sheet would come out and it would be fish fillet. You had to know the condiments for fish fillet. Then something else would come out, which would be just your regular burgers. They only get one squeeze of ketchup and one squeeze of mustard.

> I was okay, but Richard Denison was a mess. He got so flustered. I remember describing to my friends and saying I had to do this McDonald's training with a guy who has a PhD in molecular biochemistry and biophysics. He couldn't dress the buns to save his life—that whole speed thing and getting it right.

> The day dressing buns really opened our eyes to how much of the business was behind the counter that the customers didn't see and, therefore, how much ability there was to change things without having to really interfere with the very precious and highly valuable customer interface and customer experience. Indeed, we soon learned that 80 percent of McDonald's waste was actually made behind the counter, not over-the-counter with the customer. Most waste was made of stuff like the shipping packaging, coffee grounds, eggshells, and sauce dispensers.

Just as Prince and the EDF team came to respect the intricacies of McDonald's operations, our McDonald's team embraced EDF's efforts to work in our restaurants and their sincere determination to understand our business. We started to jell and roll up our sleeves as one team rather than as two sides. But we still wore the de facto uniforms that create stereotypes: I wore the suit, tie, and polished shoes of Corporate America, and EDF folks dressed more casually. Soon enough, however, these *façades* all melted away as we worked together as one task force and learned to trust and learn from each other.

Getting to know them gave us relief from our worst fears. The EDF team was not motivated to nail us. They truly wanted to reduce waste, not simply to create sound bites and hyperbole or use the raised voices that Krupp felt were counterproductive to the environmental movement. That said, EDF was determined to examine and challenge everything. Though low-key and likeable, the EDF team members were by no means pushovers.

They demonstrated their toughness by confronting head-on one of my team's fears, which was that EDF would push us into to switching to reusables (i.e., real plates and cups) in the restaurants. McDonald's business is predicated on speed, portability, and cleanliness. Disposable packaging serves this need well. We could not dream of using reusables in our operations. Washable plates, cups, and cutlery required a system of dishwashing, which required more space and labor to collect, clean, and store. EDF, on the other hand, had long been touting reusables to replace disposables in all kinds of situations, i.e., bags at grocery stores and coffee cups in offices. "For us," Prince said, "reusables were the Holy Grail. Were there opportunities to replace disposables with reusables? We felt like it was our biggest and best strategy. We felt like we had to take a really hard look at it from every angle."

I felt we needed to pursue the concept, not so much out of belief that it would work, but in order to keep open the spirit of the partnership. With that spirit in mind, Prince and the EDF team brainstormed where to go. "We thought it would enhance the customer experience. Customers would feel good about the food they are eating. It would give a halo of quality." Prince arranged a visit to another branded casual dining restaurant in the Washington, DC area. She'd never seen their behind-the-counter operations before. We were all surprised by what we saw.

The EDF team had already spent plenty of time in the kitchens of McDonald's, so they had a comparison. My McDonald's team cringed as we entered the competitor's restaurant, worried about the unknown: What if reusable dishes worked great in this restaurant?

As it turned out, we needn't have worried. Upon seeing the restaurant's big dishwasher, all of us were surprised to see how dirty, disorganized, and in disarray the area was. Prince remembered thinking how messy it was back there, noting that, "We had not expected that it would be such a mess and so different from a typical McDonald's, which is very sanitary, very clean, very organized."

It's always best to see the real world. So many pro and con arguments are philosophical. We all too often waste time debating and hypothesizing without checking out how things work in reality. There's nothing better than seeing and evaluating the real deal. With this, where we witnessed a fast food restaurant using reusable dishes, the issue of doing the same in McDonald's was mostly put to bed.

Even though this experience was a flop, EDF remained convinced that at least using reusable cups for in-store customers could work. We arranged a meeting in a McDonald's simply to watch customers' behavior with their cups.

Only 30 percent of U.S. customers at that time dined inside our restaurants. Most of our business was, and still is, through the drive-through. We learned that a good chunk of in-store customers leave soon after picking up their order, so they need their drink in a disposable to-go cup. Another set of customers eat their meal inside, but still have beverage remaining in their cup and want to take it with them. Once again, by looking at the real world, we found the truth. The idea of bringing reusables to McDonald's was finally nixed altogether.

Although that idea eventually went nowhere, we did have a lot of ideas that worked. My favorite involved carryout bags. We had developed numerous options but struggled with determining the right thing to do. We considered a brown bag made of unbleached paper, a brown recycled content bag, a gray recycled newsprint bag, an off-white wastepaper bag, and a virgin paper bag that weighed 15 percent less than the recycled bag. Which was best for the environment and for our business?

EDF provided sound science for us as we weighed this decision. They taught us the nuances of a product's total life cycle, cradle to grave, from raw material extraction to processing and manufacturing to delivery to our restaurant and finally to disposal. With this approach, we concluded that the 100 percent recycled content brown bag was the best option.

I then went to our current suppliers to produce this new bag. Amazingly, when I approached them, each one said they could not produce such a bag, giving a long list of excuses about negative impacts on cost, availability, performance, and quality. So we sought an outside supplier, Stone Container, and, lo and behold, they delivered to us an innovative recycled content bag. Suddenly the current suppliers said they could match it.

I've repeatedly observed this phenomenon at McDonald's. Suppliers tend to be resistant to change. They don't want to mess with their investment and current operations. Who can blame them? I've also met dozens of VPs of research and development in our supplier system over the years. Given the lofty title, I imagined a bunch of Einsteins developing innovative new packaging. Instead, these researchers mostly pursued continuous improvement in the existing process.

To stimulate innovation is challenging. Working with NGOs like EDF unlocked a lot of innovation. When we walked through the corridors of International Paper or Georgia Pacific, heads turned and brains churned. They knew we wanted more environmentally friendly packaging. The status quo was not sufficient. McDonald's alone asking for change was not nearly as effective as McDonald's and EDF working together and asking for change. This proved to be a powerful combination. "It was really fun to go around and talk with suppliers and see the range of openness in the supplier network," Prince recounted, adding that:

> Some hated us having us there. Others were curious, open-minded, and wanted to give more. We also knew when we walked in the door it was like the young teenage boy who finally turns to his friend in front of his girlfriend and says this is my girlfriend. He's committed. He's serious. It was the fact that [McDonald's] brought us [along] and said to [its] suppliers "EDF is helping us think about what we can do differently, or what we can do on waste management" that told us McDonald's was serious.

By the time Halloween 1990 arrived, the McDonald's–EDF team had spent three months working together to flesh out various ways we could reduce waste. Our list of projects was growing, but the nagging issue of what to do with the PSF sandwich container put us at the precipice since Roberts was about to announce the PSF recycling program.

What Is the Right Thing to Do?

Shelby Yastrow was running out of time to convince Ed Rensi that it was time to get rid of the polystyrene pest. As he later told *Rolling Stone* magazine, "That clamshell package was the symbol that everyone glommed onto. We knew if we got rid of that thing, it would be like pulling forty thorns out of our paw."

By appearance and by emotion, Yastrow seemed the underdog because Rensi took over every room he entered. He barged into meetings, stuck his head in, boomed his greetings, and interrogated us. Rensi was garrulous, smart, and opinionated. But Yastrow was his own man and could hold his own. I chuckled when he told me a story about his start at McDonald's.

Yastrow began his tenure at McDonald's during a meeting with the vice president of individuality. What a job and title! James Kuhn created that title for himself in 1975, and he was instrumental in creating incentive programs that included offering an eight-week sabbatical for every ten years an employee was on the job and presenting the President's Award for the best performers. He also wrote a book in 1997 titled *Management by Hassling*, a tongue-in-cheek effort to make managers more personal in their work style.

When Yastrow left his law firm in 1978 to work at McDonald's, he arrived at Oak Brook with a full beard. The individuality officer said the beard wouldn't work within McDonald's headquarters. Yastrow shaved it off to get along. But he was a true nonconformist at heart, keeping his desire to challenge the status quo just beneath the surface, not too visible but ready to emerge in ways that would advance change in an otherwise staid corporate environment.

Yastrow used this prowess to pounce upon a newer development related to PSF. Most of the debate about PSF was waste related. But a new argument against PSF was beginning to emerge, literally rearing its toxic head. Some external critics were shifting their arguments to how PSF was made from styrene, a carcinogenic substance.

Yastrow hunted down the head of the toxic chemicals division of EDF, Ellen Silbergeld. Silbergeld had not been party to any of our work together, but she was brought in on a conference call with the top brass at McDonald's, including Yastrow and Rensi, to discuss the recycling announcement. "I told them that I thought the real problem was styrene," recalled Silbergeld, who left EDF in 2000 to teach toxicology at Johns Hopkins University.[15]

"I acknowledged McDonald's effort to set up a national recycling program, attempting to recover polystyrene materials and then recycle them," she continued. "And then I said from my experience as a toxicologist, it's not a good idea to reprocess PSF into styrene and then make it back into something else like polystyrene."

Silbergeld recounted how the EPA and World Health Organization had already evaluated styrene as a carcinogen, with possible exposure to workers. She ended her conference call presentation thinking no one took her warnings seriously. She said, "I never expected anything would happen, even though I was really impressed that I was taken seriously. The next thing I know, McDonald's made a decision to phase out."

I was happy to hear from her that the whole discussion with our management team was "sensible and frank, not an antagonistic conversation that I sometimes had with the chemical industry."

In fact, that discussion was the last straw for Rensi. "When another ugly head got in the middle of it—this notion that styrene causes cancer—that was the moment I decided we can't let this happen," he said. "Because it is one thing to talk about landfills; it's something else to get talked about as kids may get cancer from eating Big Macs."

If the decision were based purely on sales, Rensi would have held out longer. "In fact, this PSF issue didn't bother any of our customers," he said. "Not Big Mac sales, Quarter Pounder sales. It never changed one darn bit. There was no economic reason for us to change."

Rensi's assessment was right. PSF didn't impact short-term McDonald's sales, but it did impact McDonald's reputation.

McDonald's market researchers had concluded that the PSF controversy had no direct impact on sales. Customers were coming anyway, yet brand and reputation have enormous value. They can either help improve or erode sales in the long term. Indeed, there is a fine line between profits and reputation. "The publicity was bad," Rensi acknowledged.

Rensi was not convinced of the styrene cancer scare, but he finally relented. He said, "Ultimately that is an acid that will eat away at you. So I got to the point where I said, 'Okay, science loses.' And we're going to change to cardboard boxes."

McDonald's announced its decision to phase out of PSF sandwich containers on November 1, 1990. In the press release, Rensi, said that "[a]lthough some scientific studies indicate that foam packaging is environmentally sound, our customers just don't feel good about it. So we're changing."[16]

Leaders within companies in a variety of fields and industries still struggle with similar environmental scientific issues today, with science a way more gray art form rather than a black-and-white, indisputable conclusion. Scientific results often are inconclusive or interpreted in different ways. I often find that company leadership is overly steeped in facts, figures, data, logic, and all the physical science of an issue. Companies too often spend too little time on the emotional and perceptual side, ignoring social science.

Yastrow assessed the heart of the problem: "The whole key to this stuff is that people think with their hearts and their bellies and not their heads." Companies most often deal with attack campaigns logically, with their minds, very rationally. Every communication has to pass through a cadre of lawyers' hands, where it is further sanitized and left devoid of any human feeling. Their opponents are using emotion, heartstrings, and storytelling. It is a foregone conclusion that emotion wins.

The PSF industry responded emotionally to the McDonald's decision. "This is an environmental attack on the throwaway, fast-food life style and the company with the highest profile," said John Giroux, president of the Amoco Foam Products Company, a subsidiary of the oil company and a supplier of foam packaging to McDonald's. "This is not about polystyrene."[17]

Amoco was blasting McDonald's, yet in his statement, Giroux hit the core of the problem, which related to the symbolism of polystyrene. Their industry never understood the heart of the issue, instead dealing only with the mind.

"McDonald's Surrenders!"[18] trumpeted the newsletter for the Citizens Clearinghouse for Hazardous Waste, a grassroots group based in Falls Church, Virginia, that for three years had coordinated many of the nationwide "McToxics" protests against McDonald's. Members picketed stores, fought for local ordinances against Styrofoam, and organized "send-it-back" campaigns to return used packaging to McDonald's headquarters to protest the symbol of "the throwaway society."

Regardless of whether McDonald's surrendered or instead opted to be a leader on the issue, in convincing Rensi that the emotional argument would win the day, Yastrow's knowing-the-heart strategy worked. McDonald's earned high praise from many in the environmental community.

I asked Rensi if, in hindsight, it was the right decision. He said it was. "You can't win PR wars like that. You just can't win."

I don't think "PR" captures the depth and proper meaning of consumer sentiment. To label the issue as simply one of PR insults the feelings of consumers who might not understand all the physical science but have intuitive beliefs that are on a much higher level than mere PR. Call it values or ethics. Companies continue to underestimate the power of consumer values while NGO activists know how to connect to these legitimate concerns.

Mike Roberts was disappointed that he couldn't pursue the alternative national recycling path. He said, "I was supporting being the leader of attempting to create a nationwide, maybe eventually a worldwide, recycling movement. You know, I thought we could be the leader." However, he was realistic. He understood that dropping the PSF clamshell "removed McDonald's from the center of the storm."

What does this mean for companies facing these issues today? Should we just give in to every campaign? Of course not. The only way to win a war with activists is to play offense, not defense. If you wait for the crisis to hit, it is too late.

Was McDonald's decision to eliminate the PSF clamshell rather than trying to recycle it the right thing to do? At that time, I was adamant it was. PSF was excessive packaging, made from a nonrenewable resource, including benzene and styrene. It could last forever as litter on our land and in our waterways. Many customers didn't like it. We had suitable, more customer-friendly alternative packaging.

My discussion with Roberts challenged me, though. Society today still has a huge problem recycling plastics, with low recycling rates for most forms of plastics. So was Roberts right about the need to jumpstart leadership on plastics recycling despite the enormous challenges?

After all, some of the facts validate that paper packaging is more polluting than PSF in its manufacturing process, and it will stay forever in a landfill, too, given that landfills are made airtight. Scientifically, it was not clear which was better: paper or PSF.

How long should a company keep fighting for something it believes in? What if the customer is wrong? Is that even possible in a business culture where the customer is always right?

As with most complex, multidimensional issues, science has a broad range of interpretations. Much depends on the value you place on various impacts. If you put a high value on using nonrenewable sources, your vote is against PSF. If you put a high value on overall efficiency, your vote is for PSF because it is so light, with less material to make, transport, and dispose.

I believe the decision is proportional to how important the issue is to the core of the business. In our case, PSF was not crucial to serving Big Macs, although using disposable packaging is essential. McDonald's preserved the business need to use disposable packaging by switching to another substrate: paper. The drop-off in the consumers' eyes for speed of service, sandwich temperature, and appearance was infinitesimal. Why fight for something when the consequences to your business are not substantial?

I emerged from this experience with my own formula to help guide decision-making for what is both the practical and the right thing to do. Though not black and white, it provides a good framework:

$$Effort = Importance\ to\ business \times Importance\ to\ society$$
$$\times Our\ ability\ to\ make\ the\ change$$

I'll explore more issues in this book that will put this formula to the test.

No Beige Solutions

Worries about EDF taking credit for the PSF phaseout and departing with a win in their pocket turned out to be unfounded. "The move really opens the door to further changes," said EDF senior scientist Richard Denison, in a public statement.[19] Nothing made me happier. My anxiety that EDF might pull the plug on our broader waste reduction action plan after a big win like this was relieved. We could now continue our partnership to comprehensively reduce waste throughout McDonald's system, not just quit after the PSF decision.

The task force continued to come up with dozens of ideas to reduce waste. We met often. Shelby Yastrow would stop by now and then, but for the most part he detested meetings. He believed that not much gets done in meetings. He always encouraged me to get down to brass tacks and visit people and places where we could learn what was going on in order to make good decisions.

Yastrow detested committees even more. He said, "If a committee is formed to choose the color of the carpeting, I can guarantee that it will be beige." I was managing this team, this task force committee, so I took this direction to heart. None of us wanted to develop a beige set of waste reduction initiatives.

The task force culminated in April 1991 and released a joint McDonald's/EDF report, a one-hundred-sixty-page "Waste Reduction Action Plan"[20] that detailed the forty-two initiatives addressing the environmental Three Rs: reduce, reuse, recycle. These initiatives ranged from having our suppliers use thinner gauge containers in shipments to our stores (reduce) to testing reusable shipping containers (reuse) to separating and recycling our trash (recycle). We figured out how to avoid the use of bleach in the paper we used, how to help our company employees separate their trash for recycling, and how to change delivery routes to conserve fuel. Other changes included the following:

- *The power of just one inch.* We shaved one inch off our paper napkins, saving 3 million pounds of paper annually.

- *White is not always right.* We switched to napkins that could be made from 100 percent office waste and newsprint. We had to break down the marketing norm that white is bright, clean, and safe and admit that it was acceptable for napkins to have darker spots. We did the same for all of our tray liners.

- *Composting fast food works.* We conducted significant pilot tests in which we collected McDonald's garbage and composted the organic matter. An estimated 90 percent of McDonald's waste then (and now) is organic. The remainder is plastics found in some of the coatings, cups, and condiment packaging. I marveled at the sight of weeks of McDonald's garbage piled in heaps dumped in rows at a composting facility. In a matter of days, a steady steam puffed from the rows as compostable fry cartons, wraps, and food remains decomposed into a usable soil amendment. Composting of restaurant waste has yet to take off in today's world, but I know it works. I am convinced that, as technology progresses and landfill costs escalate, the restaurant industry will change from garbage to composting.

In addition, we created a policy that set forth our company's belief in our role on the environment for the generations to come:

- Effectively managing solid waste

- Conserving and protecting natural resources

- Encouraging environmental values and practices

- Ensuring accountability procedures

My biggest disappointment was in not being able to convert the company to using flexible paper bags for french fries. The amount of paper savings would have been enormous: about an 80 percent reduction. I couldn't convince our marketing leadership to change. Everyone loved our fries. We owned the category. The red box for McDonald's fries is iconic. Marketing said, "Let's not mess with success." Even though we tested it thoroughly with consumer success (most consumers didn't even notice the change in packaging), we never made this a global standard.

The McDonald's–EDF partnership was a huge learning experience about the power of the ripple effect—and served as a launching pad for future EDF initiatives. Jackie Prince recalled that, "Your team telling us that when you decide to add a slice of tomato on a sandwich, you had to notify the tomato industry three months in advance: That was a real eye-opener. That's when we understood the scale." As the partnership started, Prince thought the work we were undertaking was only for one company. "We had no concept of the kind of leverage a company like McDonald's has over so many different industries and suppliers."

Our Waste Reduction Action Plan morphed into a de facto set of new packaging and waste management norms for the entire food service industry. Eventually, using brown bags and grayer, smaller napkins; integrating postconsumer recycled content into cartons and other packaging; and recycling used oil and corrugated boxes spread across most restaurant businesses.

Looking back at the task force decades later, Fred Krupp, normally low key and deliberate, elevated his voice with enthusiasm when he recounted what he felt this partnership accomplished. "I'm not prone to hyperbole, but in this case, I may slip into it because it's really hard to overstate how much the EDF and McDonald's partnership has meant and how it's impacted the whole future of environmentalism." Krupp gives credit to McDonald's. He said, "The fact that McDonald's was exceptionally open to EDF's embedding ourselves in the operations allowed us to create this first proof point that, if we work together, both business and the planet can thrive."

In many ways, Krupp led the way to mainstreaming sustainability. He had a vision that environmentalism need not be a tree-hugging experience for the elite. "To the middle-of-the-road average American, the McDonald's work accentuated the idea that there didn't have to be a war over these issues," he said. "It's like the lesson I learned from Charlie Walker, that if people lowered their voices and worked together, these problems are solvable."

His conclusion: "This work became a ray of hope, an openness of possibilities and potential, an upside of a whole pathway that didn't even exist before."

Krupp and EDF, together with the Pew Charitable Trusts, went on to form the leading-edge Alliance for Environmental Innovation, which led to EDF's current-day corporate partnerships. Krupp noted that, "If McDonald's hadn't done so much, I doubt we would've been inspired to partner with FedEx, KKR, Walmart, and all the other partnerships we're so proud of today."

The EDF partnership worked like an MBA school case study on how to make transformative change in a corporate environment. I wanted to undertake more of this type of work—even though I really didn't think of it as work. It was a passion, and it was fulfilling to have such meaningfulness in the work you do—so much so that I became enamored with the idea of heading McDonald's environmental efforts. The work of doing well in business while doing good for society had gotten into my blood.

With that, I set up a lunch at a Chinese restaurant with Shelby Yastrow later that summer. I had heard that Roberts was getting promoted and moving on. I wanted in. I liked working for Perseco, a dedicated supplier to McDonald's, but I wanted something bigger. What's bigger than McDonald's?

As I finished my wonton soup, I took a deep breath and nervously blurted out what I desired. "Shelby," I said, "I would love to work for McDonald's, and for you, to head up this work for McDonald's directly, not as a supplier. What do you think?"

His eyes opened wide as he replied, "Bob, I want you on my team. Give me three months, as I need to move some people around to get you in the door, but count on it." I was thrilled to think that I would be joining McDonald's, with its big brand, fame, and huge system. I was excited about what I could do.

Everything had come full circle from a year before when, at Halloween, the fate of McDonald's reputation hinged on whether to dump the PSF or recycle it nationally. One Halloween later, on October 31, 1991, I sat in the White House Rose Garden with my partners from McDonald's and EDF, swelling with a sense of pride because, together, we had made a meaningful impact. We listened as President George H. W. Bush bestowed the "The President's Environmental and Conservation Challenge Award for Partnership"[21] to our two organizations.

My neighbors once thought I worked for an evil company. Now I had departed the doghouse and arrived at the White House, transformed to working for a leadership company with a stellar reputation for environmental conservation.

During the event, I shared a poem with the McDonald's–EDF team. I had come to like and respect my EDF colleagues. I trusted them. They were fun to work with. Time and time again, I would be reminded that once you sit down with your supposed enemies and listen to them, they could become best friends with you.

Excerpt: "Ode to the Waste Reduction Team"

Richard, John, and Jackie,

Working with you, we were lucky,

I suppose we all drummed to a different beat,

But what we had was really neat.

Krupp's cadre of keen experts in solid waste were sent,

To meet Shelby's shrewd champions to help in their 3R management,

And the little melting of minds,

Found much in and out of work that binds.

Being a part of this task force,

Put us all on a special course,

And we achieved quite a feat,

Despite the critic's heat.

EDF, McDonald's—an odd couple,

The wall of waste trying to topple,

It gave us a blueprint for the future,

And a way to make it grow and nurture.

And when it's long gone,

And as the pages biodegrade from the Rolling Stone,

We'll recycle this endeavor forever,

The people, the character—all a true treasure.

On November 29, 1991, about one year after the pivotal PSF decision, Uncle Shelby hired me as director of Environmental Affairs. Yastrow would soon give me another audacious assignment that I was again wholly unqualified to lead and knew nothing about, told in the next chapter: animal welfare.

Postscript: Shedding 300 Million Pounds

During the course of the 1990s, the McDonald's–EDF Waste Reduction program grew from forty-two initiatives to more than a hundred within the entire McDonald's system. The stereotype, both within McDonald's and the public at large, was that being green added cost. In reality, we didn't spend a nickel on these efforts. We just spent more time and focus. We learned that doing the Three Rs of reduce, reuse, and recycle reduced our use of materials and resources and saved us money, for the most part.

The savings allowed us to pay more for recycled content when needed, as the economics of the recycled market fluctuated up and down.

On December 21, 1999, ten years after Fred Krupp and Shelby Yastrow bucked conventional wisdom about corporate–NGO partnerships, each determined to make change happen in his own unique way, McDonald's announced its environmental progress during the decade of the 1990s.[22] The following are some highlights:

- Eliminated 150,000 tons of McDonald's packaging by redesigning or reducing the amount of material used to make straws, napkins, sandwich packaging, cups, french fry containers, and numerous other items.

- Purchased more than $3 billion worth of products made from recycled materials for use in the operation and construction of McDonald's restaurants. These goods include construction blocks, booster seats, tables, trays, roof tiles, bags, and many other quality products made from recycled glass, rubber, plastic, and paper.

- Recycled more than 1 million tons of corrugated cardboard, the most commonly used material for shipping products to McDonald's 12,500 restaurants in the United States, decreasing restaurant waste by 30 percent.

How to Establish Partnerships

Based on the confidence we gained with the McDonald's–EDF experience, McDonald's would go on to forge more than twenty-five partnerships that made a positive impact on various issues. Often, during meetings about how to turn the tide about some thorny issue, someone would ask, "How can we create an EDF-like partnership?"

When establishing a partnership, it's important to consider some key questions and issues:

- Do you have a C-suite sponsor? It's important to have an influencer at the top in your corner.

- Are you putting your best people on the team? (Not just your PR and Public Affairs people.)

- Don't rush. You might be in a crisis, but you need enough time to listen, learn, explore, and engage with relevant stakeholders. (The McDonald's/EDF project had a six-month timeline.)

- Pick an NGO partner with high credibility. Make an NGO your best friend.

- Do you have clear, SMART (specific, measureable, achievable, relevant, and time-bound) goals?

- Commit in writing the parameters of the project.

- Collaborate with your suppliers and truly engage them to find solutions.

- Open your doors and provide full access with your partner. This transparency will serve as a springboard for transparency to a host of other stakeholders as well.

How to Choose a Partner

- Don't pick a patsy. Choose a partner that will challenge your organization.

- Evaluate partnership choices on a scale of 1–10, with 1 meaning very corporate friendly and 10 meaning very radical.

- Work with NGOs in the 5–7 range who are:

  - fiercely independent and widely credible;

  - collaborative and knowledgeable about business and market forces; and

  - practical rather than dogmatic.

- Don't forge partnerships at the 1–4 range, with too "corporate friendly" groups.

- Don't align with the radical, either, at the 8–10 range; you'll just spin your wheels with groups that want to tear you down.

- Give up total control. It takes courage to invite a truly independent NGO into your business, but it is the best way to get people to believe in you and in the results.

2

The Battle for
Farm Animals
How Animal Welfare Is Transformed

Fig. 2.1: Dr Temple Grandin Is Given the Keys to McDonald's
Animal Supply Chain.

The Dying Pig in the Aisle

I visited my first animal slaughterhouse in the fall of 1997: a pig facility. I was there to assess how to start an animal welfare program with an unusual partner, Dr Temple Grandin, who was renowned in her field of animal science—and autistic. I was anxious as I entered, not knowing what to expect.

The plant manager directed us into what he called the barn, which was actually a steel and concrete facility the size of a football field with thousands of pigs in multiple pens. I had never liked the term "factory farm," a derogatory term used by modern agriculture critics to paint a dark picture of such large facilities, but the reality was I felt like I was in an animal factory, not a barn.

About an hour into the tour, I saw a forklift operator ignore a half-dead pig lying in the aisle, running over its legs. I squirmed. The sight brought me back to a book I had read in high school: *The Jungle* by Upton Sinclair. Though what I observed around me was not the same squalid conditions Sinclair described, I still seethed. How could that person be so callous? Didn't he see the pig as a living creature? Or did he see the pig as a widget, a production piece?

Seeing the dying animal, Grandin's eyes jutted out in disgust. She pumped her arms and legs as she leaped to a position kneeling beside the pig as if it were part of her family. She emphatically called for the foreman to take care of the pig.

This was the beginning of my admiration for the most inspiring leader of change I have ever encountered. After seeing Temple Grandin on the ground, becoming one with the animals, experiencing her overt passion and love of animals, I knew something special was unfolding.

The World's Biggest PR Disaster Spurs Change

I was with Grandin because my boss at McDonald's, Shelby Yastrow, had handed me a another big, bold, and baffling assignment late that summer: Figure out how to develop an animal welfare program for our meat suppliers.

My only knowledge of livestock came from watching *Bonanza* on television on Sunday nights as a kid growing up in the 1960s. I grew up on the south side of Chicago, disconnected from animal agriculture, even though my home was only a few miles from the setting of *The Jungle*, the Union Stockyards, Chicago's center for meatpacking, where Chicago became known as the "hog butcher for the world." This meatpacking district started to disappear just after World War II, and the stockyards finally closed for good in 1971.

At the time Yastrow tapped me for this new assignment, I was serving as McDonald's director of environmental affairs, and my work focused mostly on packaging, recycling, and energy management—not on farm animals. Yastrow was general counsel and had become the architect of McDonald's transformation from environmental villain to hero, chronicled in Chapter 1. He had championed a major turnaround of McDonald's environmental program and reputation, and he had the confidence of the senior leadership team.

Now the 1990s were presenting another societal issue: animal welfare. The triggering event was a long, complicated, high-profile trial in the United Kingdom, dubbed "McLibel."

In 1990, McDonald's sued two London Greenpeace (not associated with Greenpeace International) campaigners who were passing out leaflets accusing McDonald's of a long list of wrongs related to nutrition, litter, human rights, rainforests, recycling, waste, and animal welfare. McDonald's head of United Kingdom wanted to stop London Greenpeace from continuing to slander the company. I don't think he anticipated the ramifications of giving these two people such a public platform.

The McLibel trial in England started in 1995. It was like the very worst of today's reality shows. McLibel exposed every wart of McDonald's, including many animal welfare issues with suppliers, such as hens and hogs crammed into sterile, steel cages.

I was one of the first to provide testimony in the Royal Courts of Justice, mostly to answer questions related to McDonald's environmental practices. Yastrow had advised me to be short and crisp in my answers and to answer only what was asked and nothing more. However, as I observed the first few days of the trial and the interchange between the defendants (who were representing themselves) and the witnesses, I realized that the American Perry Mason approach that Yastrow had suggested wouldn't work. In England, the courtroom atmosphere was more like a discussion, a dialogue. I would come off as an ugly American if I answered too succinctly. So, I carefully responded to questions about environmental packaging efforts, which was much easier than discussing what were at the time McDonald's nonsubstantive policies and programs about animal welfare.

Although the trial was based in the United Kingdom, the power of the emerging digital age created the first international Internet-based public campaign. The two individuals who created the millions of leaflets distributed throughout the United Kingdom, Helen Steel and Dave Morris, were savvy in leveraging the Internet and creating a website called McSpotlight to spread the word far and wide about their thoughts regarding "What's Wrong With McDonald's." Its introductory paragraph started its sharp anti-McDonald's rhetoric:

McDonald's spends more than $2 billion every year world-wide on advertising and promotions, trying to cultivate an image of being a caring and green company that is also a fun place to eat. Children are lured in, often dragging their parents behind them, with the promise of toys and other gimmicks. But behind the smiling face of Ronald McDonald like the reality: McDonald's only interest is money, making profits from whomever and whatever they can, just like all multinationals. The company's sales are now $40 billion a year. The continued worldwide expansion of fast food means more uniformity, less choice, and the undermining of local communities.

Today, transparency and sharing of daily minute-by-minute information is the norm. Back in the 1990s, such was not the case. McSpotlight was among the very first transparency efforts that travelled the globe through the new channels of the burgeoning Internet.

Although it's difficult to think of it today, imagine the unconnected world transforming to a connected one. Just a few decades ago, there was no Internet, no Google, no Facebook, no Twitter, no smartphones. As the Internet grew and became ubiquitous, we at McDonald's were not ready, neither nimble enough nor culturally prepared to deal with the ways in which the Internet was changing the dissemination and consumption of information. Looking back, even with a more concerted, sophisticated effort in place to communicate via the Internet, I don't know how McDonald's could have communicated its way out of what became a monumental PR disaster.

Many labeled the McDonald's decision to sue the two unknown, rag-tag London Greenpeace leaflet campaigners as the "world's biggest corporate PR disaster."[23] Indeed, the trial was an embarrassment for us at McDonald's. In her book *No Logo*, Naomi Klein summarized the agony well:

> Over the course of the trial, Steel and Morris meticulously elaborated every one of the pamphlet's claims, with the assistance of nutritional and environment experts and scientific studies. With 180 witnesses called to the stand, the company faced dozens of humiliating moments as the court heard stories of food poisoning, failure to pay legal overtime, bogus recycling claims, and corporate spies sent to infiltrate the ranks of London Greenpeace. In one particularly telling

incident, McDonald's executives were challenged on the company's claim that it serves "nutritious food": David Green, senior vice-president of marketing, expressed his opinion that Coca-Cola is nutritious because it is "providing water, and I think that is part of a balanced diet." In another embarrassing exchange, McDonald's executive Ed Oakley explained to Steel that the McDonald's garbage stuffed into landfills is "a benefit, otherwise you will end up with lots of vast empty gravel pits all over the country."[24]

The longest and most expensive civil case in U.K. history finally ended in mid-1997. Although the findings overall favored McDonald's, the court determined that McDonald's was "culpably responsible"[25] for cruel practices with broiler chickens, layer hens, and sows (i.e., mother pigs). Technically, McDonald's won the legal battle, but the company lost the PR war. With the finding of "culpably responsible," Yastrow believed it was time to do something tangible about animal welfare. His long-time back-and-forth interplay with a rumpled but shrewd animal activist was about to create a solution.

A Rumpled Activist, a Big-Time Lawyer, and an Autistic Animal Scientist Change Animal Agriculture History

The McLibel case shined a spotlight on alleged animal abuse within McDonald's vast supply system. McLibel alone, however, would not have pushed McDonald's toward taking up proactive policies on animal welfare.

Just as McDonald's was transforming into a recognized environmental champion due to its high-profile partnership with the Environmental Defense Fund (EDF) in the early 1990s, a new battle was percolating about the treatment and rights of farm animals. This battle was led by Henry Spira, head of the bare-boned Animal Rights International organization. Spira had led a successful engagement with Revlon in the 1980s about cruelty-free animal testing for cosmetics. Now he had his sights set on McDonald's.

Peter Singer collaborated with and supported Spira. Singer, author of *Animal Liberation* (1975), the first treatise setting forth principles and a philosophy of animal rights, knew Spira and his strategies well, noting that:

> His policy was that, initially, you went there (working with corporations) talking about positives that would come out of it. Henry liked win-win situations. So this would be something that McDonald's could do that it could feel good about, that it would get good publicity about, and that would be good for animals and basically good for the corporation.[26]

Spira knew how to mix in a bit of fear as well, as he had with Revlon and Perdue, the chicken company, in previous years. "Henry would show that there was a stick as well as a carrot lurking somewhere in the background," said Singer. "At first, maybe the stick would not be waved too obviously, but I think that was there."

Spira pleasantly nagged Yastrow many times in the 1990s. He was not belligerent. Spira always looked like he just got out of bed, with crumpled clothes and uncombed hair. Despite his rumpled appearance, he matched Yastrow with his sharp wit, intellect, and classiness. Their communication (mostly by letter) lasted for several years, exasperating both of them.

In a 1993 letter, Spira wrote: "Is it at all unreasonable after four and half years to ask McDonald's for a clear position with regard to enforcing humane standards and facilitating the implementation of improved methods, including a time table?"

McDonald's delay was not intentional. Animal treatment was McDonald's suppliers' responsibility. How could McDonald's intervene in a part of the supply chain (i.e., the slaughterhouse) where it had no procurement relationship?

From the 1993 letter, another four years passed with no tangible progress from McDonald's. Then, in a letter dated March 3, 1997, Spira wrote that, "You seemed incensed by our February 7th letter in which you say that I'm not playing fair. What's at issue here is not McDonald's good intentions. Rather, the problem is the vast gap which exists between the intent of the humane standards program and the reality."

When Yastrow shared his response, I was at first shocked by how blunt he was in his response to Spira. In August 1997, Yastrow wrote to Spira, in part stating that:

> I assure that I'm not being duplicitous, nor am I planning a scenario "which drags on forever." At the risk of having my intentions misconstrued to you, please remember that this

issue is all-consuming to you, but it is only one of the many issues to us; I say this not to minimize the importance of the issue, but to explain that my plate is already quite full and I can't abrogate all my other responsibilities just to accommodate this issue.

Though initially startled, I came to admire Yastrow's honest, forthright communication. He was the ultimate realist, and he believed that sharing news the "other side" did not want to hear was as important for credibility as telling them the good news. Yastrow was not into corporate speak. He believed, as I believe, that people will not believe you if all you tell them is what they want to hear. Indeed, within McDonald's, animal welfare was not the center of the universe, as it was to Spira, and Yastrow felt it only fair to let him know this.

Yastrow listened to Spira, and cared about the issue, but he was stymied in taking practical actions because McDonald's direct purchasing power did not reach the facilities that raised, transported, and processed animals. McDonald's purchasing connections were with facilities that purchased raw meat and converted the meat into hamburger patties.

In present-day market share, McDonald's uses about 2 percent from the overall global beef marketplace, making it one of the largest restaurant buyers of beef, yet not big enough to dictate changes, especially upstream in its supply chain.

Henry Spira and Peter Singer thought long and hard about how they could propose a reasonable solution for McDonald's to take tangible actions on animal welfare. They were worried about the hurdles. Singer said, "It seemed for a while as if there was some talk and a few words on paper, but nothing really was changing. We were worried about that, about being fobbed off and not getting any real changes."

Singer described Spira's determination. He felt it was really important to get McDonald's to lead the food service industry, in much the same way that he had influenced Revlon's leadership role in the cosmetics industry. But Spira dreamed of an even bigger multiplying effect, "because McDonald's just is involved with suppliers that supply such vast number of animals."

During one of Singer's visits to Spira's New York City apartment in early 1997, they talked about the idea of proposing that Yastrow work with the emerging, charismatic, brilliant, and autistic animal welfare expert Dr Temple Grandin. What they hatched in that small apartment would change animal welfare history.

"Henry had the idea of proposing to Shelby that Temple be brought in to do an audit of the slaughterhouses," said Singer. Spira was looking for someone who could be acceptable to McDonald's, and that had to be someone who was a not a vegan who was going to say, "This has got to stop." But he knew that he also needed somebody who could not easily be portrayed as just selling out to McDonald's. Grandin had that integrity and sincerity. Spira and Singer spoke to Grandin about it. She liked the idea.

In June 1997, Yastrow had just learned of the McLibel verdict and its looming implications for McDonald's. He believed that McDonald's could no longer be hands-off and simply rely on its suppliers when it came to sourcing humanely raised animal meat. So, rather than write another letter, he set up a time to meet Spira at his home base in New York City. That conversation set in motion major changes in animal agriculture. Yastrow noted that:

> Henry told me about Temple, and really wanted to find an ally who was very well respected, didn't have red flags surrounding him/her, someone who everybody liked. Henry was trying to get us to do more for animals for years. Henry recommended Temple Grandin. Henry was very honest and forthright. I respected him.[27]

Yastrow was enthused by the discussion with Spira and Singer. Finally, he had identified a way to take action. Yastrow recommended to Mike Quinlan, McDonald's CEO, that the company pursue a dedicated position on animal welfare and work with Dr Grandin to audit our meat suppliers. Quinlan approved.

Next, Yastrow went to Colorado State University in Fort Collins, Colorado, to visit Grandin. Spira had told him that Grandin "was kind of a different woman." She had autism. The normally well-prepared Yastrow wasn't ready for this. "I'll never forget the circumstances," he said, "because that morning I got sick and ended up having a kidney stone attack and spent the night before I met Temple in the Fort Collins hospital emergency room."

Yastrow arrived for their meeting feeling weak and a little cautious. "Temple couldn't have been nicer," he said, adding that:

> I did not know what to expect. I didn't. 'Cause at the time, you didn't have Google. Knowing she was autistic, which—I am ashamed to say—I didn't really understand at the time. So I

went to her office and she came out very erect, wearing jeans and a kind of cowboy rodeo shirt with all the studs and everything, and the bolo tie. It was not my picture of a university professor.

Yastrow quickly became enamored with Grandin's style, directness, and ideas.

Grandin recalled wondering about her meeting with Yastrow, pondering questions like "What will it be like to meet with an executive of McDonald's?" and "What should I say to him?" Grandin said that she remembers thinking that "this is really going to be big door for opening up some real change."[28]

Grandin explained the pressing animal treatment problems to Yastrow in her typical staccato style way of talking: piercing, direct, and passionate. She recalled that "I started to explain to him how there were a lot of problems with animal slaughter. Those were the bad old days. Broken equipment all over the place. Real rough handling of animals."

Grandin went on to explain the American Meat Institute (AMI, now the North American Meat Institute) objective scoring system, which she had developed in the mid-1990s. Janet Riley, a veteran leader within AMI and senior vice president of public affairs, joined AMI in 1991, young and open-minded. She led an animal welfare committee because the issue was considered more PR than substance at that time.

Riley was impressed when she read Grandin's 1996 report of meat plant audits. "Temple said that animal welfare could be measured objectively," she said. "It did not have to be just a subjective evaluation. I thought that really made a lot of sense to me." With that, she brought the objective scoring methodology forward to the management team at AMI. "Internally, there were a lot of raised eyebrows, and I remember someone saying to me, 'Do you really think we're gonna count moos?' and I said, 'I actually do.'"[29] Grandin and Riley started to work together just before the first meeting with McDonald's.

Grandin knew the limitations of the audit tool. Producers didn't see the need for it as an ongoing measurement and management tool. "Remember, back then there was no third-party auditing or any demands about animal welfare by customers prior to this point," explained Grandin. "In meeting McDonald's, basically, I thought, 'Well, I've got the power of the Golden Arches behind me'."

Grandin spent the morning with Yastrow, showing him things she was doing with corral designs and educating him about what could be done. Yastrow witnessed in action the respected and trusted leader he was looking for. Here she was, beloved by the animal rights community, a woman who knows how animals think and act, yet she loves beef and eats meat, and her work with the meat industry on designing animal handling facilities had earned her the trust of the ranchers and producers of cattle, too. Yastrow told Grandin that:

> You can help McDonald's, but here's the deal. We get criticized for our treatment of animals, as anybody does who has 30 million customers a day [that's in 1997; 70 million a day in 2018]—that's a lot of animals. I can sing to high heaven that we don't have a direct way to do something about it—we buy from independent and direct suppliers who simply make hamburger patties. Their suppliers deal with the animals. But that's not good enough. I want to do something to take concrete action.

Yastrow envisioned repeating the success McDonald's had enjoyed back in 1990–1991 in working with the EDF on reducing waste. In that partnership, McDonald's gave EDF open access to the company, its experts, leaders, data, and supply chain for packaging. It worked. His gambit was a big win for the environment, eventually reducing 300 million pounds of waste during the decade of the 1990s. The landmark partnership was a big win for McDonald's business, too, whose reputation was enhanced (including recognition by the White House for Environmental Excellence in 1991) while making all these changes to packaging without adding extra cost.

At the end of their morning together, Yastrow decided to replicate the EDF strategy, giving Grandin open access to the company. "I thought this was the perfect entrée for her to make a difference instead of just going out to the garden club," he said. Grandin would be given the muscle of one of the largest companies in the world. Yastrow offered her a proposal: "Tell us how we are doing. Tell us what we should be doing. Tell us what we're doing wrong. You have *carte blanche* access wherever you want all over the world."

Entry into the Golden Arches thrilled Temple. She welcomed the challenge of taking her research ideas and intellectual, blue sky audit and measuring system for animal behavior and applying them to the practical business of McDonald's extensive supply system.

That's when Yastrow handed things off to me to make the strategy happen. I wondered if and how I could translate my positive experiences working with various environmental groups since 1991 to this situation.

The NGO people I had worked with were skilled at what they do. Most important, I learned that the NGO advocates were most often good people with values I shared. I had become friends with the EDF team. I also had developed relationships with others like them at the National Audubon Society, National Wildlife Federation, and Conservation International.

Yastrow had always told me that change happens through trusting relationships. He led by example and through his constant advice to me. I recall his mantra of saying "Before you get out and get stuff done, get to know the key people, their families, their interests. The work will get done only if you have their trust, and trust begins at the personal relationship level."

I had built a lot of strong relationships among various NGOs. But the animal activist mind baffled me. I could see the logic of protecting the planet and reducing waste, which was the work I led with EDF. But now I was dealing with people who thought that animals were on a similar level as human beings, with similar rights. I read Peter Singer's book about animal rights, and it confounded me even more. His opening chapter title is "All Animals Are Equal." That's not how I thought. I didn't believe that humans were equal to cows and pigs.

I have always tried hard to put my mind, soul, and heart into the shoes of the social/environmental activist. I take what they do as sincere, driven by their passion. I want to respect their viewpoint. I believe this opens doors for dialogue, compromise, and solutions. If we think of the NGO as only an adversary and enemy, all we create is conflict without progress.

It's important to understand "the other side," just as the other side has to understand your viewpoint. Who says your side is 100 percent spot on? But as I dug into the animal rights issue, I could not identify with their philosophy, even if I could totally understand animal welfare (treating animals with respect, with no abuse, neglect, or cruelty). So I put my heart into animal welfare.

I had to get to know Singer and Spira, so I set up a meeting with them in New York City. My goal was to let them know that we were enlisting Grandin to audit our meat facilities and that we were hiring a full-time animal welfare director. I was very anxious. I wondered how I could have a real, authentic conversation with two people who believed in a vegetarian society. I'm an unabashed meat eater. I work for the biggest meat-serving restaurant in the world. I feared they wanted to destroy our business.

I had brought along to this meeting a colleague of mine who works in supply chain. He ordered practically every meat product during our breakfast, including eggs and sausage. I had intentionally chosen only pastries—in deference to their vegetarian mindset. I thought it important to show respect for those I was meeting with. I asked my colleague after breakfast if he ordered and ate all that meat intentionally, to make a point. If he did, I would give him some credit for taking a stand. However, he hadn't thought about it. That negligence bothered me. If you are going to offend the other party, at least do so intentionally. I don't blame him. What he did is not uncommon: an innocent insensitivity to the mindset of people who are different from ourselves.

We ended up having a respectful and fruitful discussion. I committed to them that McDonald's was serious about leveraging Dr Grandin to change animal welfare practices with our suppliers. I promised to keep them posted on our progress.

Temple Grandin Woos McDonald's Suppliers

The task to implement an animal welfare program rested upon McDonald's supply chain. It was one thing for Shelby Yastrow, with the backing of McDonald's CEO, to devise a strategy. But it was another thing to make it happen.

I had first worked extensively with McDonald's supply chain team on packaging issues a decade earlier. But I also knew success with green, eco-friendly packaging changes did not translate into creating motivation to address the treatment of animals. Packaging was largely within the control of McDonald's wishes. If McDonald's wanted recycled paper as feedstock for its packaging, we had direct suppliers who could do this. Live animals, however, were a couple steps removed from our direct meat suppliers. So we had to think of creative ways to motivate upstream suppliers to get involved with this issue.

McDonald's had built its strategic approach to supply chain management in a unique, collaborative, and long-term fashion. Suppliers were partners, true collaborators. Handshake agreements were the norm. Trust was paramount. Thinking of the long-term benefits to ensure a safe, affordable, high-quality supply system was always top-of-mind.

McDonald's has never been a transactional purchaser. Ray Kroc built a system based on success and profit of its franchisees, and the same went for its suppliers. Kroc never wanted an independent supply system, and he had no desire for vertical integration. He wanted suppliers who were dedicated and passionate about the mission and vision of McDonald's restaurants worldwide. Kroc wanted the job of McDonald's staff to be running great restaurants—and to let suppliers be the experts on beef, potatoes, fish, and other foodstuffs.

The philosophy of McDonald's three-legged stool—i.e., owner–operators, suppliers, and company staff—is ingrained in the company culture, with the understanding that each leg of the stool is interdependent on each other in order to serve customers with quality, service, cleanliness, and value (QSC&V). No one could be with the company but a few months before realizing that QSC&V was part of the DNA of McDonald's, zealously pursued and rigorously followed.

McDonald's supply chain leadership thought that the issue of animal welfare fit best into the quality assurance (QA) segment of the supply chain system rather than the procurement side. The thinking was that animal welfare standards fit with the mission of QA, which oversaw McDonald's quality and food safety standards at the meat slaughterhouses and processing plants.

Paul Simmons led the QA supplier teams, and he was assigned to be my partner to create an animal welfare program with Temple Grandin. Simmons's temperament contrasted with Grandin's. He was studious, reflecting the serious nature of his responsibilities to protect and enhance food safety systems within McDonald's. Simmons was measured and practical. He stood tall and dispassionate, while Grandin was a whirling dervish, barking out opinions and ideas. According to Gary Platt, the head of QA for one of our direct suppliers of hamburger patties, Lopez Foods, there was friction between the two of them, adding that "[i]t's kind of funny to see Paul and Temple kind of go at it a little bit."[30]

But Grandin admired Simmons, who dismissed any friction as robust, scientific, natural debate. Simmons's mission was to take the blue sky, academic ideas that were still unproven into a commercial setting. "What Temple had was great system," Simmons said, "but it wasn't proven to be communicated and passed on to other people to have the same repetitive interpretation. I wanted measures that if we trained three people, they would measure in exactly the same way."[31]

According to Simmons, animal welfare standards had its roots in the National Aeronautics and Space Administration because NASA started the food safety process control evolution beginning in the early 1960s, which in turn spawned animal welfare controls and standards that emerged during the late 1990s. Back in the 1960s, NASA had asked Pillsbury to supply its needs for space flights. That is when Hazard Analysis and Critical Control Points (HACCP) originated.

Simmons said it was a way of ensuring that the food was safe for the astronauts.

According to Simmons, HACCP originally was not destined for food, but rather for the pharmaceuticals industry. But by the mid-1990s, HACCP was well advanced and integrated, not only within McDonald's supply chain, but widely throughout America's entire meat supply chain. McDonald's was a key leader in applying HACCP to meat food safety. Simmons noted that:

> McDonald's took these control point systems as a major process, applied them to the higher-risk food industry, meat products, and brought them to a reality of control systems before it became a regulatory type program. We taught the meat industry HACCP. That was something completely foreign. McDonald's facilitated training of all packers and primary suppliers on food safety practices on HACCP, which in turn gave us credibility to suppliers to listen to us—because we came with a solution.

This all happened as a precursor to animal welfare process controls. The implementation of these food process controls occurred in the late 1980s and early 1990s. McDonald's led a big shift away from the "old inspection mentality," said Simmons. "If you measure and monitor each step of the process, you are assured the end outcome would be right, instead of inspecting the end outcome and hoping your sample is correct."

What Grandin wanted McDonald's suppliers to do was simple, observable, and measureable. For instance, one person would count cows for an hour, score a sheet, tally them up, and derive a percentage that would score the supplier. Measurement included the following*:

- Missed stuns or partial stuns (using a stun gun–like device prior to slaughter)

- Falling down

- Electric prod use (a wand that actually gave the cows a small electric shock)

- Mooing

---

* Pigs and chickens had different measures.

Simmons started to work with McDonald's five beef patty suppliers, which had business partnerships with about sixty beef slaughterhouses across the United States. He and I discussed asking a McDonald's beef patty supplier to take the lead on working with Dr Grandin. We decided upon Lopez Foods, which had a seasoned, grizzled veteran QA lead, Gary Platt, who was their director of food safety and a member of McDonald's Food Safety Team. We asked Lopez Foods to figure out how to implement Grandin's vision.

Platt was quite a cowboy, according to Grandin, who was equally independent-minded and strong-willed. Platt's first impression of Grandin was: "Boy, this gal is really concerned with animals. She could see things, in my opinion, that I couldn't see. She explained she saw visions in 3D. I couldn't see stuff like that."

At first, Platt wondered why animal welfare really mattered that much. As he worked with Grandin, he began to see the business benefit and was converted to an animal welfare advocate. Platt learned to understand that less stressed animals actually produce better meat. He said that "[i]f you have a hog that's not excited when you kill them, then you have less blood splatter in the loin, which is better for us, better for the customer."

Platt was our host for the first big gathering of our extended supplier team at Lopez's headquarters in Oklahoma City, Oklahoma. Grandin's reputation in the meat industry was so well revered that everyone there was treating her like a rock star.

Despite her fandom, when Grandin first met with Platt and others on the QA beef auditing team, she sensed their reluctance about how animal welfare's fit into QA, noting that:

> I remember when some of the McDonald's auditors that were working for the grinding [patty] companies kind of going off and saying, "Well, this stuff is all a bunch of BS." But then they saw some bad stuff. That is when, boy, they grabbed ahold of it. It was like running a hundred touchdowns.

The opposition and resistance to animal welfare audits slowly faded away as tangible business benefits surfaced. In short, more content animals made their processing easier and more efficient, and sometimes the quality of actual meat improved, too. Temple recollects how the suppliers converted:

> The other thing that happened is that the auditors themselves— these were the food safety auditors for the grinders—were

skeptical at first. But when they started doing it they'd go, "Oh, wow, we can really make some change." And they just started taking off with it because they saw how crappy the plant was. And then when they came back and they saw how nice it worked when it was nice. Instead of 20 percent of the cows mooing and getting zapped with electric prods now coming in and seeing how quiet it could be.

Another key member of McDonald's beef HACCP team was Erika Voogd. She was from one of McDonald's biggest beef suppliers: Otto and Sons Industries. She recalled her feelings after she received a letter from McDonald's stating that we were being asked to start measuring animal welfare:

> I read the letter, and it talked about counting moos and counting slips and falls and counting stunning and everything. And I wasn't completely sold on the idea at the time. I thought, "Wait a minute. We're here for food safety, and now we're going to talk about humane handling? I really don't get this."[32]

Voogd experienced her animal welfare conversion during her first trip to facilities in Texas, where there was a beef plant with a poor quality cattle V restrainer, a device used to comfortably hold the animal just prior to being slaughtered. Voogd explains:

> The plant had an old V restrainer. The way it was set up, it wasn't really designed at all to meet the needs of the animals, and so they were frightened and they were trying to climb out. There was a tremendous amount of fear in the eyes of the animals. When they were stunning them, they were requiring re-stuns. It was a dramatic episode for me because I got to feel it really from the standpoint of the animal and the moment of slaughter.

Sure enough, the QA folks were developing more sensitivity to and caring for the way animals were treated. No longer were animals considered widgets. Later that night, back at the hotel with Dr Grandin, Voogd reflected on her experience with Grandin:

> I said to Temple, "This is really not the picture we want kids—you know, moms taking their kids to McDonald's—this

isn't the picture that we want people to be thinking of when they're thinking of a McDonald's hamburger." And it really convinced me to be onboard with what we were doing.

Grandin and I took dozens of trips together, and I watched her address various problems with optimism and insight. Rather than focusing on the idiosyncrasies associated with her autism, I saw her talent and good intentions. Janet Riley also saw Grandin's talent, describing her as "[b]rilliant. Sometimes you get a professor up there who is incredibly smart, but maybe less practical, up in the clouds. People became to understand why she had this unique connection and ability to understand how animals were thinking."

People on all sides of the animal welfare issue admired Grandin, a rarity for such a controversial topic. Suppliers and animal rights people both believed her to be objective and fair. It was clear that she wanted animals to be treated with respect even while accepting their death as a source for food protein. Grandin defined respect as keeping the animals free from abuse, neglect, and cruelty.

I became invested in this definition as the right thing to do. This was the least we could ask of our suppliers. The most difficult decision we had to make at McDonald's was how tough to be when plants totally flunked the audit. Should we drop them as suppliers? There were no easy answers. Grandin shared her thoughts on the issue:

> One of the first things that happened when started doing a McDonald's audit is people had to fix all that broken stuff. A couple of plants got kicked off your approved supplier list and, boy, things got serious really fast. I saw more change near '99 and early 2000 than I had seen in my entire career prior to that. ... It brought all kinds of nice things. Plants didn't maintain it and they didn't supervise their employees. One of the things the audits did is it forced plants to maintain their equipment and supervise their employees. Word got out in the industry that we were serious.

Our collective work with Dr Grandin led to animal welfare standards, training, and audits becoming the new normal for the meat industry. Animal welfare went from something considered tangential to being accepted as a core principle of running a sound business. There were many changes, small and large, with technologies, hardware, and designs that helped with animal welfare, but the most dramatic change concerned people.

Grandin enlightened meat suppliers on the issues of animal welfare. They in turn willingly created a culture of animal care. Grandin always said that better animal treatment starts and ends with the managers and bosses. She was right.

As with what McDonald's accomplished with EDF on waste, McDonald's and its suppliers made major shifts on animal welfare without any costs passed on to McDonald's. As people came to care more about how animals were treated, as more of them were trained in the proper ways to treat animals, and as animal care was made part of everyone's job descriptions at the animal handling facilities, improvements emerged at a rapid pace. The animal welfare audits showed positive improvements: Fewer cows fell, animals moved more efficiently and quietly through the facility, and stun guns were better maintained and kept in proper working condition.

Most physical changes were not major investments. For instance, getting rid of the electric wands that zap animals in order to move them along on the way to slaughter was a minor expense. During my first visits to plants during 1988–1989, zapping animals was standard practice. Grandin used animal behavior science to convince suppliers to instead use plastic bags or flags to move the animals. It worked. Today, these facilities are as quiet as a library, with animals moving along naturally. And, best of all, these changes scaled beyond McDonald's supply chain to suppliers around the globe and across industries.

Erika Voogd has been on this journey since the late 1990s, and she still works with meat suppliers today. She summarized the impact of these changes: "It's very peaceful. You don't hear the vocalization. You don't see the slipping and falling. You don't have double stuns. You get higher quality meat. You don't have bruising. You don't have tense animals."

Would these changes have occurred had McDonald's not taken the lead? Changes were inevitable, but McDonald's accelerated the pace, impressed the seriousness of the issue, and improved the acceptance of the science-oriented principles that encompassed the work. Indeed, Grandin believes that there was a pre- and post-McDonald's era when it comes to animal welfare. "I saw more progress with McDonald's in the industry than all my previous twenty-five years of work," she said. "McDonald's was the heat. I bent the steel. You softened it for me."[33]

Riley agreed, noting that:

> McDonald's was tremendously influential. People often like to say, "If you are big, you are bad," and the converse can be true, too. If you're big, you can be good, and when you are both big and good, you have tremendous influence. And I think that is exactly what happened with McDonald's on this issue. I just don't think it would be where we are today if McDonald's hadn't embraced it.

Hard Knock Nuggets

The Three Ps: Passion, Patience, and Persistence

Dr Temple Grandin showed me the secret sauce of leading change. She has the remarkable ability to balance passion, patience, and persistence. No matter the detours and arduous process that it took to make animal welfare a mainstream priority for the animal industry, Grandin balanced a relentless passion with a remarkable patience backed by tenacious daily persistence.

While others, including me at that time, saw these characteristics as opposing chaotic forces, Grandin practiced them simultaneously. She inspired me to do the same, and the Three Ps of passion, patience, and persistence became my daily mantra. Here are some tips to get into that same mental state:

- Let passion be the engine that runs your system at 100 mph, even though it's as quiet as an electric car. Don't be obvious, and don't wear it on your sleeve. People naturally will sense your genuine commitment. And never let up on your passion. It's the fuel that propels change.

- Many of us are blinded and bounded by our overflowing passion, rubbing colleagues the wrong way, not relating with peers, and pushing our own agenda instead of helping others achieve theirs. When others don't get on board, we can become cynical and pessimistic. That's why we need patience.

- Patience doesn't mean passiveness. Patience helps you realize that nothing big is going to happen in your organization without the time needed to engage and connect with internal and external stakeholders, truly listening and adapting to their input.

- Connections lead to good relationships and trust. You cannot lead unless your colleagues trust you. So when you go to meetings, go ahead and push to get decisions made, but learn something about the other person along the way and keep building that relationship.

- We will fail often. Don't blame others. Figure out how you and your team could have done better, and then keep pursuing your goal with those lessons in mind.

- "Two steps backward." That's what I always heard from colleagues who became frustrated by setbacks. I would show them that, over the long stretch, we had also taken three steps forward. Leading change is not for those who need daily, instantaneous reinforcement.

- Remember that integrating sustainability into the core of the business is a multiyear, culture-change process. Be happy with small wins, which eventually will add up to a big shift.

- Persistence is essential to keep things moving. We can't lollygag and wait forever. I once had a boss who, in an annual review, gave me demerits for doing too much internal vetting. He wanted me to get more stuff done. That's why we need Grandin-like relentless persistence.

- Persistence in the face of conflict is particularly challenging. We might face all types of outside attacks or internal debates. Consider the conflict an opportunity. Don't consider conflict to be a bad force. It's good and needed. It's difficult to imagine anyone getting any better without facing and overcoming some conflict.

- Persistence and patience require a positive and optimistic mindset. It's easy to become negative. Let out frustration quickly and get back on the positive track. People want to follow committed, enthusiastic leaders.

As you embrace the Three Ps of passion, patience, and persistence, you will experience freedom and mental relaxation that will drive your ability to influence others to the next level. The Three Ps form a circular path that always comes back to the passion that drives leadership for corporate social change. Passion inspires us to go against the status quo, to be the one in the room to question a current practice and to advocate for environmental and social progress and breakthroughs.

3

The Battle of Extremism: McCruelty

Meat Is Murder

Fig. 3.1: PETA Launches Ugly Campaign.[34] *Source:* Courtesy of People for the Ethical Treatment of Animals.

The McLibel United Kingdom civil trial was no sooner over in 1997 when People for the Ethical Treatment of Animals (PETA) set its sights on McDonald's. PETA was preparing a McCruelty Happy Meal campaign.

PETA's penchant for shock tactics puts our McDonald's team on high alert. While it certainly was a new challenge to deal with Henry Spira and Peter Singer and their sophisticated brand of animal rights activism during most of the 1990s, now McDonald's was confronted by a group that used the unexpected and the extreme to gain attention. We knew our hands would be full—for years to come.

The timing of PETA's efforts overlapped with McDonald's decision to engage with Temple Grandin. PETA in 1997 demanded McDonald's implement seven wide-ranging changes:

1. Give chickens at least 1.5 square feet of living space.
2. Stop selling eggs from hens housed in battery cages.
3. Require improved standards for chicken transport and slaughter.
4. Stop using genetically altered birds.
5. Choose birds that do not suffer from painful leg deformities.
6. Purchase pigs only from farms which provide their breeding sows with room to move around outdoors, and which do not confine them indoors to cement cells.
7. Include a vegetarian burger at all McDonald's restaurants.

PETA particularly zeroed in on laying hens (eggs), describing their conditions as:

> Hens are then shoved into tiny wire "battery" cages, which measure roughly 18 inches by 24 inches and hold up to 10 hens, each of whom has a wingspan up to 36 inches. Even in the best-case scenario, a hen spends her life crowded in a space about the size of a file drawer with several other hens, unable to lift a single wing. The birds are crammed so closely together that although normally clean animals, they are forced to urinate and defecate on one another.[35]

PETA was smart to focus on laying hens since it seemed that they figured that the visual of these birds crammed in small cages would get a lot of attention from the public.

They got my attention as well. When I first visited a laying egg facility to find out the reality of its operations, I basically found that PETA's claims were accurate. I went through the massive warehouse-type structure with aisles and aisles of cages that stretched beyond 100 yards with the cages stacked on top of each other to 20 feet high or more. The laying hens were really squished, with no room to spread their wings or move around without a tussle.

I also didn't like the smell of the facility. The stench was like a filthy bathroom that hadn't been cleaned in a long time, with a strong ammonia smell. I couldn't wait to get out.

As PETA escalated its campaign against McDonald's, they pulled out their full arsenal: demanding letters to our leadership, tough phone calls, graphic anti-McDonald's messaging on their website, speaking out at McDonald's shareholder meetings, passing out flyers to neighbors of McDonald's CEO. PETA also engaged with the media, resulting in widespread coverage in print and television media.

My own experiences with them were unnerving. I was schooled thus far by NGOs that were advocates, yet acted honorably and were civil and collaborative. Not so with PETA.

My most startling experience occurred in 2010 when I headed to a University of Michigan podium to give remarks to an eager audience of about two hundred fifty MBA students involved with Net Impact, an organization dedicated to helping students with a passion to make a social impact through business. As I took the microphone in hand, I saw out of the corner of my eye a young, crazed woman rushing to the stage. She was screaming, piercing the room with her frenzied, high-pitched ranting: "Meat is murder! McDonald's murders animals!"

She jumped right up to me and took the microphone from my hand. I stepped far aside and let her do her thing. She was deafening all of us with her screeching. Then a young Net Impact intern summoned the guts to approach the PETA person and help escort her out of the auditorium. As he did so, the room became as quiet as a prayer room. As she defiantly strutted out, the silence smothered the room even more. Then, a male student in the upper left-hand side of the auditorium yelled, "I love McDonald's!" The room exhaled as the audience laughed and energy flowed again.

PETA had been doing similar stunts with other McDonald's executives, so I was not completely surprised at being accosted like this, but I was on edge. Who could know what a wild activist like this might do?

Turns out PETA activists could do all sorts of things. When I first went on Facebook, for example, I didn't set up my privacy settings right, and my entire Facebook profile and all my posts were public. Before I knew it, several of my nephews and daughters were receiving nasty messages from PETA.

My conversations with PETA were unpleasant as well. It wasn't because I disagreed with their proposals. I had empathy for many of their concerns. Rather, it was their in-your-face style. They made their demands in a condescending way, making me feel attacked and defensive.

Not satisfied with responses anymore from McDonald's after two years of rocky, back-and-forth communications, PETA launched, in the summer of 2000, a coordinated "McCruelty's Unhappy Meal" campaign that *USA Today* reported as:

> ... featuring a stuffed toy that look like Ronald McDonald's holding a bloody butcher's knife. "Our goal is show kids what actually happens to the animals that McDonald's raises and kills," said PETA's Bruce Friedrich. He continued saying, "to let kids know that if people eat at McDonald's, they are promoting cruelty to animals."[36]

Of course, PETA's mission of animal rights and vegetarianism collided with the mission of McDonald's, serving beef, chicken, fish, and pork sandwiches.

The conflict peaked when Jack Greenberg, McDonald's CEO at the time, declared during a shareholder meeting in 2001 that PETA would not be satisfied until all that McDonald's sold was beans and tofu. The McDonald's audience cheered and clapped, a rare sight for a normally staid crowd.

PETA was effectively controlling the agenda against us. What could we do to gain control? We needed to figure out a way to stymie or neutralize PETA.

Another dilemma was how to differentiate between addressing a worthy and legitimate issue, yet one that was delivered by what we viewed as dishonorable means.

How to Develop a Counterstrategy?

During the stretch of time that PETA was unleashing their unorthodox tactics, we were making measureable progress with our beef and chicken suppliers, which were implementing Temple Grandin's animal welfare audits at their slaughterhouse facilities. Because of this success, I started to think about how we could replicate this type of collaboration for other emerging animal welfare issues, including the laying hen issue.

Since it appeared to me that McDonald's would be facing such issues for the long term, we needed an approach to define our own actions, rather than simply reacting to the agendas set by others, including PETA.

My partner in McDonald's U.S. supply chain was Bruce Feinberg, who was hired in 1997 to head up U.S. quality systems. Paul Simmons, who was our lead with Dr Grandin, reported to Feinberg, who was extraordinarily supportive of Simmons's animal welfare work. Feinberg was what we needed. He had come to McDonald's predisposed to deeply caring about animals. His boyhood dream was to be a veterinarian, and he earned a degree in animal science from Penn State.

Hired away from a competitor, Feinberg viewed McDonald's as the benchmark for all things quality. So when he began at McDonald's, he expected a solid animal welfare approach. But that wasn't what he found: "I was a little surprised when I came in, only to find out that, no, a lot of the stuff we really hadn't figured out yet," Feinberg said. He recognized what was in front of him, adding that, "[t]he good news was that the door was wide open for leadership, for people to express opinions and formulate some of these early programs."[37]

I supported Feinberg in every way I could. We both knew that complex issues were brewing and that they were getting messy thanks to PETA's edgy and sensational demonstrations and campaigns. As Feinberg accurately reflected, "Back in those days, hardly a week would go by when we weren't confronted or contacted by PETA. It was the days of mudslinging contests. It was down in the ditches. It was talking about blood and guts."

Feinberg and I decided to do two things to start playing offense and determining our own destiny:

1. Develop a set of principles to direct our work on animal welfare.
2. Establish a blue-ribbon panel of animal welfare experts to advise us.

Develop a Set of Principles

I believe in setting a vision, a North Star, a set of principles to inform and inspire the company, its suppliers, and other stakeholders to work together to create solutions. I drafted such a set of principles, which Feinberg and others refined, that identified what McDonald's stood for regarding animal welfare (see Sidebar).

Critics often argue that principles are soft and don't accomplish anything. Not true. I believe that companies need to start any initiative with a solid grasp of the principles, values, and beliefs that drive the organization. Principles are the bedrock upon which a company lays a foundation to internalize the motivations for addressing the problem. Without principles, a company and its people swat at flies because everything is fleeting, fluctuating, and dependent on circumstances.

> ### McDonald's Animal Welfare Guiding Principles (2000)
>
> 1. Safety: First and foremost, McDonald's will provide its customers with safe food products. Food safety is McDonald's number 1 priority.
> 2. Quality: McDonald's believes that treating animals with care and respect is an integral part of an overall quality assurance program that makes good business sense.
> 3. Animal Treatment: McDonald's believes that animals should be free of cruelty, abuse, and neglect and embraces the proper treatment of animals and addressing animal welfare.
> 4. Partnership: McDonald's works continuously with our suppliers to audit animal welfare practices, ensuring compliance and continuous improvement.
> 5. Leadership: McDonald's will lead our industry by working with our suppliers and industry experts to advance animal welfare practices and technology.
> 6. Performance Measurement: McDonald's sets annual performance objectives to measure our improvement and will ensure our purchasing strategy is aligned with our commitment to animal welfare issues as a responsible purchaser.
> 7. Communication: McDonald's will communicate our process, programs, plans, and progress surrounding animal welfare.

Establish a Blue-Ribbon Panel

From experience, I knew that we needed outside experts to help us with our animal welfare initiatives, both to understand the science of what to do and to gain credibility. Working with outside experts worked with EDF and waste. It worked with Dr Grandin in developing our breakthrough program for animal welfare audits. Now the issues we faced related to animals were broad and multifaceted, across pigs, cattle, poultry, and laying hens. We needed a host of expertise.

I thought we needed a blue-ribbon panel of experts because the term connotes the best of the best, experts beyond reproach, the most preeminent. I've always believed that finding the right experts is a big part of my job. The better people I can find, the easier the task to make change and get the public to believe what we do.

I knew Grandin was our first choice for what would be called McDonald's Animal Welfare Council. She accepted immediately. She gave us the platform to recruit others.

As I conducted research to find other experts, I came upon a group of academic animal welfare scientists who already were advising the United Egg Producers (UEP), the organization that represents the vast majority of the egg producers and develops policies and programs for the egg industry. UEP had selected top experts to develop animal welfare guidelines and standards for their national membership. Their advisors included Dr Jeff Armstrong, dean of animal science at Purdue University at the time (now President, Cal Poly University); Dr Joy Mench, professor of animal science at the University of California, Davis; and Dr Janice Swanson, associate professor of animal science at Kansas State University (now with Michigan State University).

Thankfully, each of them was willing to work with us. As we began our work together, I found them to be bright, caring, and selfless. I started to see this when we agreed that McDonald's would pay only for their travel expenses (i.e., we offered no honorarium or other payments for their time). I thought they might balk at this, but they did not hesitate. Their motivations were solely to make a difference. I highly respected them for this. They each took a lot of grief from animal rights critics for teaming up with McDonald's. They were helping the enemy, a symbol of factory farming. Despite the pressure on them, each spent many hours helping us. Not once did they ask for money.

Dr Armstrong was the chair of the UEP Scientific Animal Welfare Committee. He said he joined because of McDonald's work with Grandin, noting that "McDonald's was clearly the leader in moving animal welfare forward in their supply chain and doing it right and basing it on science. And this is exactly the same pathway that I believed academia at large needed to take."[38]

Dr Mench was a preeminent expert on laying hens. She quickly gave McDonald's a lifeline on all things to know about laying hens, including how the more restrictive cages evolved. According to Mench, commercial cages were developed in the 1930s, but they didn't come into widespread use in the egg industry until the 1950s.

I thought the reason for cages was productivity—to get hens to lay more eggs. Not so, according to Mench, who said that:

> The idea of putting them into cages was to keep them from getting diseases, particularly associated with pecking the ground that had feces in it because they would get parasites from that. Also, the cages protected them from predators, and the cages kept the eggs clean, and all laid in one place rather than laid places where you had to go searching for the eggs.[39]

So, food safety and hen health were the instigators of battery cages, not efficiency. "The major cause was coccidiosis [an intestinal disease]," said Mench. "To get the hens up out of the soil and out of the litter. Coccidiosis used to kill a lot of poultry."

Mench and the other experts began working with us in early 2000. They agreed to McDonald's Animal Welfare Council's scope of work outlined as follows:

- Assist McDonald's and its suppliers meet the goals described in McDonald's Animal Welfare Principles.

- Provide information, advice, and expertise on germane issues.

- Have access to key management and suppliers.

- Make recommendations to McDonald's and its suppliers.

- Meet formally twice a year and participate in visits to suppliers to review actual programs and progress.

When the council first met, we immediately dove into the laying hen issue. The UEP committee had been working on related issues for more than a year. Our experts came to us having already studied the scientific literature. They had developed many of its conclusions based on their review, so our time to consider the facts was expedited, especially on forced molting (i.e., the withdrawal of food and water for seven to ten days in order to prolong the hen's productive life for egg production).

According to Mench, the impetus of the UEP work stemmed from groups like the United Poultry Concerns, an NGO dedicated to the "compassionate and respectful treatment of chickens, turkeys, ducks and other domestic fowl."[40] The organization also questioned the practices of forced molting and beak trimming, the latter of which refers to trimming the hens' beaks to prevent them from pecking at each other. The trio of Mench, Armstrong, and Swanson came to us with their recommendations to address forced molting and set standards for beak trimming. However, the space issue was one that was largely unexplored.

UEP soon migrated to studying the housing space issue, with their expert advisors ultimately recommending a direction to increase the cage space from an industry average of about 48 square inches per laying hen to 67 square inches. The space issue was the most sensitive to the industry because changes would require more investment to cover the costs related to installing more cages and building larger facilities. Therefore, UEP was considering a long phase-in period.

Then McDonald's entered the equation.

The McDonald's team saw the need to provide more space and decided upon 72 square inches, based on input from the Animal Welfare Council. I was amazed and surprised at how quickly we came up with our decision. It took just a couple of months. I heard internal discussions that the price tag for McDonald's U.S. business was more than $10 million annually. The extra cost came primarily from the price associated with accommodating more cages and more space. Instead of five to seven laying hens per cage, the cages would now hold no more than four.

I remember talking to our head of global supply chain at the time, Tom Albrecht, and he didn't hesitate one second. He said it was simply the right thing to do. Albrecht said the hens were too crunched and that their living conditions were not humane. We needed to change and bear the costs of that change. I was so impressed with Albrecht's stance. If there is a stereotype of purchasing professionals having no heart, this is absolutely not true.

In August 2000, McDonald's announced that it would purchase eggs only from suppliers that provided more room in their cages (an average of 72 square inches) and supported new standards for beak trimming. It was the first announcement of its kind, and it made headlines. As *The Washington Post* reported:

> "We are very appreciative of what the company has done, and think they are doing the right thing," said Steven Gross, who has served as a negotiator for People for the Ethical Treatment of Animals (PETA) in its two-year discussions with McDonald's. "Other companies in this field have been dragging their feet and, frankly, we think this decision will have the salutary effect of waking them up."[41]

Despite the positive press and the positive feedback from PETA, the suppliers of laying hens were resistant. I remember going to a large meeting of the UEP membership to talk face to face with them in order to explain our motivations and seek their support. But I ran into a buzz saw. UEP members were enraged at McDonald's. They thought we were out of bounds. It was not McDonald's responsibility to set standards. They argued that McDonald's does not raise the hens and so it doesn't know what is best for their business or for the animals.

I tried having a dialogue with them. In front of me I saw neck veins pulsating. Their emotions high, they were spewing angry questions and comments. I got nowhere with them in trying to find some common ground.

McDonald's announcement included a timeline calling for the new space requirements by the end of 2001. As we approached twenty-seven current, local regional egg suppliers, I was shocked when all of them refused to change to these new standards. They were turning down McDonald's 1.5–2 billion eggs a year, about 2 percent of the U.S. egg market.[42] And it wasn't due to cost because McDonald's was willing to pay for the changes. Rather, their decision was based on rejecting McDonald's role as a de facto regulator. As a result, McDonald's was forced to seek a new supply of eggs, which it achieved by working with Cargill.

Indeed, McDonald's announcement would launch long-term effects across the industry. Mench recalls the impact of McDonald's announcement: "Once McDonald's did this, the interest in the other retailers was obvious. McDonald's really made a big splash," she said. "We don't have any laws regulating the treatment of animals on farms, and as long as we don't have any laws, someone has to step in and do that."

The ripple effect started to take effect. In a span of just a few months most of McDonald's competitors announced similar policies and standards. For example, Burger King announced a week later upping the space per hen to 75 inches. I never learned why they added three more inches to their standards.

In any event, McDonald's did not make the move for a competitive advantage, so we were pleased with others' quick adoption, and we hoped that adoption of these new standards would level the playing field for the necessary industry investment.

Indeed, the standards eventually became the industry norm over the next five to seven years. The extra costs incurred by McDonald's ended up being an investment in change that created a domino effect. As a result, the costs of increased housing size for laying hens were normalized for all. This was a key lesson. We learned that, as a market leader, when we change, many others will follow, and what originally is viewed as an added cost becomes an embedded industrywide cost later on.[*],[43]

Mench was happy about the changes because they brought forth immediate laying hen benefits. According to her, the benefits were the following:

- Mortality rates of hens decreased.

- Egg production actually increased.

---

[*] Right after my retirement in March, 2015, McDonald's announced a further commitment on eggs. By 2025, McDonald's USA and Canada would transition to cage-free eggs.

- The hens now had room to turn around and lie down.

- The lower ammonia levels benefitted both workers and hens.

Public Relations *Piñata*

What's the best way to respond to a PETA type organization? Lay low and wait it out? Provide minimum statements? Or take on PETA aggressively?

Walt Riker was the leader of McDonald's communication response, a tough one to weigh the pros and cons, especially since the way the campaign unfurled, and the way the media amplified PETA's message, McDonald's was on the immediate defensive.

"PETA focused on cheap publicity, and they were very effective in getting a lot of attention right off the bat," said Riker. "It's a blindside hit. You're kind of knocked backwards due to the immediate blitz of media interest because of PETA." Though taken aback by PETA's over-the-top accusations against McDonald's, Riker decided to take them on. "I engaged on a level that probably was not in the playbook of your typical McDonald's response."[44]

Indeed, Riker was accustomed to the *piñata* political scene, serving as Bob Dole's communication director. "My first instinct, having been in major league politics for 13 years, was to hit back just as hard." So Riker talked tough:

From *USA Today*, June 20, 2000:

McDonald's calls the campaign an "ugly distortion" of the truth, designed to frighten children. "McDonald's is absolutely committed to animal welfare and won't tolerate any kind of abuse in that area. We're committed to being leaders and thing we're making progress."[45]

From the *Lakeland* (Florida) *Ledger*, June 15, 2000, quoting McDonald's Riker:

"Their message is very much like their fake Happy Meal box. It's an ugly distortion. And even worse, it's portrayed in a revolting and grotesque way that's designed to frighten children. I can tell you from McDonald's point of view is what they (PETA) are saying is simply not true. It's tasteless and disgusting."[46]

Riker did interview after interview, especially for local radio and newspapers. He found a receptive audience. "They wanted our honest response instead of some mealy mouthed rhetoric. People calling into these local radio shows were a 100 percent behind us."

My own experience with the media over many years was similar to Riker's assessment. Most of the time, the journalist has a preordained storyline that is not favorable to McDonald's, and is just looking to talk to McDonald's, or for that matter, any big brand, and put their point of view at the end of a story.

Riker's experience was that McDonald's starts the communication process deep in the hole. He said, "The frustrating part and the biggest challenge was that academics, critics, special interest groups, even comedians, were given a 100 percent credibility. They are all given full credit, and all-of-a-sudden we were on the defensive."

I admired Riker's bulldog approach. In the end, McDonald's got a lot of credit for the laying hen decision. "The laying hen issue was one of the biggest media stories that I ever saw at McDonald's." Riker fought the battle and prevailed. He broke down the stereotype that big is bad. He helped forge a contrarian success story, where big is good. As Riker says, "It showed that McDonald's, working with good faith, third-party experts, could make a difference on a scale that no one else could."

Does PETA Deserve Some Credit?

As McDonald's made tangible progress with its suppliers on animal welfare, PETA declared victory. McDonald's reasoning for these changes was perhaps best captured by Riker: "PETA had nothing to do with any of this. They took themselves out of the discussion two years ago and we have moved away from PETA."[47]

When I gave speeches and answered questions from agricultural groups who thought we are simply kowtowing to PETA, I explained that we were doing no such thing. I countered that PETA was good at bringing forth an issue important to consumers, but that the consumer is really the force for change. Bruce Feinberg agreed, noting that:

[t]he tipping point was really consumer based. Consumers were really more interested and more demanding, wanting to understand what was going on with their food. They started to ask for more transparency. How are the animals raised? They expected McDonald's to act on their behalf and do the right thing.

But did PETA really have nothing to do with McDonald's decision?

If PETA's claims were only half-baked, it would have been easy to dismiss them. But a picture of the crammed hens in the cages spoke the truth to the consumer and to many involved at McDonald's.

I've always advocated that if you are not comfortable with a certain practice shown in a picture or story in *The New York Times*, then you ought to change the practice. This was the case for our internal McDonald's stakeholders. We thought the practices surrounding laying hens were not the right thing to do.

While I certainly did not enjoy dealing with PETA, and although I found their tactics and ethics unsavory, I do ask myself a couple of questions: "Is there a place for the PETAs of the world?" and "Does PETA deserve some credit for ushering the change?"

The upside of activism is shining a light on important issues. Good activists work on affecting emotions, creating messages and campaigns that tug at the hearts of people. They set the stage for others to find solutions. Was PETA such a group? Or did their brand of activism extend too far into extremism, venturing beyond civility and legal and ethical boundaries?

I don't necessarily mind activist antics, as long as they stay within legal and ethical boundaries. For example, I thought Greenpeace showing up at our U.K. restaurants (see Chapter 9) dressed up like chickens to promote their report, "Eating Up the Amazon," was brilliant. Greenpeace did not damage our restaurants nor treat anyone with disrespect.

Michael Specter wrote a superior profile of Ingrid Newkirk, president and cofounder of PETA, in an article published in 2003 in *The New Yorker* titled "The Extremist."[48] He profiled the woman behind PETA's creation in 1980 and the thinking behind the brazen broadside campaigns PETA has launched in the name of animal rights. Specter wrote that:

> People for the Ethical Treatment of Animals describes itself as an "abolitionist organization," and its thirteen word mission statement (at that time), while simple, is breathtaking in its ambition: "All animals are not ours to eat, wear, experiment

on, or use for entertainment." PETA believes that animals, and by this it means all animals, from crustaceans to chimpanzees, are on earth to occupy themselves and for no other reason. That humans take advantage of other animals in any way, simply because we are stronger, smarter, PETA sees as the abiding moral outrage of our time."

"… from the start, PETA was more radical than any of the other more established animal welfare groups." And Newkirk loved the attention and stirring the pot. He quoted Newkirk: "We are complete press sluts. It is our obligation. We would be worthless if were just polite and didn't make waves."

PETA, the Humane Society of the United States, and other animal rights organizations succeeded because they brought forth issues that made companies and their consumers uncomfortable. Animal producers did not experience the consumer backlash against animal agriculture, which emphasized efficiency and highly intense housing conditions. For example, though I cringe at the derogatory term of "factory farming" for modern animal agriculture, I believe it portrays some truth.

Paul Simmons, leading the day-to-day animal welfare audit program, was quite aware of PETA's brand of activism, noting that, "The overlay of activism was based on all emotion, and most of it was grounded in not having animals as food, to be honest." Simmons did not like how PETA twisted the truth:

An animal activist group will have a video of an animal kicking or something on a shackle that's completely unconscious, and they will take that to a news media to make fundraising and whatever they say, "Look how these animals are being tortured." And it was bad science, bad communication.[49]

Simmons said McDonald's animal welfare team was highly motivated to get to the truth: "We were passionate about this. Let's clear the facts because it was being polluted out there with bad information. Our neighbors talk about this. Our friends talk about this. They don't have the facts. So this actually helped bring the facts to the table."

I believe it is hard to give any credit to an extremist-type organization. Specter pointed out that such extremism "raises the question of whether PETA's shock tactics and abrasiveness might be so unsavory that they offend many of the people the group wishes to attract." Even Singer, a philosophical soul mate to Newkirk, states in the Specter profile: "Publicity is a tactic that has worked well for them. Ingrid constantly risks offense, but she seems to feel it does more good than harm."

Temple Grandin also has noted her concerns with today's activists vs the leaders of the past, such as Henry Spira. Temple said, "Henry Spira was a very affective activist. He was an old labor negotiator for the Maritime Union. Henry knew when to lay the hammer down, when to back off. Another thing about Henry Spira is his word was good."[50]

Grandin is not so forgiving when it comes to some of today's tactics, especially those that mix a vegan agenda with that of animal welfare. She said:

> What's happening now with the activist groups is they're going more the vegan approach. It's "let's work to get rid of the meat industry, not fix it." What worries me now today with activists is everything is getting too abstract. You're getting a kid that's coming out of law school, never actually had a real job. So all the issues are abstract. They don't even know what's going on out on the ground.

In tracing the progress on animal welfare, as with any larger social movement and cultural shift, no one leader or organization drives change. It's a confluence of many forces. As Specter wrote in *The Extremist*:

> It has been argued many times that in any social movement there has be somebody radical enough to alienate the mainstream—and to permit more moderate influences to prevail. For every Malcolm X there is a Martin Luther King, Jr., and for every Andrea Dworkin there is a Gloria Steinem.

I believe this is consistent with McDonald's experience. Without the noise PETA was making and without the media spreading the word about the issue, I have no doubt that the momentum for change in laying hen conditions would have been slower. Without PETA's agitation and aggression, the runway would have been too short and bumpy for Grandin and Mench to launch their reasonable and scientific methods for changing the world and for changing McDonald's (and others') animal welfare practices.

Hard Knock Nuggets

Ideas to Neutralize the Extremist

1. Develop a counterstrategy.
   - The biggest lesson by far from this story about PETA against McDonald's is how important it is to partner with credible experts, who can help the company in two ways:
     - Assist in developing tangible actions to address the real issue at hand.
     - Stand up for the company's efforts because not too many people will believe the company.
2. Set up advisory groups.
   - Determine when to sunset the council.
   - Establish term periods for council members. What if you are stuck with an unproductive council member? What happens if things change?
   - Don't assume you need to compensate council members. The best and most credible financial setup is to pay only travel expenses. This preserves the independence and credibility of your council members. This worked for some of the councils we set up, but not all. For instance, we felt we couldn't get the best global nutritional experts without paying an honorarium ($7,500 each annually in the mid-2000s).
   - Be transparent in what you pay your council members. External critics are wary of organizations that hide how their funding works. They might not like you paying third-party experts, who, in their minds, tarnishes their independence, but it is far worse to not be open.

3. Don't settle for a mealy toast communication effort.
   Riker struck back and talked tough in order to counter the PETA campaign. You don't always want to take on the enemy, largely because doing so can give them more attention. However, when you do pick your battles, go for it.

   - Acknowledge the larger issue at hand as being legitimate.

   - Be humble; be willing to truly say, "we're not perfect" and "we can do better."

   - Argue your case with facts and third-party voices.

4

The Battle to Be Proactive
Happy Meal Toys and the Ups and Downs of Anticipatory Issues Management

The General Life Cycle of an Issue

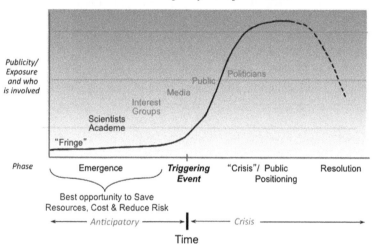

Fig. 4.1: The Anticipatory Issues Management Model Provides a Playbook for Offense on Emerging Issues.
Source: Courtesy of Dr Deborah Anderson.

The AIM Evangelist Meets the Global Safety Officer

Mike Donahue was watching the BBC one night in early 2000. The network aired a story about the danger of phthalates in toys. Phthalates[51] are softening chemical agents that make plastic more pliable. Phthalates are a possible endocrine disrupter, with children a particularly at-risk age group.[52] The story showed a toddler sucking on a plastic teething ring.

"I put phthalates on the AIM chart," Donahue said. "We've got this in our Happy Meal toys. It could be a problem."[53] So began McDonald's first foray in anticipatory issues management (AIM).

In his role as McDonald's director of government affairs, Donahue had been a close partner of mine during the antipolystyrene foam days in the late 1980s and early 1990s. We worked together to fight against legislative bans on the polystyrene foam container. Donahue was the company's lead lobbyist for a reason. He prided himself on his ability to persuade and be an appropriately loquacious advocate for the McDonald's brand.

His experience in government affairs convinced him that McDonald's needed to graduate from being the victim of the external issues that affected McDonald's to a proactive player forging solutions ahead of a crisis. Donahue presented the business case for doing so to McDonald's management. The company authorized him to create a public and community affairs department (PC&A) in 1999. I was one of his first internal recruits.

My mentor, Shelby Yastrow, had retired in 1998, and my role as senior director of environmental affairs was moved over to worldwide supply chain, where I reported to Tom Albrecht, the top global supply chain officer.

When Donahue approached me about joining his new group, I relished the opportunity. I thought PC&A would provide a broader platform for corporate social responsibility (CSR) at McDonald's beyond supply chain. Plus, I fully bought-in to the concept of playing offense rather than playing defense. While Donahue was on a crusade for the company to adopt a more proactive stance on public issues, he didn't have the compelling model—or framework to do so.

I found him the model.

I ran across an article by a former executive of Procter & Gamble, Deborah Anderson, who created a proactive emerging issues management model called anticipatory issues management.[54] The AIM model resonated with me because our past decade of history clearly demonstrated how we waited too long to confront issues. The list was long: arguments that we were filling up landfills with our packaging waste and polystyrene foam; claims from some environmentalists that McDonald's was using beef from the Amazon[55]; accusations from environmentalists accusing McDonald's of using ozone depleting CFCs in our foam packaging[56]; PETA demonstrations at our restaurants and annual shareholders' meetings claiming abusive animal slaughtering practices; and campaigns coming from a converted public health advocate, Phil Sokolof, who was campaigning against McDonald's and other fast food restaurants for "poisoning America with high cholesterol menus."[57]

I met with Donahue and gave him the article by Anderson and told him that the AIM model should be the model we use to manage emerging issues. Donahue said, "I remember the day as clear as a bell. I think I carried it in my briefcase for three, four months. One day I was on a plane and finally the time needed to read it, and I went nuts."

"Nuts" to Donahue meant he became evangelical, with a zeal unmatched by any other leader I've known in my career. His zeal propelled him to make AIM a fundamental new approach for McDonald's to proactively manage trending societal issues that could impact our business. When watching that BBC piece on phthalates in toys, he placed his first big AIM bet on addressing the phthalates in Happy Meal toys. He went to Joe Beckwith, the senior vice president of global safety with the AIM model in hand. Donahue and I both realized that it would take a tried and tested executive skilled in the no fluff operational speak for the company to change from a reactive to a proactive culture.

Beckwith was the perfect champion to introduce the AIM model, as he was a thirty-year McDonald's veteran who had earned accolades and respect during his rise up the ranks from a store trainee in 1969. When Donahue approached him about AIM, Beckwith said, "I thought it was great. I was up to my eyeballs with the CSPC [Consumer Product Safety Commission] on playground safety, and going there to testify every quarter and having to give injury reports quarterly to the CSPC."[58]

In 1999, the U.S. Consumer Product Safety Commission (CPSC) and McDonald's Corp. announced that the restaurant chain had agreed to pay the government $4 million in damages for failing to inform CPSC of playground injuries at some of its restaurants. The settlement resolved a dispute arising from enforcement of the 1995 Playground Equipment Reporting Agreement between McDonald's and the U.S. government. The injuries involved the Big Mac Climber, a metal platform resembling a hamburger.[59]

Donahue explained the AIM model to Beckwith (see Fig. 4.1). What AIM illustrated was that by waiting and ignoring for public issues to go through a natural evolution—from initial knowledge and awareness to saturation through fringe groups and academics—an eventual crisis occurs in which activists, media, lawyers, and politicians become involved. By that point, solutions typically become costly and inefficient.[60]

The AIM model shows that if you wait for the triggering event (such as the *Mobro* barge described in Chapter 1, which launched a media craze about the dangers of running out of room for trash), you've lost your chance to address the problem in a rational, scientific, and economical way. This model explains the advantages of taking on and solving societal issues when they emerge, before the hoopla of media, politicians, and lawyers turns it into something unmanageable. At the point of emergence, you should analyze and assess the issue and seek solutions, while you have the time and resources to do so in a noncrisis climate.

Donahue warned Beckwith to avoid a triggering event affecting the Happy Meal. He showed him how Mattel, Gerber, and Hasbro were all dealing with triggering events in their businesses.[61] Teething rings were the center of attention, and the toy brands were scrambling to manage phthalates in their products. He got Beckwith's attention and passion when he asked, "how long will it take before a TV camera crew shows up at a restaurant and video tapes a child with a Happy Meal toy in their mouth?" Beckwith went to work with a vengeance.

With poor results from the various reactive steps Beckwith had attempted regarding playground safety, he was more than receptive to AIM. He started to pursue the idea of quickly getting rid of phthalates, before McDonald's was linked to the health scares associated with this endocrine disrupter. When he approached marketing, however, they thought he was overreacting. Some people joked about reverting to wooden toys. Nevertheless, Beckwith persisted. Donahue said:

> The first time I used the AIM process was with Joe [Beckwith]. I said, "This is going to be a triggering event." I showed him a media piece on teething rings, and within two weeks, Joe ordered the suppliers—even though they were telling him they couldn't make toys as bright, that they wouldn't be as pliable—he pushed them to be more innovative and found out those were just passive-aggressive resistance, and in record time he got it done. The result was an opening bell that became a clarion call for McDonald's to be more proactive on socially responsible issues.

Beckwith was a down-to-earth, burly guy who cracked jokes despite the serious nature of the work he led. He was determined, too. This determination is what lent him the authority to get phthalates out of toys despite resistance from suppliers and marketing.

When Beckwith was offered the global safety officer position, he met with senior management and laid it on the line with his concern that they not "shoo him away" when it came to substantial safety issues. He had seen that too often, when officers brought something to management and then "they sent you to get more facts, sent you out to research it further. They never said no. They just shooed you away."

Beckwith told CEO Jack Greenberg and the other McDonald's department presidents that:

> I will not be shooed away. I will not bother you with trivial stuff, and I will bring you solutions. There's a lot of what we'll need to do that won't make us money or have a return for the company, issues like playground equipment, food safety issues, OSHA issues, or environmental issues. I'm going to bring you unpleasant stuff. I'm going to be a thorn in your side, but that's the job you're putting me into.

Greenberg and the top execs agreed, providing Beckwith the leeway to make the toy change. As it happened, other, safer softening agents were available, but they had not been tested in toys and were available only in small quantities. It took a year to set up a supply of alternatives.

As Donahue and I approached our internal colleagues from various departmental functions involved with this public issues (e.g., legal, supply chain, communications, operations, government relations, marketing), we gathered enthusiastic support.

We created an AIM cross-functional team, our equivalent to the working relationship between the FBI and the CIA. We combed the globe for emerging issues that might impact our brand, operations, and/or supply chain. We put these issues on our radar screen and began to prioritize them and create action plans. We had finally found a process and a framework to become proactive. The fact that we finally had a formal AIM team made it much easier to forge internal solution discussions. AIM was not a panacea for all issues and problems, though. First, it can be easy to miss emerging issues. Second, departments within the company might not even think systemically about decisions they make.

The Limits of AIM

For example, in Summer 2006 I started to receive the most letters ever addressed to me, all slamming the McDonald's Happy Meal featuring

Hummer trucks. Environmentalists thought this was horrible, since Hummer vehicles were criticized as over-the-top gas guzzlers. They argued that including the toy in Happy Meals made McDonald's look hypocritical since we touted our energy efficiency efforts. *The New York Times* reported the issue:

Would You Like a Gas Guzzler With That?

When General Motors introduced the three-ton, 11-miles-to-the-gallon Hummer H2 four years ago, it redefined American extravagance. But now, with gas prices hovering at $3 a gallon and threatening to go higher, sales of Hummers are declining as Americans become increasingly conscious of gas mileage.

McDonald's, however, appears not to have gotten the message. This week, the restaurant chain started putting toy Hummers in children's Happy Meal boxes, calling it the "Hummer of a Summer" promotion. Television and radio ads, which started running this week, feature a family riding in a Hummer on the way to a McDonald's.[62]

I approached marketing leadership and asked if they had considered the consequences of the Hummer marketing effort, given that some people thought the Hummer was a prime example of wasteful, over-the-top energy use. What I heard was disheartening. No one in marketing had even thought about the Hummer's negative association. How could that happen? Don't they read the newspapers? This is what happens when you are myopic in your work: You don't see other possible connections.

Internally, I was vocal about my displeasure that marketing didn't even consider this. If you do such a promotion, I argued, you should have both knowledge of the critics and a plan to deal with them. We had none. Externally, I defended McDonald's publicly in what I thought was a sincere way, noting that the Hummer was for fun, just a toy. I detailed my response to the criticism in a weekly CSR blog, "Open for Discussion," which I maintained for several years:

… I polled my staff that have or had children. One of them said her children enjoy the little Hummer replicas as toys, just as many kids like toy trucks, regardless of make or model. She drives a Mini Cooper, walks with her children to get groceries, bicycles with them on weekends, etc. Another said her grandchildren absolutely love the toy Hummers—that they're fun.

Of course, there's nothing scientific about this poll, but I think it makes an important point. Looked at through children's eyes, the miniature Hummers are just toys, not vehicle recommendations...[63]

Not everyone in the environmental community was happy with my response, one saying that I was "being either naïve or disingenuous." I didn't agree, but I did believe that, by not looking ahead at what could happen, we inadvertently created an unnecessary event that tarnished our brand. It showed how AIM works for all functions of a company.

Although AIM works across departments and divisions, the work done using this model can be overlooked. There are no heroes when you prevent a problem before it becomes a critical issue. The proactive solution does not have the hoopla that resolving a crisis does. Those who solve emerging issues, early, before the crisis point, are invisible. However, heroes are made in successfully handling a crisis. They get President's Awards. Beckwith describes this phenomenon well:

> Someone in the company solves a problem way ahead of time. The issue's gone. Nobody ever knows about it. Then there's no way to measure it. It's simply handled. There's never recognition for the person leading change because nobody ever knows how big an issue it would have been or could have been.

Indeed, identifying issues to put on the AIM radar list is easier than actually solving those issues. Doing something about it is a business challenge, mostly due to the impracticality of addressing every emerging issue, each with an unknown future. Even Beckwith admits to that thinking. He said, "There's a side of me, operationally, that says, 'You can't get involved in every single issue.'" Even if in doubt, Beckwith advises to at least develop a what-if scenario:

> Certainly, you can weigh things when they're out in the fringe area as to whether or not something like that could ever have an impact on you. If you think it may impact the company, at least then you can begin to put a plan together for what you would do. You may never use it, but if this becomes a big, mainstream issue, you won't be caught by surprise.

Hard Knock Nuggets

Getting Ahead of Issues

I thought then, and still believe now, that the practice of not proactively handling emerging social and environmental issues is a major flaw throughout the business world. Time and time again, companies prove that it's wait, wait, wait for the crisis. Then, by golly, the company leaps in, galvanized with orders from on top to form a SWAT team to solve it. Time is crunched. Science is discounted. There's a rush to placate public perception. Excessive costs are ignored. Their brand is tarnished. And the solution is most often temporal and half-baked.

Instead, companies of all types can succeed by taking proactive measures to deal with issues before they become a crisis and cause panics throughout the organization. Here are a few tips for doing just that:

- **Develop an AIM radar map:** Ensure that there is a cross-functional team identifying and monitoring issues on a regular basis.

- **Develop solution scenarios:** Not every issue is going to impact your business, but for those that have reasonable odds of doing so, create, at a minimum, an assessment of the issue with recommendations to implement change if things hit the fan.

- **Listen and explore:** It's useful to explore issue characterization (what people on all sides of an issue think about it) by talking with external, relevant stakeholders. You will be surprised what you learn when you hold conversations beyond the four walls of your office.

- **Don't be afraid to ask the experts:** Some argue that talking with external stakeholders is akin to opening Pandora's box. If you show you are concerned about an issue, you may stir them to act against your company. I believe that the risk of staying insulated against complex issues is far more risky. Outside experts, chosen wisely, shows your company cares, puts a human face on the company, and creates the potential to have constructive dialogue. Most companies can't hide from problems anymore anyway with all of today's transparency requirements.

5

The Battle of the Waistline and Brand Health

The Obesity Dilemma and a Healthier Happy Meal

Fig. 5.1: McDonald's Happy Meal (2018).

There's a Hole in the Roof

Throughout the decade of the 2000s, report after report showed how more and more children were becoming either overweight or obese. McDonald's was at the epicenter of the flurry to find blame.

Critics argued that Happy Meals were making children obese. The clamor of McDonald's culpability regarding the childhood obesity dilemma weighed heavily on the mind of Jan Fields, president of

McDonald's USA. As she chaired a November 2010 meeting of her newly formed Brand Trust Team (BTT), we debated what to do about the Happy Meal. For example, the city of San Francisco was considering banning McDonald's Happy Meals unless it was made healthier.

The Happy Meal problem was a part of a much larger society crisis, as obesity rates were climbing across all ages and genders. Food companies such as McDonald's were challenged to improve the nutritional profile of their food.

I had dealt with many complex issues in my role at McDonald's, but this one topped all. I believed that determining how to handle obesity was one of the most complex societal issues McDonald's would ever face, for a few reasons. First, experts disagreed about what the causes and solutions were for the obesity epidemic. Second, our experience so far showed that healthier food menu items were hard to sell at the volumes McDonald's business model needed. Finally, I wasn't convinced that any change by McDonald's could change the entire industry, as our work in waste and animal welfare did (Chapters 1–3). I'll explain more later.

What we did know was that the business implications were enormous since kids and families were a big slice of what defines McDonald's success. Attacking the Happy Meal was a missile targeted to the heart of McDonald's business. McDonald's nutritional image for the entire corporation was front and center when Fields became president of McDonald's USA business in January 2010.

Fields was a classic underdog success story. She started working a fry station as a part-time worker and full-time mom in 1977. Thirty-three years later, after working her way all the way up the McDonald's ranks, she became one of the most powerful businesswomen, ranked number 25 in *Fortune*'s Most Powerful Women 2010 list.[64]

Up to this time, I knew Fields only by reputation, and everything I had heard was good. I had heard she was an energetic, blunt, direct, and funny, and a genuine people person. She asked me to join the BTT—the first of its kind at McDonald's focused on brand trust. To me, the need to bolster McDonald's brand and reputation was the primary McDonald's business driver when it came to corporate social responsibility (CSR), so I was thrilled to be on this team. Our brand's "emotional" attributes had been in the tank for a decade. McDonald's studied many attributes of the brand's health with our consumer in a very detailed way. Several of the long-term (impacting revenues three years out) fell in the bucket of CSR (including being ethical and responsible, supporting worthwhile charities, sustainable packaging, concern for kids' well-being and concern for societal issues). The results were categorized by their strength of association for McDonald's. Red indicated less than a 35 percent association; Yellow indicated 35–65 percent; and Green indicated more than 65 percent. Most of the CSR attributes ended up as Red. Since McDonald's brand is paramount to its success I believed that, if we addressed improving our brand health, the natural outcome would be to step up our CSR strategy and programs, both in its substance and communication efforts.

At this BTT meeting, I looked around the room at a dozen of Fields's top officers, all of whom impacted McDonald's external reputation, including restaurant operations, human resources, legal, supply chain, marketing, menu, and government relations. My previous conversations with those in the C-suite were usually due to a big problem or crisis. Now I had a real seat at the table to directly influence McDonald's leaders to do more on CSR. Leading CSR is a lot about influencing others, like a conductor who connects with and motivates the musicians in an orchestra.

At this BTT meeting, I observed Fields, her lively banter and inquisitive questions on full display. She had plenty of chutzpah. She knew how to stir the pot, get to the nub of core issues, and lead the team toward action.

Fields knew that the U.S. business was in the midst of an excellent run of sales and guest counts for a number of years:

> We had positive sales, positive guest count, great cash flow; everything was going really, really strong. But as I looked at the information underneath the financials, including customer feedback, I saw this real question about food and our values. Where does our food come from? What are our sustainability practices, such as our animal welfare and forestry policies? There were a number of different emotional brand attributes that really rated low.[65]

So Fields decided to place a big bet on fixing these reputational issues before they hit the cash registers and affected the bottom line. She took the philosophy of the anticipatory issues management framework, whose formal structure ended in 2006, to its highest platform.[66] "When I became president, one of the priorities that I saw was this need to fix the roof while the sun was shining," she said. "We have a hole in the roof, but the sun is shining. And I started attacking these things that were not going our way."

Fields was about to lead the BTT into unchartered territory, managing brand issues as inextricably linked to business success. The soft issues of food sourcing, nutrition, the environment, people, and community were, hopefully, on their way to sharing importance alongside traditional hard operating measures such as daily guest counts, sales, and speed and accuracy of service.

Fields directed the BTT team to have a razor focus on food and people. She said, "With food, we knew we needed to do something about Happy Meals, and our responsibility to children."

An Avalanche Hits the Happy Meal

Karen Wells, head of menu, gave a briefing to the BTT of her recent trip to San Francisco where she testified at a hearing about banning the Happy Meal toy unless the meal was made healthier, with fewer calories and less sugar, fat, and salt. Outside McDonald's, she felt alone, with no external friends, no support at all. When it came to health and obesity, we didn't have too many allies.

I never considered the Happy Meal healthy per se, but I never considered it unhealthy, either. In a 2005 public report my team developed for our board of directors, we listed all the nutritional components of the two most popular Happy Meals. One consisted of 34 percent of the daily requirements for calories for a six-year-old girl; the other 31 percent. Fats ranged from 26 percent (for the hamburger meal) to 44 percent (McNugget meal). I thought that was decent for a kid's meal.

McDonald's rolled out the United States' first Happy Meal in 1979. It came with the standard hamburger or cheeseburger option, as well as french fries, cookies, a soft drink and, of course, a toy. Chicken McNuggets were added as a Happy Meal option in 1983. Otherwise, the Happy Meal has stayed the same for three decades. Kids are not easy to feed. Any parent can attest to this. Why do you think macaroni and cheese is such a staple at home? We had tried all sorts of healthier meals for children, with no success.

We were successfully stuck on hamburgers and McNuggets because kids loved them—and their parents loved that they loved them. They were a treat. Yet although we served 70 million customers a day (in 2018), people tended to feel guilty. There were many reasons for this guilt, but chief among them was the feeling for the Happy Meal customer that the meal was not good for their children. Indeed, an important brand health measure that we monitored asked customers if they felt "good about eating our food." This measure had been scoring in the red zone for several years.

In addition, and in fact most concerning, was the decline in Happy Meals sales. In 2011, Happy Meal and other child meal sales were down 6 percent, from 1.3 billion to 1.2 billion orders.[67]

The BTT had faced a Himalayan-sized obstacle build of accumulated negative assaults on its food in the past decade (see Sidebar below). We felt we were at the center of a war on two fronts: one was about obesity; the other stereotyped modern agriculture as factory farming. These twin issues fostered campaigns, legislation, books, movies, and various op-ed pieces, which all felt like an avalanche.

McDonald's had become synonymous with junk food. It was the ultimate insult to us. Junk food references were not only about food devoid of nutritional and quality ingredients but also food devoid of good sourcing practices toward people, the environment, and animals. Fields often said in her public speeches that, "McDonald's became synonymous with things like Kleenex was for tissue. McDonald's was the symbol for bad food or bad behavior."

2001–2010: The Dark Decade for McDonald's

During the 2000s, McDonald's faced a mountain of accumulated negative criticism about our food. From Eric Schlosser's accusatory book *Fast Food Nation* to Morgan Spurlock's mockumentary *Super Size Me*, from issues with obesity and calorie counts, to various lawsuits, the corporation was fighting on several fronts.

2001: *Fast Food Nation* Details the Dark Side of McDonald's and Fast Food

This book fast became a *New York Times* bestseller, especially popular as recommended reading for college students. The book began inculcating young people to the stereotypes that McDonald's sells unsafe food that comes from factory farms, exploits workers, and destroys the environment.

Indeed, Eric Schlosser stated his purpose at the end of the book's introduction: "I've written this book out of a belief that people should know what lies behind the shiny, happy surface of every fast food transaction" he wrote. "They should know what really lurks between those sesame-seed buns. As the old saying goes: You are what you eat."

2002: Two Obese Teenagers Sue McDonald's

This lawsuit was similar to the hot coffee lawsuit in the 1990s. It was frivolous, but—wow—did it get a lot of attention.

Two teenagers blamed McDonald's marketing practices, meals, and their lack of accessible information to make good nutritional choices for their obesity. Their attorney, John Banzhaf, said, "When we're suing on behalf of children, it's hard to argue that a six-, or eight-, or ten-year-old child has to take full responsibility for their decisions when they're lured into McDonald's by the toys and the playground and Happy Meals and the birthday parties."[68] Although this lawsuit was dismissed the next year, the strategy to argue that McDonald's was luring helpless kids into overeating was very similar to the advertising for tobacco products, and it became a formidable narrative picked up by many activists.

2003: The Surgeon General Calls Out Obesity as an Epidemic

This report reverberated across our country and our company. The U.S. surgeon general put an official stamp on the emerging obesity epidemic. It would accelerate the greater scrutiny of food companies, including McDonald's, and what actions we all would take to help solve the problem. As Surgeon General Dr Richard Carmona declared in July 2003[69]:

> The crisis is obesity. It's the fastest-growing cause of disease and death in America. And it's completely preventable.

1. Nearly two out of every three Americans are overweight or obese.
2. One out of every eight deaths in America is caused by an illness directly related to overweight and obesity.

> America's children are already seeing the initial consequences of a lack of physical activity and unhealthy eating habits. Fortunately, there is still time to reverse this dangerous trend in our children's lives.
>
> Looking back 40 years to the 1960s, when many of us in this room were children, just over four percent of 6- to 17-year-olds was overweight. Since then, that rate has more than tripled, to over 15 percent. And the problem doesn't go away when children grow up. Nearly three out of every four overweight teenagers may become overweight adults.

Carmona also laid out a call to action, declaring we must reduce and eliminate childhood obesity in America, through:

- Increased physical activity;
- Healthier eating habits; and
- Improved health literacy.

2004: McDonald's Settles Trans-Fatty Acid Lawsuit

In 2002, McDonald's announced a phase-out of artery-clogging trans-fatty acid (TFA) cooking oil for MacFries. Instead, the company would locate a healthier option. McDonald's set a target date of eighteen months to complete this initiative. Unfortunately, we failed to meet this deadline for a host of complicated reasons. The transition was more difficult than we imagined, largely because our primary supplier had to plant additional fields of canola seeds to meet our demand. We ended converting to TFA-free oil by 2006 in the United States.

A class action lawsuit penalized our good intentions. The gist of the lawsuit was that McDonald's failed to live up to a promise it made in September 2002 to customers that it would reduce its use of trans fats. Plaintiffs claimed in the lawsuits that McDonald's did not take sufficient steps to inform the public that it had not changed the oil. McDonald's settled in court for $8.5 million.[70]

The handling of TFAs severely hampered my future work on CSR and sustainability, for good reason. McDonald's got punished for trying to do something good.

2004: *Super Size Me* Movie Creates Negative Buzz

Morgan Spurlock released a popular mock documentary, satirical movie, *Super Size Me*. It depicted his thirty-day diet consisting of only McDonald's food. This diet was excessive, running at about five thousand calories a day, during which Spurlock led a sedentary lifestyle. He sat and ate, gained weight, and became unhealthy. No surprise. Five thousand calories a day without exercise would make anyone unhealthy, especially considering that the recommended daily allowance of calories for adult men is two thousand five hundred.

Even so, Spurlock's mockumentary created a big buzz everywhere. It seemed like everyone saw it—and believed at least some of it.

2005: Marketing to Children Battlefront Opens

In 2005, the Institute of Medicine (IOM) of the National Academy of Sciences released a critical critique of food advertising to children. Since McDonald's was one of the largest advertisers to children, we became part of this debate. As such, the IOM study launched a threat to our business. McDonald's relied on connecting to kids and communicating to them through marketing, so losing this ability created consternation.

The IOM report was called "State of Food and Beverage Marketing to Children and Youth: Influence on Diets and Health".[71] It called out children's marketing as a force putting children's health at risk:

> The commercial advertising and marketing of food and beverages are
> intersecting factors that influence the diets and diet-related health of

children and youth. The review indicates that, among many factors, food and beverage marketing influences the preferences and purchase requests of children, influences short-term consumption, may contribute to less healthful diets, and contributes to an environment that puts their health at risk.

2008: Calorie Counts on the Menu Board

In July 2008, calorie counts became a requirement on menus in New York City restaurants and coffee chains. Any restaurant chain with more than fifteen branches nationwide was required to post calorie information in a similar font and location to the item's price. Later, in 2010, Congress passed a national law requiring chain restaurants with twenty or more outlets to list calories and other nutrition information on menus and menu boards.

We were worried about the impact of this transparency. Some of us thought it would make matters worse. For example, customers might be scared away by the five hundred± calories in a Happy Meal. Others thought it could help level the playing field and expose other food chains with calorie counts as McDonald's.

2009: Corporate Accountability Launches Campaign

In 2009, Corporate Accountability International, a small NGO that defined itself as "stopping transnational corporations from devastating democracy, trampling human rights, and destroying our planet," launched a multiyear, full-throttled attack on our brand via their "Value [The] Meal Campaign." They demanded that McDonald's stop marketing to kids; to stop using sponsorships that appealed to children and teenagers; to stop manipulating public health policy and nutrition science; and to provide complete, accurate, nonpromotional information about the health risks of fast food. On a similar tack, in April 2010, the nonprofit began calling for the retirement of Ronald McDonald, saying the venerable mascot fueled childhood obesity.

Corporate Accountability pulled all sort of stunts to get attention. For example, their activists would line up at our annual meetings in May to make emotional arguments about how we were using predatory marketing practices to make kids fat.

2010: Let's Move! Shakes Things Up

Let's Move! was a public health campaign in the United States, led by Michelle Obama, announced in February 2010. She indicated that the campaign would encourage healthier food in schools, better food labeling, and more physical activity for children.

The initiative had the initially stated goal of "solving the challenge of childhood obesity within a generation so that children born today will reach adulthood at a healthy weight." Let's Move! wanted to decrease childhood obesity to 5 percent by 2030.[72]

Once the obesity epidemic hit in the early 2000s, I soberly realized that McDonald's would be under the spotlight until obesity rates decreased.

Soon after the Surgeon General's 2003 obesity callout, I landed a key part of a team created to develop our company strategy on nutrition. We called our effort balanced active lifestyles (BALs). The initiative came about when Jim Cantalupo came out of retirement in 2002. He took over a company in deep trouble. Wall Street was writing us off. Our stock dipped to an all-time low of $12 per share. I remember a *Bloomberg* story depicting McDonald's as "Hamburger Hell"[73] and predicting the demise of our business. We were all on pins and needles. It seemed like our business was in a nosedive.

Cantalupo was a savior for McDonald's business. He turned us around by strategically shifting our focus to getting better, not bigger. This meant he got rid of several partner brands that were a distraction, such as Chipotle, Pret à Manger, and Boston Market. He ripped up the historical growth plan that centered on building more restaurants and collecting rent and royalty fees from franchisees. Instead, he told all of us that we would grow by increasing our sales and profits in existing restaurants, so we could concentrate on better operations and better food. His strategy energized all of us, including me.

When Cantalupo was CEO, we were at the beginning stages of the assault against the Happy Meal. I remember a few of us from the BAL team approached Cantalupo with a proposal on how to explore ways to improve the nutrition of the Happy Meal.

Cantalupo looked at us with his intense eyes, squinting with concentration. He spoke from his heart about how McDonald's needed to lead on the children's obesity issue. I remember him so adamantly caring about the health of kids, our core customer bloc. He felt we had a proactive role to play. He didn't want to play defense. He gave us approval to move ahead with ideas and strategies to address obesity. He ended up putting my boss, Ken Barun, in charge of leading McDonald's efforts to deal with food and nutrition, and, for a few years, I ended up spending the majority of my time learning about nutrition and supporting BAL's three priorities:

- Offer more choice and balance in our menu;

- Provide ways to educate consumers on nutritional aspects of their choices; and

- Promote physical activity.

We tested many things, but nothing seemed to sell enough to stick. Going beyond the traditional hamburger/McNugget, french fry, soft drink Happy Meal was truly difficult.

Cantalupo died of a heart attack in 2004. His eventual successor, Jim Skinner, continued to champion within McDonald's more choice, information, and physical activity. I remember he gave a 2005 heartfelt Business for Social Responsibility conference keynote speech and humbly acknowledged McDonald's difficulty in cracking the code of providing healthier food that people would still purchase in enough volume to be viable. He gave McDonald's a score of A for effort and a humbling C-minus for results. I was impressed with both Skinner's assessment and candor.

The Unhappy Meal: From the Edge of a Cliff to Society Friendly

CEO Jim Skinner was a vocal champion within McDonald's to do more and play a role, emphasizing personal responsibility, too. He supported Fields and the BTT as we deliberated on what to do about the Happy Meal.

Could we figure a way out of this mess? The past ten years of academics, NGOs, nutritionists, and various opinion leaders describing McDonald's as a central obesity villain created a huge wall to hurdle.

Fields took on the nutrition challenge with gusto, and she was a vocal crusader for resurrecting the McDonald's brand. She had changed her own personal lifestyle in the past few years. She had shed weight and became a regular jogger, with almonds always handy at her side.

She wasn't afraid to make decisions. I so welcomed that. It seemed that my corporate life had become a series of meetings to get approval on policies or programs that scores of people could reject. With Fields and the BTT, I felt liberated from the bureaucracy that often accompanies becoming a larger company.

As the BTT started to create its priorities, the Happy Meal topped the list of what we needed to address. Steve Levigne, head of strategy and consumer research, described how Happy Meal sales were down for the past five years, about 5 percent per year. "That decline is almost like falling off the edge of a cliff," he said.[74]

Levigne described four reasons for the precipitous decline.

First, "Our prices kept going up."

Second, McDonald's created its own internal competition by launching the Dollar Menu. "I have this option on Dollar Menu that I can feed the kids."

Third, "A trend started at that time where a lot of parents were going to Panera, or Starbucks, with their kids. Not getting kids' meals. But they were going there for themselves, and then the kids were eating there too."

Finally, "We were hearing from moms that, 'Hey, we need something else. We need something healthier. We need more variety.'"

Neil Golden was the U.S. chief marketing officer, fearless with his opinions, with a wry sense of humor. Golden also "saw a tsunami that was on its way." He had begun to represent the brand as part of external groups such as the Federal Communications Commission Taskforce of Childhood Obesity and Media and the Council of Better Business Bureau, who were examining the impact of food marketing practices on childhood obesity. "People were questioning the merits of McDonald's engaging, or for that matter any marketer engaging, children directly."[75]

Finally, to cap the perfect storm of a declining Happy Meal, Golden recognized that the nutritional composition of the Happy Meal should be enhanced in order to be more in line with guidance from nutrition experts and evolving expectations from parents. The business threat, for example, was significant because McDonald's owned the kids' business. According to Golden, McDonald's Happy Meals represented more than 50 percent of all kid meal businesses in the United States' quick service segment. Because of our dominance, it was difficult to rally support from other fast food restaurants. Their kids' meal business was either small or nonexistent.

Up to this time, the McDonald's food strategy on nutrition was to offer more choices, such as milk, juice, or soda. I supported that strategy. We are not the food police. Who are we to force people to eat in a certain way?

For example, kids could choose apple slices instead of fries. With the images and aromas of McDonald's fries all around them, do you think children would jump for joy to choose apple slices? As Golden said, "moms were telling us 'I don't want to be the bad parent particularly when I'm taking my child out to eat.'" Golden was a champion of the idea endorsed by the entire BTT, that the bottom line was that:

> the Happy Meal is a powerful brand. It means so much to so many people, but it's losing its relevance. So we had to find a

way to give it relevance so that kids would feel good about it, moms would feel great about it, and opinion leaders would implicitly endorse it.

Golden proposed something radical for McDonald's, which would be the first substantive changes to Happy Meals in twenty-five years. First, eliminate choice. Apples would be the default in every Happy Meal. In essence, McDonald's was making the choice for families and their children. Second, the portion size of the fries would be reduced from two hundred thirty calories to a kid-sized one hundred calories. This was extraordinary. We never tailored food for kids. Happy Meals were always a bundle of items off the core adult main menu, such as hamburgers and McNuggets. Third, with every purchase, we would donate a penny to Ronald McDonald House Charities, which helped families find comfort and a home away from home in challenging hospital settings.

"How could McDonald's critics argue against all of this?" asked Golden. All members of the BTT agreed that making this decision was best for our business—and best for our customers and their concerns about health.

On July 2011, Fields made the public announcement on *Good Morning America*, saying that "[w]hat we're doing is offering fruit to every child that comes into a McDonald's, so it is an automatic. We recognize the importance of fruit in a child's diet." CBS News summarized the change[76]:

> McDonald's will reduce the amount of fries in each Happy Meal from 2.4 to 1.1 ounces and add a quarter-cup of apple slices. Consumers may also get pineapple or orange slices, raisins, and carrots, depending on the time of year. Previously, McDonald's had offered kids' meal customers a choice between fries and apples with caramel dipping sauce

> Although it might not sound like much, replacing some fries with fruits can trim over 100 calories from a Happy Meal. For example, a hamburger meal that used to contain 590 calories will dip to 470 calories—measurements that factor in a kid will order the default soda instead of other options the company is introducing, like fat-free chocolate milk. Kids can also opt for more fruit instead of the fries.

> Some experts applaud the changes.

> "These types of incremental improvements in popular meals can have a broad impact on public health," said Dr Adam

Drewnowski, director of the center for obesity research at the University of Washington, in a written statement. "Better to improve the diets of many than to seek perfection for the few."

Fields gave a lot of credit to Michelle Obama for this, and for her Just Move! initiative, which brought the issue of obesity into the light. "I respect that she truthfully did bring an issue to light that was there," Fields said. "Children are growing up obese, inactive, and that has to change."

Michelle Obama made a positive statement regarding these changes, noting that:

> McDonald's is making continued progress today by providing more fruit and reducing the calories in its Happy Meals. I've always said that everyone has a role to play in making America healthier, and these are positive steps toward the goal of solving the problem of childhood obesity. McDonald's has continued to evolve its menu, and I look forward to hearing about the progress of today's commitments, as well as efforts in the years to come.[77] There were, however, some detractors. For example, one of our constant critics, Dr Marion Nestle, a preeminent nutritional expert from New York University, continued her jabs at our efforts. During a segment on CBS News, she said that:

> It's a step—a tiny step in the right direction. I don't happen to think that potatoes are poison, and I think it's great they're giving out fewer of them because they're fried. But what I'm hoping for is a default Happy Meal where everything that's in it [is something] parents don't have to worry about.[78]

Various opinions on the changes we made to the Happy Meal raised some important issues. Some negative feedback, for example, came to consumers who balked at the kid-sized portion of fries. But one of the biggest questions we had was "Did this Happy Meal change benefit McDonald's business and have a positive impact on society?" From a business perspective, Golden reported to the BTT that the Happy Meal saw improvements in sales and in perceptions:

> The Happy Meal went from a perceived symbol of questionable nutrition to a symbol of good, because the nutritional composition was good and balanced better.

The only real resistance was the smaller portion of fries, and it was from parents who said, "I like the larger portion of fries because I eat some of them, and now there's not as much for me to eat."

The societal scorecard was more difficult to calculate and assess. On one hand, McDonald's was addressing arguably the most important societal problem linked to our business. As far as I was concerned, childhood obesity trumped climate change, sustainable beef, and recycling. On the other hand, McDonald's real impact was relatively small, with external limitations to creating transformative, scalable change. Sure, we reduced calories in an average Happy Meal by 20 percent. That is good and significant. We also addressed a real need: childhood obesity. We were on our way to making fruit fun for kids. At that time, McDonald's impacted 100 percent of the approximately 700 million annual Happy Meals consumed by kids in the United States.[79] We were doing our part. However, the average child visits McDonald's a bit less than three times a month. McDonald's serves three of their ninety meals a month.

A young child may need 1,800 calories a day. That's 54,000 calories a month. With our changes to the Happy Meal, the child who comes to McDonald's was now eating about 1,400 monthly calories from McDonald's, less than 3 percent of their total diet.

Unlike what we did with waste, animal welfare, and laying hens, the changes we made to the Happy Meal did not lead to any systemic change in how children universally eat. McDonald's had lots of restaurants in the United States (twenty-six thousand in 2011) but there were close to a million others to choose from as well. It wasn't like the EDF Waste Reduction task force partnership where our moves were replicated and multiplied by most companies.

McDonald's certainly has a role to play in addressing obesity, yet it requires a huge societal village and a vast network of government, academic, community, corporate and NGO collaborators, and change agents. In my view, McDonald's is a needed, responsible player within this network, but McDonald's alone is not going to turn around the obesity trend.

Adding to the challenge, eating too much food is only half the problem. In my lifetime, I have seen the dual evolution of cheap, abundant food combined with a remote-control, sit-down society. According to the World Health Organization, "More than 80 percent of the world's adolescent population is insufficiently physically active."[80]

Nevertheless, McDonald's tried hard to make food changes—and we failed frequently. For example, we developed many salad entrées. I thought they were delicious. But selling them was a challenge. During one BTT meeting, our head of operations reported an average of just seven salads sold per day per restaurant. We had the same experience with veggie burger tests. Every test of really good veggie burgers had dismal sales results. That's not viable. By way of comparison, we typically sold roughly one thousand two hundred hamburgers per restaurant per week.

The one sustaining success is that the healthier Happy Meal evolved even more. Two years later, in September 2013, McDonald's did more to enhance the nutritional profile of the Happy Meal. McDonald's found an NGO partner, the Alliance for a Healthier Generation (AHG), which modeled the characteristics of other successful partnerships we built with the Environmental Defense Fund, Conservation International, and Dr Temple Grandin. McDonald's committed to additional big changes in its joint announcement with AHG:

- Provide customers a choice of a side salad, fruit, or vegetable as a substitute for french fries in value meals. (Salad, fruit, or vegetable option varied per participating market.)

- Promote and market on menu boards and in-store and external advertising only water, milk, and juice as the beverage options in Happy Meals.

- Utilize Happy Meal and other packaging innovations and designs to generate excitement for fruit, vegetable, low- or reduced-fat dairy, or water options for kids.

- Dedicate Happy Meal box or bag panels to communicate a fun nutrition or children's well-being message.

- Ensure that 100 percent of all advertising directed to children includes a fun nutrition or children's well-being message.[81]

This was a big deal. Most impressive to me was that we were taking soda off the kids' menu. They still could choose it if they like, but it was not an overt choice. The marketed options now were juice, water, or milk. This impressed me because we forsook the higher profit margins of soda. We truly were doing this to do the right thing.

I commend the AHG to collaborate with McDonald's. They had the courage to break from the pack that viewed McDonald's as a nutritional villain. AHG was independent and they challenged us, yet they also were flexible and positive in their approach. Actual progress was made. I am convinced that if other public health NGOs and academics adopted a similar approach, our society would be making a bigger dent in curbing obesity.

The Death and Resurrection of Brand Trust

The work I did with the Jan Fields's BTT was one of my favorite periods at McDonald's because it elevated CSR and sustainability to the C-Suite of McDonald's USA business. Together we achieved major steps in building brand trust. In addition to the revised Happy Meal, the BTT developed several strategies to improve both what we do and how we communicate what we do:

- All white meat chicken for McNuggets
- New premium roast coffee made with 100 percent Arabica beans
- Paper-based cups to replace polystyrene foam
- National Employment Day, during which McDonald's pledged to hire a hundred thousand people within the next year (2011)
- A national listening tour by Jan Fields to show openness and transparency
- A new sustainability team established for McDonald's USA, with new dedicated headcount, led by Dan Gorsky, in addition to his role of leading our U.S. supply chain
- Approval of an environmental strategy to address energy, waste reduction, recycling, and supply chain impacts

I believed the BTT was turning the brand around. But in early 2012, according to Steve Levigne, head of strategy and consumer research, the pressures of gaining short-term sales comps brought an end to the BTT. Levigne said, "[y]ou know, this was never designed to get comps immediately. This was a long-term brand health initiative." After two years, with the underperforming financial results in the U.S. business, McDonald's disbanded the BTT. The death of the BTT crushed me. Fields was light-years ahead of what these social issues meant for the business.

To this day, I still don't understand why this all happened, but other dynamics were at play because Fields was fired soon thereafter (in mid-November 2012). Fields displayed her usual chutzpah upon leaving, causing an internal stir when she told *Fortune* that, "[e]veryone has a date stamped on their ass and they're the only one who can't see it."[82]

Fields wouldn't do the politically correct thing and go out without a whimper or even with an insincere "I want to spend more time with my family" statement that others before Fields had used. It was that straight-shooting style that made me so enjoy working with her.

But BTT was not entirely dead because, concurrently and at a global level, McDonald's was redefining its brand ambition. I served as a member of that team as well. CEO Don Thompson charged the brand ambition team with energizing our internal system around a set of core aspirations that would define what McDonald's stood for. Thompson said that:

> [w]e had some underlying data that really did show that, functionally, we were a fabulous brand. Convenience. Strong in consistency. But we weren't known for the softer side of the brand, that emotional connection, in enough ways. When you get measures like that, it's only a matter of time before you're going to have some challenges.[83]

Thompson envisioned this new brand ambition as galvanizing the McDonald's system through its roots and rich heritage. But it took a while to get there. After a year's work, we produced our end product. I loved what we created. I thought it captured a future for the company that was both ambitious and possible. I also believed that it captured the true beliefs that all of us in global brand, communication, marketing, and CSR leadership positions sincerely believed to encompass everything McDonald's could be and should be:

2012 McDonald's Brand Ambition

Our purpose goes beyond what we sell. We're using our reach to be a positive force.

For our customers. Our people. Our communities. Our world.

Good Food

We promote choices. Real ingredients. Great taste. Transparency.

Good People

We create opportunity. Encourage diversity. Offer training. Facilitate teamwork.

Reward achievement.

Good Neighbor

We champion happy, healthy kids. Keep families together through Ronald McDonald House Charities. Commit to reducing our footprint. Using less energy. And recycling more.

Thompson described the new McDonald's brand ambition initiative as "a *Back to the Future* of what McDonald's was founded on." He said the brand ambition was about "[b]eing a good neighbor through Ronald McDonald House Charities, and through supporting local schools, and supporting local teams, and being a great hirer of people. We want to have really well-trained, well-positioned people who had some upward mobility in society."

Of course food remained front and center for us. "Though we understood we were not considered gourmet cuisine," Thompson said, "our food came from great farmers and suppliers. We took a lot of care in the quality and production of our food."

I was excited that our CEO was talking so prominently about sustainability as a key part of McDonald's brand ambition. As Thompson said, "[w]e were discussing how we could be even stronger citizens of the sustainable world."

This exciting new brand ambition initiative was launched at McDonald's biannual worldwide convention in 2012 with much fanfare. Indeed, the initiative set the stage for creating the first ever sustainability strategic framework (see Chapter 12). Soon, the visibility of "Good Food, Good People, Good Neighbor" was omnipresent in messages, exhibits, communication pieces, and sessions—and in spirit.

Brand and Business Inextricably Linked

- **Fix the roof while the sun is shining.** That's what Jan Fields said and believed. She put that proactive philosophy into action through her BTT. Too many leaders wait for a crisis to hit before taking action. Fields's brand trust vision was the right strategy, but she was not given enough time to deliver. Everything I have learned from the brand experts at McDonald's is that it takes three to five years to change brand perceptions. The McDonald's USA BTT lasted but two years. I believe a core solution to McDonald's growth was prematurely eliminated.

- **Make corporate reputation as important as sales, profits, and customer visits.** Managing corporate reputation is often a sidelight in a company. Put a team on it. Set strategic, tactics, and measurements and demand accountability just as you would for the sales team.

- **Serve a social purpose.** Even large institutional investors want more than profit. Who better to quote than Larry Fink, CEO of BlackRock, the largest institutional investor, in his January 2018 letter to all CEOs in their portfolio.[84] As Fink says:

Society is demanding that companies, both public and private, serve a social purpose. To prosper over time, every company must not only deliver financial performance, but also show how it makes a positive contribution to society. Companies must benefit all of their stakeholders, including shareholders, employees, customers, and the communities in which they operate.[85]

This trend of large mainstream investors putting corporate purpose and profit on parallel tracks is only going to grow.

6

The Battle for a Sustainable Supply Chain
From Silence to Sustainable Fish, Less Polluting Hogs, and Better Lives for Tomato Pickers

Fig. 6.1: The Filet-O-Fish: McDonald's First Global
Sustainable Menu Item.

Getting Beyond Ragtag Corporate Responsibility

It was blazing hot in Orlando, Florida, on April 30, 2002. Inside the cavernous convention hall, the air-conditioning was in overdrive, making it frigid indoors. I stood at the back of the hall as the vice president of global quality assurance was doing something never done before. The slender Ken Koziol walked to the podium ready to introduce the concept of sustainability to the huge McDonald's supplier audience.

Were they ready to hear the message and clarion call from Koziol? Were they ready to add what he termed a "fourth element" to

109

McDonald's supply chain? As Koziol spoke, I focused on the audience in order to gauge the reactions of the five hundred owners and top executives who pulled the supply chain levers of McDonald's beef, chicken, potatoes, and beverages.

Koziol described how, together, we would make sustainability a fourth element of supply chain, on par with the fifty-year history of McDonald's commitment to quality, service, and value. He was not introducing a new program; rather, he was advocating for a cultural and mindset change among the supplier community. By making sustainability a cultural issue, he was unleashing the arsenal of supplier talent and resources toward proactively solving societal problems that were both business problems and business opportunities.

Koziol was my first boss when I assumed environmental responsibilities at McDonald's supplier dedicated to packaging (Perseco) described in Chapter 1. We both chuckled about how, back then, in 1998, we knew diddlysquat about environmental matters. Koziol was one of the best forward-looking, big-picture leaders I have ever encountered. No wonder six years later he became senior vice president of innovation; a few years after that, he was promoted to be the top global operations officer.

Koziol had been senior director of U.S. supply chain management during most of the 1990s, and he witnessed the same reactive style of management that had long frustrated me. He described the typical unsophisticated approach we had embraced during this time frame: "The first we heard of issues were from NGOs and the news stories," he said. "For the most part, honestly, we had no idea about them. The first thing we would do is go figure out if we were even involved in this and what it was."[86]

You would think that after a decade's worth of attacks on our company coming from external sources, not to mention McDonald's visible size, scale, and brand power, there would be a more thoughtful, strategic approach to emerging societal issues. There wasn't, though the AIM process was contemporarily evolving (Chapter 4). I believe we thought these pressures were temporal. We were convinced that we were good people doing good work. Plus, the upstream impacts of our supply chain were outside our control.

McDonald's supply chain wasn't alone in scrambling to figure out where supply chain responsibility begins and ends. Nike was ahead of us, and they were getting into more public trouble than even we were. During the same 1990s, Nike was attacked for supporting "sweat shops" that made shoes and apparel in China and elsewhere in Asia. Initially, Nike didn't know how to handle this outside pressure. Their business model was to contract its manufacturing to suppliers. Since they did not own the factories, they didn't see it as their responsibility to manage the social conditions of their suppliers' workers, who were earning meager wages and living in sordid, crowded, dormitory-style housing.[87]

For retailers from Nike to McDonald's, the decade of the 1990s was the dawn of a new era marked by a spotlight on the full supply chain, all the way to the source, which often was multiple steps away from the finished product. Before this time, it was conventional thinking that retailers were not responsible for goods made overseas. The era of transparency had yet to come.

In other words, McDonald's struggle to define its responsibility for the whole stream of supply chain impacts was on par with the struggle other major retail brands were experiencing. We were all trying to figure it out. McDonald's was a more visible and accessible company for scrutiny than most others.

As Koziol stepped into his new role in 2000, he was determined to change the sporadic approach to handling social and environmental issues that were affecting the supply chain. "I wanted to stop playing defense. We had no offense," he said. "There was no sense for where to go, what to do, how to think about it, how to build a strategy."

Koziol's assessment matched mine. The work I had been helping to lead during the past decade was enriching and meaningful, but it was ragtag. I was proud of the big steps that we had taken on waste reduction and animal welfare, as described in Chapters 1–3. However, we did all of that work in reaction to societal pressures. Our work was not yet proactive, as discussed in Chapter 4.

This lack of strategy created an internal perception that we had no real plan. Externally, our battles and victories were considered to be one-offs. These initiatives earned some attention for a bit, but then the issue dissolved like the fizz from a soda, forgotten the next month and next year because they were not connected to a larger framework or narrative that we could constantly reinforce and build upon. The laying hen announcement was a prime example: a piece of big news that quickly faded away.

Remember that the concept of a sustainable food supply chain was virtually nonexistent at that time for the entire food industry. That made it difficult to find an external partner to help us discard our ragtag efforts to tackle societal issues in lieu of adopting a broader, more strategic approach. Even today, most NGOs are focused on a specialty cause, and rightly so, whether animal welfare, the environment, human rights, diversity, and so on. It's difficult to find a broad-based NGO that deals with all societal and cultural issues.

When Koziol was promoted, I decided to take a shot and invite an NGO based in Sweden, which I had found and followed nine years earlier during a trip to McDonald's Sweden. Something remarkable was happening there, and I wanted to see first-hand. Mats Lederhausen was leading a business turnaround success story there by leveraging socially- and environmentally-minded operations and supply chain initiatives to motivate McDonald's staff, appeal to more customers, and turn the business around.

The Next Step: The Natural Step

The gestation process for a sustainable supply chain for McDonald's began in the early 1990s. What I saw and heard in Sweden launched my strategic sustainability quest.

Mats Lederhausen, the spirited, thirty-year-old managing director of McDonald's Sweden, was the first leader within McDonald's to see the practical business upside of corporate responsibility. In 1992, Lederhausen invited us to Sweden to show off their environmental program and introduce us to The Natural Step (TNS), a novel NGO that inspired him to see sustainable business as the way of the future. TNS did not focus on any one narrow concern; rather, it stressed the big picture and prioritized educating business leaders about the broad concept of sustainability and about how to apply these principles to everyday decision-making across core operations.

Lederhausen's father, Paul, had started McDonald's in Sweden, opening its first restaurant in 1973. Lederhausen grew up within McDonald's, loving the American brand. Later, he went to university, served in the military, and worked at Boston Consulting Group in London. When his father needed help to stem a long sales slump, Lederhausen took over the reigns.

During the 2000s, he rose to the top tier of management at McDonald's Global. He was a mentor to me, and working with Lederhausen set me on a transformative path, similar to his own journey. Like me when I had graduated from college years before him, Lederhausen had no particular inclination to think too much about the planet and its ecology. Then he met Karl-Henrik Robért, founder of TNS. Lederhausen noted that:

> When I first got introduced to The Natural Step in the early nineties, they helped me understand what sustainability means and that our current ecological system is unsustainable.

Our current economic system is spending resources faster than our increasingly reduced ecological system can replenish. This affects our ability to sustain life as we know it on this planet.[88]

Lederhausen's thinking was ten, maybe twenty, years ahead of others in seeking a cohesive strategy regarding sustainability, especially with his counterparts at our Oak Brook headquarters, who, as he recounted, "thought we didn't have an environmental problem. There was denial, basically."

Soon, McDonald's Sweden ran its distribution trucks with fuel from its used french fry oil. They committed to using renewable energy, phased out antibiotics, and recycled most of their waste. (Remember this was the early 1990s; even today, companies tout doing these things.) Consumers responded positively to these new initiatives. In fact, McDonald's Sweden's customers loved this side of McDonald's, and sales rebounded, which is exactly what Lederhausen's father had asked him to accomplish.

> This experience really took hold over me. I had the fortune early in my career to see the power of "doing good" and being part of the solution. I saw how it affected our people—how a purpose bigger than just selling hamburgers actually got people animated. Our people worked harder, worked smarter, and it ultimately connected with our consumers.

> I got really enamored with this idea of "Why wouldn't more businesses do this?" It makes sense for the world. It makes sense for McDonald's. It's a win/win/win thing, and since then that's my religion.

His conversion came from this deep-seated practical experience. He didn't arrive at this epiphany intellectually or spiritually. Explaining why he changed, he said, "One of my favorite quotes when it comes to change is that people are more likely to act themselves into a new way of thinking rather than to think themselves into a new way of acting."

The turnaround of McDonald's Sweden's business, so much tied to doing good things, was quite radical compared to McDonald's traditional, conservative, and more functional business approach, so much so that I believe most at the Oak Brook home office discounted it to a Swedish cultural oddity. Though Sweden was a small market for McDonald's (by 2016, there were 220 McDonald's restaurants in Sweden—equivalent to the state of Oklahoma with 217 in 2016).[89]

Nonetheless, it really affected me. It was the first time I saw a proactive strategy to be a good corporate citizen effect positive business results.

Historically, the best McDonald's ideas have started in a local market, usually with an innovative franchisee, rather than at the home office. That's how the Egg McMuffin, Filet-O-Fish, and Big Mac started. Lederhausen was the innovator who introduced sustainability into McDonald's business in Sweden, laying the groundwork for McDonald's global business to adopt this thinking—albeit slowly several years later as we both took on greater responsibilities at McDonald's.

Karl-Henrik Robért and the Four System Conditions

After giving us a tour of several McDonald's restaurants, Lederhausen brought us back to his home office, where Karl-Henrik Robért started to teach us TNS's Four System Conditions. I was immediately attracted to TNS because, for the first time, I found an NGO that wasn't singularly focused, but was big picture and holistic. TNS was the first NGO I encountered that used the holistic language of sustainability. Robért described the TNS four key system conditions (see Fig. 6.2):

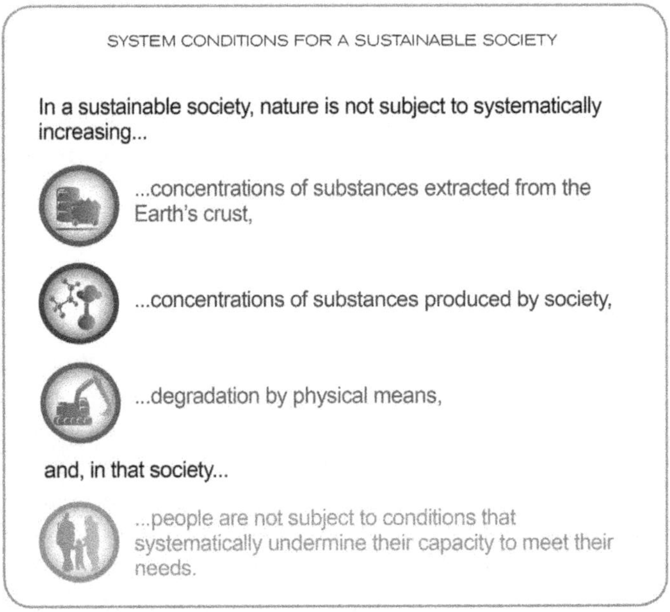

SYSTEM CONDITIONS FOR A SUSTAINABLE SOCIETY

In a sustainable society, nature is not subject to systematically increasing...

...concentrations of substances extracted from the Earth's crust,

...concentrations of substances produced by society,

...degradation by physical means,

and, in that society...

...people are not subject to conditions that systematically undermine their capacity to meet their needs.

Fig. 6.2: The Natural Step's Four System Conditions. *Source:* Courtesy of the Natural Step.

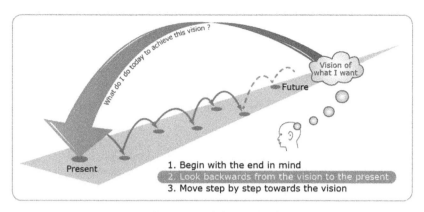

Fig. 6.3: The Natural Step "Backcasting."

Robért then used the intriguing term "backcasting" (see Fig. 6.3). I really liked the idea of envisioning the future we wanted and then returning to the present to see how to move forward toward that end state.

The last element of the TNS model was its "funnel" (see Fig. 6.4), which showed how we could create a better world through innovation.

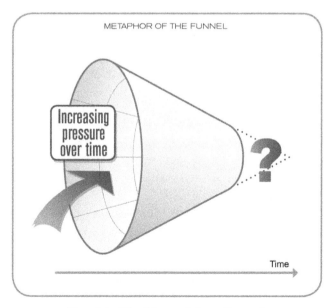

Fig. 6.4: The Natural Step Funnel.

I found all this intellectually stimulating. It was big picture. It was objective. It provided a pathway for strategic solutions that were optimistic and business friendly.

The Fourth Element of Supply Chain Introduced to Chilling Silence

TNS exposure was a great learning exercise, but I couldn't see a way to leverage TNS to help McDonald's adopt the approach beyond Sweden. Sustainability, across most of the business, was still a peripheral, far-off notion perceived as do-gooder philanthropy, not as good for the bottom line.

In 2001, Koziol was leading a big part of McDonald's global supply chain (i.e., quality assurance). Given he was such a kindred spirit, I thought the timing was perfect to invite TNS to our home office to see what we could do together.

TNS's U.S.-based chief scientist entered McDonald's Oak Brook oasis just after we made the laying hen announcement in 2001. Tall and gangly, George Basile's long strides gave him an aura of confidence, like he had arrived to conquer. Despite his PhD in biophysics from the UC at Berkeley, and teaching at Stanford University, Basile didn't seem like an academic type. He seemed more like a former athlete. He talked rapidly, as if on a race. He was smooth in his phrasing, speaking rapidly when he wanted to emphasize a point, as though he was sprinting for the last fifty yards of a marathon.

Basile was joined by the executive director of TNS's U.S., Catherine Grey. She was the calm to George's storm. She seemed at peace, almost meditative. When Grey spoke, it was with a soft question that had a deeper intent. She listened like an owl on a tree limb. You didn't always know her thoughts, but you knew she was turning them over in her mind.

By chance, as the two of them entered the elevator at our campus, they bumped into Koziol, who greeted them, hesitated, and added, "Who are you guys? What are you doing here?"

Basile started to explain sustainability, literally during a 20-second elevator pitch. Basile recalled that "Ken was looking at us like we are talking some language from some other planet." Then Koziol got off the elevator, gave them a smile, and said, "That's interesting." And then he left. George says he found out later "that's 'interesting' was sort of McDonald's speak for 'what the heck are you talking about?'"[90]

Later that morning, we all got together, and TNS explained to Koziol and me their philosophy and framework. TNS described the Four System Conditions, the funnel, and backcasting.

Basile left that meeting with an opinion that this "was all a stretch for McDonald's." His assessment was that McDonald's "supply chain had been built around a very understandable zero-failure model."

Basile captured McDonald's essence at the time: Food safety defined quality. Many, including me, believed that McDonald's had the best food safety standards in the business. Jack in the Box's E-coli scare, when forty-four people died in 1997, rocked the quick service restaurant sector. The BSE crisis (mad cow) hit Europe in the mid-1990s and threatened McDonald's core menu. McDonald's was obsessed with food safety and good at it, which gave McDonald's an edge to gain the trust of consumers.

In addition, Basile thought McDonald's suppliers were too insular, not thinking of their broader responsibilities to manage their suppliers. He said that:

> McDonald's had deep, trusted relationships with a relatively small set of suppliers for its scale. Many of the sustainability challenges that McDonald's faced weren't in its own house. You had the obesity issue, and things like trans-fats, sugars, and especially environmental issues that were beyond your own control. They were down the farm, or outside the existing scope. It was clear that McDonald's was going to have to profoundly change their supply chain relationships. It was almost like asking the company to change who they are.

McDonald's supplier community was small. Our top fifteen suppliers represented 80 percent of our business. Remember, it was McDonald's suppliers that made the hamburger patties, the buns, and the Coke products. They made the final product, but they did not raise the cows, grow the wheat, or refine the sugar. Further upstream, McDonald's suppliers had hundreds if not thousands of suppliers, but they were not on McDonald's radar screen, particularly back in the 1990s.

Finally, Basile thought McDonald's was in a state of denial, unable to understand the core reasons for those that thought ill of the company. He noted that:

> As I worked with the McDonald's supply chain folks, they were just stunned at the level of animosity against the corporation. They were like, "Gee whiz, we sell burgers and french

fries and Coke. We're not nuclear terrorists." Bad news came from every corner. From the perspective of the McDonald's team, who did not have a sustainability lens to help them understand the origins of some of the perspectives, correct or not, there seemed to be no method to [the activists'] madness. People were mad about how the chickens were treated. People were mad about how the cows were raised. People were just pissed off about everything.

As Koziol digested the TNS system, he underwent an epiphany. Koziol recalled how incredibly influenced he was by the engagement with TNS: "From that moment on, it was the tipping point from going from defense to offense," he said. "We were playing defense on every front. It was like swatting flies, and there were just too many of them, and it was too crazy for us."

Koziol walked out of the meeting with a whole different understanding. He was into business tangibles, tools, measures, and scorecards, and so he liked what he saw: "The Natural Step sustainability method gave us a currency," according to Koziol. "It gave us a way of evaluating all our actions through a lens that gave us a relative value metric. Are we net better or net worse?"

Until this seminal meeting with TNS, Koziol looked at the emerging sustainability efforts in a similar way as I did: the activists were too preachy and asked for an impossibly perfect environment. Koziol's experience was that sustainability issues boiled down to:

> Don't touch anything. Don't do anything. Don't open your doors in the morning. Don't grow food, raise animals. Don't spray chemicals. Don't use water. I mean everything is don't, don't, don't. You can't feed a lot of people that way. Modern agriculture doesn't work that way, and business doesn't work that way.

> Instead of responding to other people's issues, we could create our own agenda for our own reasons that we felt were good for our business. TNS created a continuous improvement mindset. How do you show up every day and make things a little better, and a little better, and still better? That certainly fit the McDonald's MO and culture, too.

Koziol was so excited about the TNS-informed sustainability strategy that he began to think about how to introduce this new discipline to the entire supplier community. And this brings us back to the beginning of this chapter, when Koziol presented to the supplier community during a special meeting at the 2002 Worldwide Convention what we had learned from TNS. Every two years, McDonald's hosted this huge, worldwide get-together with its family of owner–operators, company leaders, and supplier principles for upward of 15,000 people.

As a partner working with Ken, I was exuberant. I, too, saw the potential in embedding this emerging sustainability framework into the core of supplier expectations. Programs, projects, and strategies come and go, but integrating something like sustainability into the mindset, structure, and reward system of our supplier community could unleash unbridled innovation and solutions.

As Koziol and I prepared for the supplier summit, we both knew the audience had had no exposure to sustainability. Plus, with all the societal issues landing like bombs on McDonald's brand, the going mentality was to see this as nuisance noise, detached from McDonald's business.

As Basile put it, referring to the top people running our company and our suppliers—all reared in the 1960s and 1970s—"this was just the latest in another wave of ridiculous do-gooders attaching societal blame to McDonald's. There was a 'this too shall pass' mindset at the top of McDonald's and of our supplier leadership."

Koziol compared the mentality to a child growing up:

> Wherever you grow up is always where you're from. So they grew up in the 1960s and '70s, when McDonald's was the darling and everybody liked them. The community was happy when they opened them in town.

> So now the same community is doing all these nasty things. And the McDonald's old-school leaders are saying, "What are you talking about? Everybody loves us. We're good. We're local, little businessmen, and we sell affordable food that's safe and consistent, and we have clean restaurants."

This onslaught of attacks framing McDonald's as a bad company that was negatively impacting society "didn't match at all with their history, or what their understanding of what McDonald's was all about," concluded Koziol.

Facing the audience of seasoned suppliers, Koziol started to communicate a fourth element (sustainability) of McDonald's supply chain. His presentation style was logical, much like hearing a scientist lay out his latest discovery. But, while he explained the funnel, backcasting, and the Four System Conditions, I could see suppliers getting restless. I saw puzzled faces.

Koziol finished to a dead-quiet audience. "I remember it was silent when I finished," he recalled. "Maybe I should try to do it in English the next time. When I was done, I mean, it wasn't even polite applause or anything. There was just stone-cold silence."

I listened to suppliers as they exited the exhibit area. The common comment I overheard was, "What was Koziol taking about?"

Despite the less-than-stellar feedback, and even though the suppliers didn't immediately sign on to Koziol's plan, "The ball was in play," Koziol said. "The fourth element was on the board. Quality, service, price, and, now, sustainability. We created a hook, a reference point, where we can go back and say, 'You remember the presentation at the convention? Now this is what we are talking about.'"

The purpose of Koziol's presentation was not to create immediate action. Rather, it was to start an awakening. The goal was to alert suppliers that McDonald's was going to be talking to various product councils and working with the supplier teams to develop sustainability agendas. "I wanted to make them aware that this was becoming a thing," said Koziol. "Your owner was here. Your president was here. You need to get after this. We're doing this."

Koziol chalked up the silence to the newness of the sustainability concept. "There wasn't Neanderthal thinking that people were opposed to it," he said, "but people didn't want to spend a lot of money on it, either. Those were times when we were pushing hard on value, and the business was under stress."

I admired Koziol's courage to enter such unchartered and unexpected territory, despite the challenges. This was the beginning of McDonald's sustainable supply chain evolution. Koziol started it by throwing a hot potato to an audience not quite ready to catch it.

Even so, sustainability finally had a seat at the table. How would it proceed? Could we get traction? Small wins? Could we make proactive progress using the TNS model? Would suppliers eventually understand and embrace sustainability?

Can We Make the Filet-O-Fish Sustainable?

After the 2002 worldwide convention, McDonald's fish team (i.e., McDonald's supply chain and their handful of global fish suppliers) convened to consider some dramatic changes in purchasing its fish. They were considering whether to stop purchasing Russian Pollock based on a new sustainability scorecard system the team had recently developed. The scorecard rated Russian Pollock (a kind of cod) in the "red" (meaning action needed to rectify) due to lack transparency of its data. Changing to a different source would be a big financial hit to the McDonald's U.S. and Japanese markets. Russian Pollock sold at about a 10 percent discount versus the rest of the marketplace, meaning an impact of more than several million dollars annually for the McDonald's U.S. business alone.

Where and how to source fish for the Filet-O-Fish marked the real beginning of proactive sustainability thinking in McDonald's supply chain. Since 1986, McDonald's supply chain leader on fish had been Gary Johnson, who was way ahead on sustainability. That's because he was among the first to acknowledge that cod, then the sole source of the Filet-O-Fish, had been so overfished during the late 1980s and early 1990s in New England that fishing for cod there was shut down. "There was a fishing industry all up the East Coast of the U.S. and Newfoundland in Canada that was very vibrant for hundreds of years," said Johnson. "Then it was overfished, and it was gone overnight. And that really resonated with me: that sustainability is really real."[91]

McDonald's did not purchase its cod from this area; nevertheless, the loss of this substantial fishery area caused havoc in the marketplace. "The pricing for cod started to go really crazy," Johnson said. He saw this new sustainability idea as core to the future of sourcing fish. He needed a stable, uninterrupted supply of fish in order to keep the Filet-O-Fish on the menu. "I had no idea what I specifically needed," he admitted, "but I knew the end result was that we had to get a sustainable assured supply of fish without harming the environment."

At the time, I had yet to learn about Johnson's sustainability bent, and I viewed him as an unlikely candidate to unlock the pragmatic possibilities of sustainability implementation. From what I knew of him, he was all business. Johnson's mannerisms reminded me of Bob Newhart. Johnson was thin on top and had a wry smile. He seemed like an exacting accountant, studying things endlessly. That perception changed when Johnson came to me for help and I learned about the backstory of New England cod disappearing.

To help Johnson, I knew from the EDF and Temple Grandin experience that we needed a trusted third party. I proposed that we bring in Conservation International (CI). CI fit the bill in my 1–10 evaluation of an NGO. They were not a corporate friendly patsy (1–3). They certainly were not radical (8–10). They were in the middle, heavily weighted with scientists. Indeed, CI had a great philosophy: "Head in the sky, boots on the ground." They were visionary, creative, and idealistic, with a work ethic of rolling up their sleeves, getting dirty in the field, and crafting pragmatic solutions.

I had kept close to CI since their founding in 1989. We partnered with them on creating a rainforest video in the early 1990s, called the *Rainforest Imperative*. CI helped defend us against bogus claims that McDonald's was deforesting the Amazon rainforest. We also worked together on the first environmentally themed Happy Meal, in 1991, called "Discover the Rainforest." With the purchase of a Happy Meal, kids received a book versus a toy. It was our company's first venture outside a toy as a premium. Unfortunately, it was a flop. Kids liked toys better.

We decided to invite CI to the 2001 McDonald's Toronto Fish Forum, the annual meeting to which Johnson invited the McDonald's global fish suppliers to review progress and talk upcoming strategy.

When Johnson let the fish suppliers know that CI was coming to the meeting to have a sustainability conversation, the fish suppliers voiced opposition. A couple of suppliers threatened not to come, asking how we could invite a radical group to our meeting. To think our suppliers thought CI as radical was really odd. Remember, though, that, at the time, we were on the heels of a major antiglobalization movement, with McDonald's as a symbol of supposed multinational companies taking over trade and commerce. I had to hand it to Johnson. He did not waver. He told these suppliers, "You're coming. And CI is coming. Let's have a dialogue."

I helped CI prepare for the engagement with our fish suppliers. John Buchanan was my primary contact at CI and one of my favorite NGO leaders. I trusted him 100 percent. He told me that Jim Cannon from their fish team was a phenomenal expert, so Cannon came to Toronto.

We didn't know at the time where this could all lead, but the first step was to raise the awareness of the sustainability issues at hand. Cannon's presentation reviewed the current status of white fish around the world—the good, bad, and the ugly. Afterward and by consensus, the Fish Forum leaders decided to work further with Cannon in order to create a task force to develop a sustainability scorecard for fish.

Cannon was perfectly cast for this role of collaborating with the rough-and-tumble leading fish suppliers. He was a top marine biologist expert, and he had a smooth listening style that was highly effective for an NGO leader. He was not cut from the stereotypical cloth of an NGO: not a policy idealistic wonk, not a stir-the-pot radical.

Cannon came out of Cambridge University and Imperial College schooled in ecology, economics, and math. He quickly learned that facts were not the problem. He said, "It all comes down to politics, and how to build political will."[92] He shifted his work to companies, where he believed there was the ability to garner the political power necessary from corporate leaders.

As his knowledge of fish continued to deepen, he did not strut out his know-how. "It takes listening," Cannon said. "I want to start where the company is at, and really listen to them, and what moves them. What their needs are. And I tailor my recommendations to what I hear."

This was in marked contrast to what I often observed from ineffective NGO leaders who try to influence the corporate sector by bringing in facts and science, which often are tied to an established agenda. They end up pushing their viewpoint on the company versus truly engaging with them and listening.

So Cannon listened a lot in Toronto and won over the tough fishermen. He bellied up to the bar like he was your very best mate. This was a sentiment shared by many of the fish suppliers. Jon Safey, then general manager of marketing for Sealord, a large fishing company, and a participant in McDonald's Toronto Fish Forum, recalled that first meeting, saying that:

> [t]he first thing I noted about Jim, apart from his Scottish accent, was that he didn't talk in an abstract fashion; he talked straight and with no BS. That was refreshing, and after a good session on the subject, Jim joined us for drinks and dinner, where he showed that he was, indeed, a good mix of Scottish and Australian. That is, he enjoyed the socializing while showing he had deep pockets (and short arms). He fitted in with the fishing industry people very well.[93]

Johnson asked Klaus Nielson, CEO of Espersen, one of McDonald's primary fish suppliers, and the team at Gorton's, another major fish supplier, to define a working definition of fish sustainability. Johnson also suggested a "stoplight" measurement scheme. Johnson gathered Jim Cannon for a meeting in Iceland with Neilson. Johnson said, "I reintroduced Jim (Cannon) to Klaus and asked them to work together and not come back with a fish sustainability scorecard unless they both agreed it could work within our system." Within a year, Cannon and the suppliers collaborated to develop mapping and guidelines for the fish scorecard, and the simple "stoplight" methodology suggested by Johnson: Red (trouble), Yellow (problems are developing), and Green (good and acceptable). The ratings were calculated based on three main criteria:

1. Biomass of the fish (was the region being overfished?)
2. Management of the fishery (did they use best practices?)
3. Transparency of the data (was the information on the fishery open and credible?)

The main source of fish for McDonald's USA and Japan, Russian Pollock, did not score well. On transparency of data, Russian Pollock was graded as red.

What should McDonald's do? Cannon was keen on giving the improvement process a chance. He didn't like to kick fish suppliers out of McDonald's supply chain. After all, their business would just go to someone else, and the poor practices would just shift elsewhere. Working with the suppliers, the team gave the Russians three years to put in place an improvement plan. They never improved. "What was their incentive to improve?" said Johnson. "They can sell their Pollock to others with their low pricing."

Johnson talked to Dan Gorsky, the supply chain lead on fish for the U.S. business. Gorsky agreed that the lack of transparent data was a problem, and he decided to shift out of Russian Pollock, despite the considerable 10 percent or more cost increase. When I heard this, I was so proud of our company. Aided by Cannon's superb skills, McDonald's took a stand and chose purpose over profit. Safey, Sealord's general manager, summed Cannon's effective style well:

> One of his key attributes is that he can walk for a time in other people's shoes, and he can translate that into action plans that can be accepted by parties that don't necessarily share common ground all the time. He manages to expand that common ground to the extent where stakeholders in the sea-food business can develop agreed targets, and plans to achieve progress, even if it is over a longer period of time.

After the Russian Pollock decision, McDonald's Europe did something similar with fish from the Baltic Sea, which had been deemed as unsustainable on the fish scorecard. We withdrew our business from them, but pledged we would return if they became more sustainable. Three years later, that is just what happened. The power and influence of McDonald's supply chain was working at its best, balancing cost, quality, value, and, now, this fourth element of sustainability.

By 2013, McDonald's took another huge step on sustainable fish, becoming the first national restaurant chain to announce that all of its fish met Marine Stewardship Council (MSC) standards. MSC was created in 1996 by the World Wildlife Fund and Unilever as a nonprofit group dedicated to creating a standard for sustainable fish. MSC also create an eco-label for sustainable fish to inform the consumer and encourage the purchase of more sustainable fish.

Dan Gorsky, who had since been promoted to senior vice president of McDonald's USA overseeing the supply chain, said in a public release:

> "McDonald's collaboration with the Marine Stewardship Council is a critical part of our company's journey to advance positive environmental and economic practices in our supply chain," said Dan Gorsky, senior vice president of U.S. supply chain and sustainability. "We're extremely proud of the fact that this decision ensures our customers will continue to enjoy the same great taste and high quality of our fish with the additional assurance that the fish they are buying can be traced back to a fishery that meets MSC's strict sustainability standard."[94]

Soon, MSC fish went global for McDonald's. McDonald's also decided to put the MSC logo on its fish sandwich packaging, and the marketing department started to add this feature to its communication efforts to consumers. As a result, certified sustainable fish became the very first McDonald's menu product to attain this distinction. I was in seventh heaven one morning when a colleague texted me a picture of a bus stop poster that displayed McDonald's sustainable fish sandwich with an advertising line that said "sustainable fish, sustainable price."

Converting a Hog Supplier From Bad to Good

I was sitting with Bobby Kennedy Jr in McDonald's home-office cafeteria (a McDonald's restaurant). He told me he loved our food. And I could tell he was: Kennedy was downing a Quarter Pounder with cheese in fast motion. His eating style was in keeping with his general being: restless, always moving.

"Is this real?" I asked myself. I couldn't believe I was actually sitting with the son of one of my boyhood idols, who was a famous Kennedy in and of himself.

After lunch, we adjourned to the Tokyo conference room, surrounded by glass. Kennedy had come to McDonald's to present a passionate plea to a group of us to stop doing business with Smithfield. In his role as head of the Waterkeeper Alliance, an NGO dedicated to clean water, Kennedy was on a crusade against Smithfield. He viewed Smithfield as a huge polluter, whose huge, confined hog facilities were out of control, often spewing waste from lagoons that often leaked or busted over to foul rivers with their nitrates and other poisons.

I was on the edge of my seat as I listened to his logic and emotional case. Kennedy's pointed thoughts mimicked a scathing indictment published in a Polish paper in October 2003. (Smithfield was looking to expand to Poland.) That article note that:

> Smithfield is one of a handful of large multinationals who are transforming global meat production from a traditional farm enterprise to factory style industrial production. Smithfield is the largest hog producer in the world and controls almost 30 percent of the U.S. pork market. Smithfield's style of industrial pork production is now a major source of air pollution and probably the largest source of water pollution in America.

> Smithfield and its cronies have driven tens of thousands of family farmers off the land, shattered rural communities, poisoned thousands of miles of American waterways, killed billions of fish, put thousands of fishermen out of work, sickened rural residents, and treated hundreds of millions of farm animals with unspeakable and unnecessary cruelty.

> With encouragement from these politicians, Smithfield built the largest slaughterhouse in the world in Bladen County, North Carolina. The plant butchers 30,000 pigs each day. By building this pig slaughter plant, Smithfield set off explosive growth of a new way of producing hogs in North Carolina—factory-style production.

> Smithfield builds football field-sized warehouses in which the company crams thousands of genetically manipulated hogs into tiny metal boxes where they are deprived of sunlight,

exercise, straw bedding, rooting, and social opportunities. A hog is as smart and sensitive as a dog. Under these crowded stressful conditions, they must be kept alive by constant doses of antibiotics and heavy metals. Antibiotic resistant bacteria and residues of these additives naturally end up in their waste.

Since a hog produces ten times the amount of waste as a human, a single hog factory can generate more fecal waste than Warsaw. One of Smithfield's factories in Utah houses 850,000 hogs and produces more fecal waste than New York City's 8.5 million people. Hog waste falls through slatted floors into a basement where it is periodically flushed into giant outdoor pits called lagoons.

While cities must treat sewage before discharging it, Smithfield's meat factories dump their liquid manure untreated onto fields which quickly become saturated. The manure then percolates into groundwater or is carried by rain into nearby streams or lakes."[95]

My heart was sympathetic to Kennedy's diatribe against Smithfield, one of McDonald's largest suppliers of pork products for the bacon, sausage, and ham on Egg McMuffins and more. My mind, though, didn't assume everything he said was the truth, so after the meeting I conducted my own research on Smithfield's track record with the U.S. Environmental Protection Agency (EPA). Indeed, the company was getting fined regularly. I counted more than a thousand fines in one year. I wondered how we could allow a supplier of ours to operate this way. I decided that we needed to visit Smithfield to assess first-hand if they were as bad as Bobby Kennedy had demonized them to be—or if Kennedy was full of bluster and blarney.

John Hayes, the top guy in charge of all of our beef and pork for the U.S. business, agreed to go with me. So did Bruce Feinberg, head of quality assurance. I thought this was a perfect group for the task: the head of procurement, the head of quality, and the head of corporate social responsibility (CSR) from McDonald's visiting a big supplier. It was ideal teamwork.

I saw a big part of my job as seeing a potential or real problem, probing into it, and stirring the pot internally to start assessing it. My style is to ask a lot of questions and to try to convince others to join me to act upon the problem. In this case, the best first step is a practical one: Visit. See. Listen. Learn. And do it together.

With that in mind, we travelled to North Carolina. Hayes* didn't like what he heard there at Smithfield's operations, noting that:

> We asked about the treatment of animals, but instead they gave us a tour that had nothing to do with animals; rather they were trying to impress us with their efficiency gains, the way they could get the animals to gain more weight quickly, and the way they handled the animals that would ensure better financial returns.[96]

I remember Hayes, Feinberg, and I argued back and forth with the Smithfield team leading us on this tour. We wanted to explore environmental and animal welfare issues. Smithfield seemed only interested in productivity. The overt consternation displayed during the meeting was the first time I had encountered such a brouhaha. Usually our meetings with suppliers were professional, with no insults or loud voices. This one got heated. "Smithfield had no idea that this efficiency talk didn't resonate with us at all," Hayes said. "We were there to understand their operations from the environmental and animal welfare perspective."

"Oh, my God," Hayes said to Feinberg and I as we left for our plane. "These guys had no clue of what they were up against."

That proved true, because no sooner was Hayes back in Oak Brook when he got on the phone with Robbie Hofmann, former owner of North Side Foods, a long-time supplier to McDonald's of finished pork products, such as bacon. North Side had recently been purchased by Smithfield. Hofmann had a seat on their board. Hayes gave him an earful about how dissatisfied we all were in Smithfield's insensitivity to animal welfare and the environment.

Hofmann worked his magic, which was to translate McDonald's concerns to Smithfield in a way to move them to where we wanted them to be. He was a dedicated long-term supplier to McDonald's, and he knew our culture and history better than most.

Within a couple weeks, Smithfield's newly promoted Larry Pope was visiting McDonald's, saying he would do something about the problem. Pope had been named president and chief operating officer in 2001, and he was on his way to replace CEO Joe Luter, who, in my mind, represented the old-school thinking of animal agriculture as being solely based on efficiency management.

---

* Hayes also played a large role in an issue regarding tomatoes, which we'll explore later in this chapter.

The Houdini of Sustainability

I had to hand it to Pope when he went outside his organization to the governmental agency policing them, the Virginia Department of Environmental Quality (DEQ), to hire its head, Dennis Treacy, to start to fix Smithfield's sustainability problems in 2002.

To Treacy's departing DEQ team, Smithfield was the poster child for a bad company; it even held the record for the largest Clean Water Act penalty levied in EPA history at the time.[97] Treacy was now transitioning to a sector that was not a "cool" business—i.e., a company tainted by the image of factory farming and industrialized farming.

Despite the demonization of the meat industry, the reality is that meat, and the protein it provides, is essential for the diets of many consumers. Another special attribute of the meat industry is that its product is not an inanimate object. Rather, it's a live animal, with trade-offs that need to be considered about how intensely to manage the animals for efficiency, animal health, and quality versus balancing efficiency with preserving as much of the natural behaviors of the animals as possible.

In order to define natural behaviors, many groups use the Five Freedoms developed by the U.K. Farm Animal Welfare Council in the mid-1960s. Given that much of animal agriculture has increased its intensity of housing the livestock, a couple of the Freedoms are a real challenge to meet. Those freedoms are as follows[98]:

1. **Freedom From Hunger and Thirst:** providing ready access to fresh water and a diet to maintain full health and vigor.
2. **Freedom From Discomfort:** providing an appropriate environment, including shelter and a comfortable resting area.
3. **Freedom From Pain, Injury, or Disease:** ensuring prevention or rapid diagnosis and treatment.
4. **Freedom to Express Normal Behavior:** providing sufficient space, proper facilities, and company of the animal's own kind.
5. **Freedom From Fear and Distress:** ensuring conditions and treatments which avoid mental suffering.

Modern animal agriculture is portrayed by some vocal critics as bad for animals, the environment, and workers; yet without modern agriculture, our society wouldn't have abundant and affordable plentiful meat products. Some advocates want animal agriculture to reflect the small, rural farming of the nineteenth century, when the population of the world hovered around 2 billion people. Now the planet's population is

7.2 billion. A much larger good production system is needed to safely and affordably feed that many people.

I relished working on finding sustainable solutions for meat because of these multifold challenges. I was convinced that big was not necessarily bad and small was not necessarily good. Good and bad practices could come from both. Given all the baggage, with regulators, critics, and leading NGOs condemning Smithfield, Treacy needed to become the Houdini of sustainability in order to escape and transcend the horrible Smithfield reputation. He told me that he was wary when hired but excited about making a difference: "Man, I might work here a day or I might be here for 10 years," said Treacy.[99] He took a leap of faith that he could really change things for the better. But that is why he chose the position: As a consensus builder, he would listen and learn, understanding how to best proceed. Even so, I wasn't certain he could make inroads with Smithfield, one of the leaders in a tough industry. John Hayes wasn't certain, either, noting that: "I remembered they hired this attorney (Treacy) who initially turned me off big time, because he was such a polished shoe attorney. If you ever use the word 'attorney' with me, my first inclination is 'this is a disaster.'"

Hayes had to eat his words when he saw Smithfield transform, admitting that, "I was completely wrong. Whether Treacy had the emotional or thoughtfulness for animals, or whether he was approaching it purely from, 'Hey, I know about this, and I'm going to fix it whether I believe in it or not.' Whatever his motivation was, he took it seriously."

I, too, saw in Treacy strong resolve and grit and a wry and clever sense of humor able to draw friends and foes alike to him for whatever idea he was pitching. Indeed, Treacy ended up orchestrating one of the biggest sustainability turnarounds I've ever seen. His story is rare because most sustainability professionals develop ways to build upon an existing program or start one from scratch. Instead, Treacy was in a deep hole as he first walked into the office in 2002. He told me he was determined to make Smithfield an environmental and animal welfare leader in his industry. He did just that. Today, Smithfield is a leader in the meat industry on many issues:

- First to announce moving away for gestation stalls for sows.

- Made a groundbreaking move in 2007 to report antibiotics usage. In its 2013 sustainability report, Smithfield showed 151 milligrams of antibiotics used per pound in its hog operations.

- Set specific targets across the scope of its operations, including reductions in water, energy, greenhouse gas emissions and waste— and it is making tangible progress.

- Rose to the top of the leader list for the meat industry, according to an NGO published report by CERES in 2016: "Feeding Ourselves Thirsty: How the Food Industry Is Managing Global Water Risk." Smithfield's score was triple its nearest competitor.

John Hayes summarized Treacy's turnaround well:

> He led Smithfield from a position where it seemed that the citizenry was at the gates with pitchforks yelling, "Kill the beast!" to a position where they were truly leading the industry, not only on animal welfare, but in how they managed water and other natural resources. They did it, and they did it in a big way that was beyond reproach, in my opinion.

Smithfield did so well that we never saw Bobby Kennedy Jr again. That's the way it should be. In 2008, Smithfield became the first supplier to receive McDonald's Supplier Sustainability Award. This turnaround exemplified the ability of McDonald's supply chain leaders to influence suppliers such as Smithfield toward adopting sustainability strategies.

Hearing From the Voice of God

One peaceful morning in May 2006, the phone rang. I answered and heard on the other end of the line: "Hello, this is Bishop Imesch."

My heart tripled its beat and pushed up on me as if it would jump out of my throat. I had never met the Bishop. This was the most unexpected call I ever received. Bishop Imesch was the top Catholic bishop for the diocese of Joliet, Illinois, which, as a Roman Catholic, is my own diocese. It was like God calling me.

After some small talk about my own parish priest recently leaving the priesthood, the Bishop turned the discussion toward tomato workers in Florida. The Coalition of Immokalee Workers (CIW) was engaged in a visible campaign against McDonald's, demanding that McDonald's work with its suppliers to provide better wages and conditions for these impoverished workers.

The CIW is a worker-based human rights organization operating out of Immokalee, Florida, less than an hour's drive to the northeast of affluent Naples. CIW was built by organizing the farmworker community, starting in 1993. The organization created a national consumer network since 2000. It worked to improve the plight of impoverished farmworkers who worked the fields, such as picking tomatoes. These workers tended to follow their work from southern Florida up the East Coast as the weather changed in spring.

The gist of my Bishop's comments was that these workers deserved a decent wage and living conditions. He asked me why McDonald's couldn't do something about it. I found it difficult to come up with a counterargument against the word of God.

I never wore religion on my sleeve, but my faith has always been important to me. I went to mass virtually every week of my life. I've listened to a few thousand sermons, many of them calling upon each of us to be humble, treat others as we want to be treated, to seek peace and justice, and to live the Beatitudes.

In many ways, these sermons and my faith helped provide me with a solid foundation to lead CSR and sustainability at McDonald's. My Catholic faith provided me with a moral compass and road map. On the other hand, I was schooled for business, with an MBA from Northwestern. I never saw the equal mixture of a business and social responsibility mindset as an oxymoron. Business cannot survive unless it serves society well.

I responded to Bishop Imesch with McDonald's key messages. "We care. We're a leader. We are working with our suppliers on a better program for the tomato workers." The Bishop listened, and then with his holy voice he simply asked, "Then why don't you pay the penny a pound more?" That question hung heavily over me.

A year earlier, in March 2005, CIW won a four-year battle with YUM Brands who committed to pay the tomato pickers more through its suppliers. For once, McDonald's was not the first target.

CIW led a simple, persuasive campaign that was extraordinarily effective at garnering support from other stakeholders, particularly the religious community. CIW was asking for a penny a pound more per worker. It was simple and direct. It seemed a nominal and simple thing to do. YUM had resisted for many years, finally announcing an agreement with CIW to pay the extra penny a pound to tomato workers.

After winning the YUM agreement, CIW turned its campaign against McDonald's (see Fig. 6.5). CIW soon organized its first Truth Tour. Hundreds of workers and protesters arrived in buses from far-flung places to protest near our Oak Brook home office.

This CIW campaign marked a milestone moment. Up until now, my work had been focused on helping our supply chain improve treatment

Fig. 6.5: Coalition of Immokalee Workers "Truth Tour"
Campaign Against McDonald's.

for animals and implement environmental programs. Now we were getting into the people dimension of sustainability.

The people side is a complicated territory for McDonald's, considering its franchised system—i.e., owner–operators, who own about 90 percent of McDonald's restaurants and who control their people, training, wages, and career development. In addition, the people issue is complicated in the supply chain. McDonald's suppliers are independent. Founder Ray Kroc purposely set up McDonald's three-legged system of company staff, suppliers, and owner–operators—all equal yet independent, working for the overall good of McDonald's business. McDonald's is not an integrated upstream. We are experts at running restaurants; suppliers are experts at growing tomatoes. So it was the suppliers' duty to develop their people policies, wages, and benefits.

Given the high profile of this CIW campaign and the potential ramifications on our business, we set up a cross-functional team to tackle the issue, as we typically would do. The team included McDonald's staff, including key supply chain leaders, communications, government affairs, legal, and CSR, the latter of which was me. It also included McDonald's direct suppliers of sliced tomatoes. Remember, we only purchased the final product. McDonald's only relationship was with our direct suppliers, most of which were processors, not growers. They in turn worked with their own supply chain of growers and producers. We were tasked with devising a recommendation.

The Power of the Slippery Slope

For the first year, I supported our team, which was creating an alternative solution to CIW's demands. I was happy that our head of U.S. purchasing was John Hayes, who was responsible for overseeing more than half the McDonald's menu, including tomatoes. He helped transform Smithfield. I envisioned him doing the same with the tomato issue. But, as I soon learned, Hayes was dead set against any capitulation to CIW. "My view was that if McDonald's got involved at [the wage] level," he said, "you would have to make the sidewalks longer outside the our home office because the people lined up for their handout would have stretched for miles."

It was the slippery slope theory, which I often had heard over the years, especially in supply chain matters. Some decisions would trigger something else and lead us down a path that was way too far away from McDonald's direct responsibility. The slippery slope was a nemesis in work. Sustainability is not about fear about what could come next, but doing what's right for society and business and taking smart risks.

Hayes's point of view permeated the supply chain team, which envisioned similar actions and pressures migrating beyond tomatoes to all produce and all products, like meat, milk, and potatoes. His argument against capitulating to CIW was persuasive:

> If you are going to the tomato-grower level, somebody that is three or four times removed from you and is hiring the people, and you're going to tell them what it is they should do, how they should treat workers, the list of problems that could be hoisted onto McDonald's would bring everybody with a cause to McDonald's door to make a difference.

> In my mind, this was a nightmare just waiting to happen. It would be a full-time job for McDonald's to fight that dam once it was broken.

I was not certain I agreed with Hayes. Bishop Imesch sure had motivated me to think this through more. If I were to influence the company to go a different direction, how would I do it? I decided that my first step was to visit Immokalee to see the real conditions and to seek the truth, examining whether CIW was on the right track or whether McDonald's was right to resist.

After I arrived at Immokalee just before dusk, I walked around the town center. I saw run-down bars, dirty streets, and long faces. The next day, I joined a working crew in the tomato fields so I could do the work and see what it was like. I wanted to get to the bottom of what these folks really made. Hayes had insisted they made respectable money, arguing that:

> I've walked the field. I met these workers. They're young. They're anywhere from their teens to their late twenties. They work their ass off, and at the end of the day, they don't make $5 an hour, they don't make $10 an hour. The young bucks are making $18 to $25 an hour, because that's how fast they can pick and harvest ripe tomatoes.

Hayes's opinion was backed by a 2006 study by the Center for Reflection, Education and Action, Inc. (CREA), which McDonald's helped pay for.[100] The CREA study examined the pay rate for the ten fastest and ten slowest pickers; they averaged forty-one buckets an hour and twenty-one buckets an hour, respectively. The fastest made as much as $18.27 an hour; the slowest averaged $9.65 an hour.

I have a skeptic eye about all studies. I know many external critics always denigrate studies funded in any way by corporations as inherently biased. To me, most studies have some bias and assumptions, whether they come from corporations, NGOs, or independent scientists and academics. The truth is hardly black and white.

I felt I needed to understand all the sides before coming to a conclusion. My philosophy on issues like this was to navigate apolitically. No matter who it was, and no matter what the politics were, I advocated for what I thought was best, both for society and our McDonald's business. I made a point of learning everything I could from multiple sources, including reports on a subject from the right, left, and center. Only then could I sort through the various viewpoints to shape my own opinion.

This search for the truth landed me amid hundreds of rows of tomato plants stretching far and wide in the blazing sun all the way to the horizon. There was no shade at all. It was at least 90 degrees outside, the heat penetrating my skin. I grabbed a basket that held 32 pounds of tomatoes. I filled the basket by bending down, picking off tomatoes from their stem until the basket was full, which took about 10 minutes. Then I walked about 100 yards to the truck, where I hoisted the bucket to a man who poured them into the trailer. Everyone in the fields did this at different speeds. This was backbreaking work.

The average piece rate was about 45¢ per basket. I calculated that, at my slow pace, the beginning rate I was on track to make was $2.70 an hour. To achieve minimum wage ($7.50), a worker would need to fill 17 baskets, one every 4 minutes.

Later that day, I roamed the town to see if I could get a look at the workers' living conditions. I peered into plenty of one-room homes and saw as many as ten people living in space the size of the family room in my house. I left the next day with complete empathy for the workers, and for their need for a better life. I was sold on the idea that they did, indeed, deserve a penny a pound more. But I was facing an internal supply chain team that felt they had a better solution to solve the problem than the one offered by CIW.

Hayes and Dan Chally, head of our social accountability program, supported a supplier led program called SAFE (Socially Accountable Farm Employees), which later became Grower Standards. This organization addressed similar issues as CIW, such as wages, working conditions, and forced labor. CIW blasted the SAFE standards, stating that:

> None of what has been announced addresses the fact that farmworkers still desperately need immediate economic relief, a raise in wages so that they can meet their basic needs and live free of the degradation that has been the shame of Florida agriculture for so long.[101]

The Tough CIW Leader

Though the McDonald's team would meet, interact, and negotiate with many of the CIW leaders over the next year or so, the person the McDonald's team, including me, gravitated to was one of the CIW's many cofounders, Greg Asbed. Hayes and Chally had met recently with this rough-and-tumble leader of CIW, who had cofounded the organization with his wife Laura and several dozen farmworker community leaders from Mexico, Guatemala, and Haiti, including Lucas Benitez. Hayes and Chally thought they could persuade Asbed to go along with the SAFE program. But it didn't exactly work out that way: Soon after their meeting, McDonald's went public in support of SAFE, which infuriated the CIW to the point that the farmworkers stepped up the intensity of their campaign against McDonald's.

Hayes didn't respect Asbed, believing him only interested in raising money and attention for CIW. I felt I needed to meet with him and the other CIW leaders to judge their intentions for myself. So I travelled again to Immokalee, Florida, nervous with apprehension of meeting a very different NGO leader than I'd known thus far. My experience was with NGOs who were fiercely independent yet willing to collaborate and bend a little in order to come to a compromise. EDF's Fred Krupp, for example, was quiet, humble, and collaborative. Jim Cannon with CI was the ultimate listener, willing to belly up to the bar with those he wanted to influence. Temple Grandin was passionate and scientific, as apolitical as a piece of wood. My only true negative experience was with PETA, which I believed practiced extremism versus activism. I worried that the CIW's style would be akin to PETA.

I met Asbed in CIW's cramped, unkempt office in the center of Immokalee. He wore jeans and a t-shirt. He was grim and offered little small talk. He made terse comments and statements. I was facing a thick wall of distrust. However, I soon learned that Asbed was cut from a different cloth, one with real activism woven in his heart. Asbed is in the 8–9 category on the NGO rating scale I had developed, a rabble-rouser but not a wild extremist. Though Asbed did not demonstrate the collaborative traits I was used to seeing, I sensed in him a lot of integrity in his purpose to improve the lives of farmworkers. For him, it was a battle that required him to be pugnacious. His family background had groomed him for this battle. Asbed's father, a Syrian-Armenian immigrant to this country, was three years old when his grandfather died. The family depended on the support of the community to survive, as did many Armenians after a third of the population was lost due to the Armenian Genocide. He recalled that:

> My grandmother survived the Armenian genocide at age fifteen and was bought and sold twice, finally to my grandfather. My father was born right after the genocide in the Syrian desert, not any kind of real place. Because they were still displaced by the genocide, they had nothing. That's always been an important part of our family history, the idea of survival and fighting for life. All this shaped the way that I saw the world.[102]

I asked if this history had led to his activism. He balked at the term "activist." I think he thought of it as a manufactured approach, zeal without substance, whereas his focus was on getting past the protests as quickly as possible so as to get to work on the day-in, day-out work of correcting injustices. He said that:

> "You know, it has always felt ridiculous to me that we have to protest just to get people to agree that farmworkers are poor and suffer some pretty horrific abuses. Picking fruit is the worst job in the country, all things considered, and everyone knows that. We as a country should have fixed it a long time ago, but instead it's the twenty-first century and we still have to waste time marching in the streets just to get to a place — a table, where we can sit in dialogue with buyers and growers — where we are going to end up sooner or later anyway. We could be using that time more constructively, working together to make the job more humane, but instead we have to fight our way there, wasting time and building enmity in the process."[103]

As we talked, Asbed's piercing dark eyes and rigid look showed a deep commitment to the cause he was leading: a better life for the down-and-out workers in the tomato fields. I like to think I am a good judge of character. Unlike Hayes's assessment, I found Asbed to be a straight shooter and sincere in his efforts to forge change for the tomato workers. He actually shunned the spotlight. He was more of a leader who remained behind the scenes, who devised strategies and campaigns, but preferred to stay backstage. I saw in Asbed a good man who I could trust, but also a hardened man who was not ready to trust me. I wanted his trust so we could forge an agreement.

I confided to Asbed that McDonald's supply and legal teams were concerned about the slippery slope. They were apprehensive about getting too close to suppliers and getting entangled in their oversight of their farmworkers' wages because doing so could lead to dilemmas with other agricultural products. But Asbed thought the reverse would be true if McDonald's didn't get involved now, noting that:

> It's a slippery slope the other way, in fact, which happens when you turn your back on the conditions of your supply chain, then suddenly all the things that can happen, like slavery and sexual assault, eventually do happen in every crop that you don't take care of, that you don't do your part to help make better.

Since the positions of CIW and McDonald's were miles apart, I thought I needed an independent facilitator to facilitate discussion on both sides and look for compromises and a win-win solution for both sides. I contacted Tom Crick at the Jimmy Carter Center. We agreed to meet at the Carter Center in Atlanta.

I planned for the meeting together with Dan Gorsky. At the time, Gorsky was a senior director, soon to be promoted to vice president of the U.S. supply chain. He was also Hayes's boss. My job was to convince Gorsky to collaborate with CIW. It was a big challenge. He believed the supplier-developed SAFE program was better than CIW's. We got nowhere during a day of dialogue with the CIW team, including Asbed and Benitez, and Crick as facilitator. The CIW wouldn't budge; nor would we. But at least we had met face to face. The opposition wasn't a stereotype anymore—and neither were we.

Another Truth Tour

Because of our impasse, CIW decided to get more aggressive publicly. They started to organize another Truth Tour. They trumpeted it as bigger than ever before and planned to bring hundreds if not thousands of supporters to our Oak Brook campus to protest during our May 2007 Annual Shareholder's Meeting. CIW was clever to partner with Lutheran, Presbyterian, Methodist, and Catholic leaders, supporting CIW and criticizing McDonald's. From a reputational perspective, we were the devil fighting the angels.

A few weeks prior to the Truth Tour showing up at our back door, my future boss, J. C. Gonzalez-Mendez, head of the U.S. supply chain, chaired a meeting with the broader team to decide what to do. There were about fifteen of us, clockwise from Gonzalez-Mendez were leaders from supply chain, communications, public affairs, and legal; near one end of the circle I sat and listened.

We rehashed the pros and cons of the strategy of sticking with the supplier SAFE program versus agreeing with the CIW approach. The overwhelming sentiment was to not give an inch to the CIW. Each person ahead of me reaffirmed sticking to the supplier plans, each arguing against caving in to CIW's demands. When my turn came, I advocated that workers deserved better pay and conditions, and that the supplier plan was not credible. Also, I said, if our goal is to remove McDonald's from this ugly campaign, I said we would never win with the SAFE program, no matter how good it was. The penny-a-pound rhetoric was too effective and convincing. The solution was a nominal cost for us (about $200,000). I argued that we should consider an agreement with CIW.

The final tally was a resounding reaffirmation to stick with the current approach. I was the lone opposing vote.

Another powerful group within McDonald's also had a keen interest in the CIW battle. Jack Daly created McDonald's worldwide corporate relations council (WWCRC) just a year earlier for exactly the dilemma we faced right now. I was Daly's right-hand man to help set it up, create agendas, follow up, and streamline decision-making. WWCRC was comprised of every key function of the company that intersects with issues that impact our brand reputation, so the council was comprised mostly of senior officers from legal, marketing, operations, government relations, supply chain, communications, and my area, CSR. By definition, WWCRC was a global group. McDonald's was very decentralized, so our culture was heavily weighted toward still allowing local markets, like the U.S. business, to make their own decisions. Many of the WWCRC members were sympathetic to the CIW situation.

I loved WWCRC. It finally gave a more formal forum for decision-making. Up to this time, I felt that deciding what to do on any public issue was like pulling teeth. Or worse yet, I felt that I was playing pinball, bouncing around to scores of people to get approval on any initiative, with any one of them having the ability to nix the decision. This created too much internal paralysis.

At the April 2007 shareholders' meeting, CIW's campaign took another effective step: They started to write letters to both our CEO and board of directors. As the issue became more public, they were directly asked why we wouldn't pay the penny a pound more. Answering that question was not easy. This in turn made them ask a lot of questions within McDonald's about why we had yet to resolve the CIW issue.

A couple weeks before the annual meeting, we finally had a showdown. The U.S. supply chain team wrote a summary letter to CEO Jim Skinner. It proposed to stay the course, stick to the current plan, and support the tomato growers' SAFE program.

I felt an obligation to put an alternative proposal in Skinner's hands. I worked with Heidi Glunz from my team to draft a different proposal, coauthored by Daly, in which the core element was to agree to the extra pay for the workers (by working with our direct suppliers, still keeping pay as their issue, not a McDonald's issue).

Within a week, Skinner sided with the Langert/Glunz/Daly proposal. I felt good about this, and, on April 7, 2007, I went south to Immokalee,

Florida, to shake hands with the CIW. The supply chain leaders, however, did not like this decision. Hayes, in fact, characterized the decision as "rolling over," saying that:

> When McDonald's caved in, they did it from a PR perspective. McDonald's ended up back in a corner, making a bad decision that benefitted no one. A small group of radicals managed to hoist this problem onto McDonald's and would not let McDonald's do what it normally would do, which is work through the supplier community, work to benefit the affected people directly. Instead, CIW rammed it up McDonald's keister.

Although Hayes and the supply chain folks remained opposed to the deal with CIW, the CIW people were elated. "We were very happy, of course," said Asbed. "Getting McDonald's to be part of the program was huge at that point. I think we probably expected it to mean it would be downhill from there." In addition to CIW, others were pleased with the result. Even former U.S. President Jimmy Carter released a statement praising the agreement:

> I welcome McDonald's commitment to work with the Coalition of Immokalee Workers to improve the lives of the workers who supply their 13,000 U.S. restaurants with tomatoes. This is a clear and welcome example of positive industry partnership. It demonstrates also McDonald's leadership in social responsibility and CIW's importance as a voice for farmworker rights. I encourage others to now follow the lead of McDonald's and Taco Bell [part of the YUM agreement two years earlier]to achieve the much-needed change throughout the entire Florida-based tomato industry.[104]

As it turned out, McDonald's two-year battle with CIW was not over. Actually, it started another battle: "Instead of prompting an accelerated rate of change toward this partnership that we'd finally been able to establish and unleash," Asbed said, "it prompted what you could call the final death throes of resistance by the growers."

Our suppliers went upstream to their suppliers to implement the wage increase of a penny a pound. They faced tremendous resistance. A kind of cold war erupted over tomato-picking wages. The growers refused to pass this money on to the workers. This was astounding. Imagine a customer like McDonald's actually publicly committing to paying more, through its suppliers, with the upstream suppliers refusing.

Public interest groups often say McDonald's can snap its fingers and forge change in our supply chain. Here is a prime example of the barriers to change McDonald's routinely encountered. We struck a deal with CIW and finally asked our suppliers to ask their suppliers to pay the extra penny a pound, noting that McDonald's would add that to the cost of buying tomatoes, but the growers rejected it out of hand.

A couple years later, the growers finally agreed to pay more. Better yet, the growers finally started to collaborate with CIW—about ten years after beginning their work with Taco Bell. It took ten years to achieve this important change. It was a change that couldn't easily be undone. New technology and social media had compelled such high levels of transparency that no longer could any part of a supply hide. As Asbed said:

> The genie's out of the bottle and it's not going back in. The ability in this information age for information in the supply chain to get out of the supply chain into the public awareness is infinitely greater than it was back when you and I were kids. It's just a different game today and it has different rules.

> It's not the Las Vegas-style supply chain management anymore, where what happens in the supply chain stays in the supply chain. It's now out there; it's transparent to all.

After a full decade, CIW had forged this change. Asbed and his coalition hung in there despite formidable resistance from several quarters. Progress did not come in days, weeks, or months. Change took years. As Asbed noted, quoting Martin Luther King: "The arc of the moral universe is long, but it bends toward justice. It sounds corny, but it's true. Ultimately things bend toward the better."

Although many activists are looking for quick fixes, change takes persistence. The CIW ended up winning a Presidential Medal in 2014 and was twice invited to the U.N. in Geneva for forums for human rights. The CIW could take comfort in the fact that its grit paid off. The farmworkers had found a way to balance a sense of urgency with the reality that achieving change is a long haul. "It's not easy," said Asbed. He added that:

> We don't have much of a choice. There is no choice but to keep fighting, especially when we have a solution that works. Having a solution fuels our perseverance.

All of this progress is happening because companies like McDonald's who said, "We need this to happen in our supply chain." The grower knows if they refuse to make those changes they're going to lose business. And that economic incentive is strong enough to have essentially reshaped an entire industry.

It's a remarkable story. When you think about it, if you could take a town like Immokalee where things were absolute hell 25 years ago, and even 10 years ago, one of the poorest towns in the country. It just languished here, in the middle of nowhere, dusty, horrible streets, with poorest people you know. And now the town has become a beaming light for the protection of human rights and corporate supply chain responsibility across the globe.

Mixed Progress With the Fourth Element of Sustainability

Four years had passed since Koziol called for suppliers to add a fourth element to supply chain: sustainability. The results were a mixed bag:

1. Integrating sustainability, though rocky at the beginning, picked up speed. McDonald's 2004 CSR public report extensively detailed how the company used TNS's principles to shape McDonald's. I was most proud that in this CSR report we publicly proclaimed a strong sustainable supply chain vision:

   Socially Responsible Food Supply Vision

   We envision a food supply system that profitably yields high-quality, safe food products without supply interruption while creating a net benefit for employees, their communities, biodiversity and the environment.

2. Demanding that our suppliers rely on sustainable fish was a great accomplishment, even though our suppliers were first reluctant to do so.
3. Persuading Smithfield to reconsider its approach to sustainability highlighted the influence McDonald's had with suppliers.
4. Failing to take a stand on the CIW issue early on tarnished our reputation. We let it drag on for two years too many.

McDonald's had taken important strides toward providing more sustainable food, but we still were not where we needed to be. The sustainability mindset was vastly improved, but it remained inconsistent. This needed to change. It would take Greenpeace campaigners dressed as chickens protesting at our restaurants to set in motion a giant step toward sustainability in McDonald's supply chain (see Chapter 9).

Managing a Sustainable Supply Chain

Supply chain is no longer just about quality, service, and value. Sustainability is now on par with these attributes that define a good supply chain.

An organization that does not have a well-defined approach to sustainability in its supply chain risks tarnishing its reputation and losing an assured supply. This also might mean missed opportunities to save money, especially with environmental resource conservation. Using less water, creating less waste, and reducing energy use can translate to a more cost-efficient supply chain as well. Consider these suggestions as you assess the future of sustainability in your supply chain:

1. **Employ a systems-based approach:** Functional leaders cannot think just about purchasing, marketing, or operations. Ensure that functional departments, such as supply chain, understand other aspects, including the intersection of products and services and societal trends and issues.

2. **Embrace the long-term view:** Adding sustainability to purchasing requires a long-term commitment and effort. For example, McDonald's sustainable fish timeline from awareness to action to results was a decade-long journey.
3. **Make it based in science:** Seek the highest level of scientific understanding possible. Use outside expertise to inform yourself and your organization, including scientists, nongovernmental organizations, academics, and industry leaders.
4. **Partner with and prod suppliers:** Collaborate with your supplier partners to integrate sustainable principles as a critical part of their service to your organization. Allow for flexibility in meeting these goals. When you face resistance, keep prodding them.
5. **Use the best sustainable change agents:** Empower your supply chain leaders to take strong stands and back them up when they do so. Suppliers may kick and scream, like Smithfield did, but the supply chain leader's blunt feedback is necessary.

7

The Battle for Values
Can You Etch Them in Stone?

Fig. 7.1: "To Do What Is Right" on the Cover of McDonald's
First CSR Report, 2002.

Squabbling Over the Importance of Values

I've always believed that the best sustainability change agents can come
from any part of the company. The unexpected sustainability hero is
someone with the will, desire, and grit necessary to rise above the status
quo. Jerry Calabrese, the rapid-fire, fireball from our accounting department was such an unlikely hero.

Calabrese was a little guy with a big personality. He had a sincerity about him that oozed truth. He could call out BS in a second or challenge someone else's thinking point blank, but he did it without offending anyone. In fact, people liked him even better for doing it: what a skill, such a rare business art form.

Calabrese was put in charge of developing a scheme to measure restaurant performance, eventually called restaurant operations improvement performance (ROIP). ROIP was all about continuous improvement. Our owner–operators were skeptical of this measurement system, considering it an intrusion into their operations, a big brother, strong-arming play from the corporate office, so Calabrese joked that it was first called RIP.

In developing these core measurements, "[w]e were asking our people—our customers and our employees—what they thought," Calabrese said, "how they were being treated and so forth, because they were the most valuable asset and the core to the company's existing Plan to Win."[105]

McDonald's had developed this strategic Plan to Win framework near the end of Jim Cantalupo's CEO tenure in 2004, in partnership with his right-hand man, Jim Skinner. It became McDonald's blueprint for success for the ensuing decade, encapsulated in the Five Ps: people, product, promotion, place, and price. The key was to focus on getting better, not bigger. This shift to building fewer restaurants in order to focus on improving customer satisfaction in order to improve restaurant performance was the key to McDonald's revitalization.

Since Calabrese was the respected numbers and measurement guru at McDonald's, it was a godsend that he was the one to lead the idea of making the company values a foundation for the Plan to Win. He said that, "[w]e wanted to make sure that the things that we were measuring were the critical drivers of the business and incorporated the values that made our company great."

When Calabrese brought the idea of codifying and integrating values into the Plan to Win, Skinner scoffed at first. "Jim was a little cautious," says Calabrese. "It's not that he didn't believe in the values. But Skinner thought it [was] going to distract from the Plan to Win." Indeed, Skinner pounded on the table, rejecting the idea to integrate values, declaring, "I don't want these. I don't want to confuse people."[106]

Calabrese just kept on with his conviction, saying that, "[v]alues are not going to harm anything. It's just going to motivate people to get focused around the key values and enablers that will drive good performance." Despite ongoing rejection, Calabrese kept at it, pushing to codify and integrate values into the Plan to Win. If Skinner was stubborn,

Calabrese was even more stubborn, and he displayed a tenacity that I admired.

In 2007, Skinner finally agreed to developing and integrating the values into the Plan to Win. He said, "We decided to put this on paper and define what kind of company we were, where our focus was, so that when people got up in the morning, whether they worked for accounting, real estate or operations, I wanted them to internalize our mission, and understand the kind of company we were and what Our Values centered around."

Revealing McDonald's Values

Skinner witnessed in real time the organic evolution of the values of the company. He started in the company in 1971 as a restaurant manager trainee in Carpentersville, Illinois (about 45 miles northwest of Chicago). He absorbed the culture that emanated from McDonald's founding leaders, Ray Kroc and his right-hand man, Fred Turner. So Skinner wasn't creating McDonald's values from a blank canvas. Instead, his goal was simply to reveal the values already on the canvas.

Jim Skinner was intimidating for many of us, including me. Once you understood him, though, he was a man of integrity, focused on results. He had no patience for puffery. The more concise you were with him, the better. He was a true champion of my work leading corporate social responsibility (CSR), as we called it when he took over as CEO in 2004. His perspective on CSR was based on doing the right thing. At big audiences, internal or external, Jim would always say, "we try to do the right thing and do things right." I was very moved to hear Skinner say this so often.

At the time, there wasn't a consistent, well-known, and well-ingrained set of values guiding all of McDonald's. For the most part, we each had our own version of company values, even though I had published a version* of McDonald's values in an earlier CSR report. Skinner turned to Professor Ed Freeman from the University of Virginia Darden School of Business to help him to formally craft a set of McDonald's values. Freeman was chosen to help because he was an impactful lecturer in McDonald's Global Leadership Development Program.

---

* Our "Core Values" were included in McDonald's first CSR report (2002). These "Core Values" were not the result of any studied internal cultural effort, but more of a communications piece.

Skinner said, "When I first met [Freeman], I thought, 'Ugh.'" I suspected that he was initially put off by the professor's large beard and frizzy hair. "I ended up liking the guy a lot," Skinner said. "He was very bright, very unassuming and quite funny guy, actually."

Freeman liked Skinner, too, saying that, "Jim and I hit it off pretty well. We are both farm boys, and we had that in common. I had a tremendous amount of respect for him. He realized he was probably the last guy to have gone from the fry cook all the way to CEO."

Skinner, schooled in the tough daily grind of a restaurant, told Freeman in his typical brusque way, "I want to say what the values are. I don't want to do any values jam or surveys or any kind of that stuff."

Freeman agreed to help. He felt an affinity to the McDonald's people he trained. "They loved McDonald's," he said. "They loved the food. These were my type of people. These weren't Harvard, Princeton Ivy Leaguers. They were regular folks who were out there trying to do something good in the world."

So two smart, strong-minded farm boys from humble roots bonded together to craft what eventually became McDonald's "Our Values."

McDonald's Our Values

We place the customer experience at the core of all we do. Our customers are the reason for our existence. We demonstrate our appreciation by providing them with high-quality food and superior service in a clean, welcoming environment at a great value. Our goal is QSC&V for each and every customer, each and every time.

As with Kroc, Skinner started with the customer. "The customer is at the core of all that we do," he said. "It's not too confusing. You remember I used to say the moment of truth and most important time is when interaction with the customer at the front counter and drive-thru. If we screw that up, all is lost."

Over the years, I must have heard Skinner refer to the moment of truth with our customers a hundred times. Kroc and Skinner had uttered types of sayings that permeated our culture. For example, as Skinner said, "If you work just for money, you'll never make it, but if you love what you're doing and you always put the customer first, success will be yours."

> **We are committed to our people.** We provide opportunity, nurture talent, develop leaders, and reward achievement. We believe that a team of well-trained individuals with diverse backgrounds and experiences, working together in an environment that fosters respect and drives high levels of engagement, is essential to our continued success.

Skinner put customers first. The company's people were a close second. "We're committed to our people," he said. "What role do they play? Everyone wants to get ahead, everybody wants to contribute, and that's why we put together the Talent Management Leadership Institute."

The leadership institute included many modern training programs to help McDonald's store managers advance their careers. Kroc had started Hamburger University (HU) in 1961 for the same purpose, but the HU curriculum had not kept up with the times. Nor had many of our other practices. For example, it was not unusual for me to have gone a decade without a performance review. I consider it one of Skinner's legacies that he put top talent in charge of human resources and of training and development. He brought McDonald's up to modern standards.

> **We believe in the McDonald's System.** McDonald's business model, depicted by the "three-legged stool" of owner–operators, suppliers, and company employees, is our foundation, and the balance of interests among the three groups is key.

Skinner also incorporated the philosophy of the three-legged stool. Some might consider this phony-baloney rhetoric. I assure you that it is not. Employees were bombarded with this philosophy, often hearing the quote from Ray Kroc asserting that "[n]one of us is as good as all of us." This meant we were all linked and mutually interdependent: franchisees, suppliers, and company staff. All three parts of the stool represented equal coowners of our brand and our future.

> **We operate our business ethically.** Sound ethics is good business. At McDonald's, we hold ourselves to and conduct our business to high standards of fairness, honesty, and integrity. We are individually accountable and collectively responsible.

Another important value concerned is ethics. Skinner saw honesty and integrity as foundational to the people who comprised McDonald's. I always felt I worked for a company that valued high standards, and it seemed that we were able to weed out those who violated them. No wonder Skinner and Jim Cantalupo signed off on McDonald's first CSR report in 2002, which had on its cover a quote I heard quite often: "We are committed to doing what is right."

We give back to our communities. We take seriously the responsibilities that come with being a leader. We help our customers build better communities, support RMHC [Ronald McDonald House Charities], and leverage our size, scope, and resources to help make the world a better place.

Giving back is another of the values. I like the way this value is phrased. This value is not only about our long-standing commitment to Ronald McDonald House Charities (RMHC) but also about "making the world a better place." The McDonald's system was dedicated to RMHC, an independent 501(3)c charity dedicated to "[k]eeping families together and near the care they need." This value came from Ray Kroc as well, who said, "[w]e have an obligation to give something back to the community that gives so much to us."

We grow our business profitably. McDonald's is a publicly traded company. As such, we work to provide sustained growth for our shareholders. This requires a continual focus on our customers and on the health of our system.

The sixth value is about satisfying our shareholders. This one struck me as odd—not really connected to values. Freeman was at odds about this one, too. He would have preferred to leave this value out or to articulate the need for engagement with all stakeholders, such as NGOs, community leaders, academics, government, and so on. But Freeman was comfortable with denoting shareholder satisfaction as a value if doing so was what Skinner needed to do in order to make this particular value a relevant business imperative rather than a squishy, feel-good thing.

We strive continually to improve. We are a learning organization that aims to anticipate and respond to changing customer, employee, and system needs through constant evolution and innovation.

Skinner and Freeman thought these six values captured everything. It struck Skinner later that they missed a key value of never being satisfied. "We're a learning organization," he said. "We are all about continuous improvement. We listen, we learn, and we anticipate and respond to the changing customer."

I can personally vouch for this value, as it seemed that no one was fully satisfied with any achievement. I say this with respect and as a compliment. It was inherent in our culture that we always thought things could be done better. If you were looking for an "atta boy" from top execs, you'd be looking for a long time as few were offered. It kept us humble, working as a team, not for ourselves, and getting things done.

Integrating Our Values

Once they were completed, it was time to get Our Values disseminated to the McDonald's three-legged system of company employees, franchisees and their employees, and suppliers. But Skinner was adamant that he did not want posters, signs, or cards touting McDonald's Our Values. He disdained marketing the values. He believed it went against the authenticity of Our Values to make them a program.

Freeman agreed. "This is not something you want to roll out," he told Skinner. "What you want is a set of conversations. If there is not a set of conversations, it's going to die a death like every other corporate values thing that happens with other companies."

As I became aware of the Our Values work, I wanted in. I wanted to help. I was excited about the notion of everyone within the McDonald's system living Our Values every day. I believed that, by doing so, we would reach the pinnacle of being a socially responsible company. I saw living McDonald's Our Values in all of our 1.9 million people and thousands of supplier personnel as the Holy Grail of CSR.

Since I believe being guided by Our Values every day is more sustainable than any CSR program, policy, or project, I called Calabrese to schedule a meeting to discuss what my team could do to get Our Values integrated into the company. I wanted my team to help put this Holy Grail in the hands of all our employees, owner–operators, and suppliers.

I knew my team was taking on a mammoth challenge. McDonald's had a roll-up-your-sleeves type of culture, where it was common to put all hands on deck to roll out a new toaster or grill system or all manner of operational stuff. We were well versed in training people on new frying procedures. We weren't so good at training our people on soft issues like values.

Another challenge was how to reach the crews in the restaurants, which were the heart of McDonald's. About 99 percent of McDonald's employees worked in the restaurants, scattered throughout one hundred nineteen countries, each of which would need to translate and understand Our Values in their own culture and context.

But the biggest challenge we faced was the continual need to train people because McDonald's restaurants had a high employee turnover ratio. Believe it or not, a good restaurant averaged 90–100% employee turnover each year at the time. That's because McDonald's is set up to have mostly part-time workers who use McDonald's for short-term, supplemental financial needs. Then they move on. How to inculcate values into this ever-shifting employee base felt like mission impossible.

What gave me hope was that Walmart was doing it already. If they could do it, surely McDonald's could do it? Since Walmart's big proclamation in 2006 that they would lead on sustainability, they have been impressing external stakeholders with their goals, actions, and employee engagement.

Walmart's 2006 announcement was like the Declaration of Independence for corporate sustainability. Walmart had unleashed a movement and jump-started the mainstreaming of sustainability. They set audacious goals, such as zero waste and 100 percent renewable energy, which took the NGO and corporate world by surprise.

Later, Walmart also implemented what was then called My Sustainability Plan (MSP). Ellen Weinreb, an independent recruiter for Walmart, summarized the initiative:

> MSP launched in 2010, urging Walmart associates in 28 countries to adopt goals concentrated on living healthier, caring for the planet, or getting the most out of life. Associates were asked to be part of the process to define the MSP focus areas of My Health (eating healthy, getting active, quitting tobacco, reducing stress), My Planet (saving water, reducing waste, saving energy, enjoying nature), and My Life (learning new skills, managing their money, making quality time, helping others).

> MSP offers associates an online space with tools to not only create, track, and stay dedicated to their goals, but also to connect with other associates via social networking such. Over 50,000 U.S. associates have signed up and used the tool, allowing Walmart to measure their associates' level of engagement and the impact of their collective actions.[107]

Walmart had one big advantage over McDonald's: They were not franchised. All employees were part of Walmart, not five thousand separate entities like McDonald's. Theirs was a top-down culture. If the CEO wanted something, their system was united in that direction.

In contrast, McDonald's culture was not top down. We were doubly decentralized, with owner–operators controlling almost 90 percent of our restaurants. Plus, we let country management run the restaurants in their countries. Being close to the local customer and making decisions within the actual marketplace was a strength for McDonald's international expansion. Indeed, it was this kind of decentralization that allowed McDonald's to adapt and excel in so many diverse markets.

However, this decentralization had a downside as well: It could be a detriment to implementing any global program or policy. Top down was not in McDonald's DNA. We believed in "freedom within a framework," where we at the corporate headquarters in Oak Brook developed an overarching direction but allowed a lot of flexibility so that local markets could adapt various frameworks to meet the needs of their customers.

I asked Kathleen Bannan from my team to head up Our Values integration. She was as scrappy as they come, small and lean, yet gritty and dogged, too. Bannan quickly put a business case together and presented it to our heads of human resources, operations, and corporate affairs.

If we were to even hope for full implementation of McDonald's Our Values, we absolutely had to engage our restaurant employees. Bannan said, "We had a whole bunch of data that we threw at them in terms of employee retention and how important it is for people to have something to believe in, what we stood for beyond operations and making a profit."[108]

Bannan prepared an implementation plan to present to top management. We didn't want this to be a top-down push. The worst tactic we could use was to prescribe. Our decentralized system rejected corporate decrees. Therefore, we recommended establishing a values activation council (VAC) made of leaders within our top ten markets and our top five emerging markets. This represented 80 percent of our business.

Senior management approved the formation of the VAC and the effort to integrate Our Values, ultimately to the restaurant managers and their staff. This set Bannan on her way to activate the VAC. She noted that:

> We established a Values Catalyst leader in each of these fifteen markets. It was their responsibility to serve as champions for Values, and to lead the engagement of their stakeholders to

develop and test market level initiatives, and to share progress with other markets. These Values Catalysts were responsible for developing an action plan as well.

Bannan did an excellent job of working with colleagues around the globe to activate McDonald's Our Values. She encouraged incorporating Our Values into employee orientation and training materials and including an example of living Our Values into recognition programs. In keeping with our freedom-within-a-framework approach, restaurants in different countries tailored their implementation to their local staff. McDonald's Australia came up with an extraordinarily creative way to share the values, putting them into plain Aussie speak (see Fig. 7.2).

After two years of work, Bannan crafted a superior brochure about values integration. Just as she finished and distributed the report, Skinner, the chief advocate and creator of Our Values, decided to retire. In March 2012 Don Thompson took over as CEO. He had been a

McDonald's Australia

McDonald's Australia led the System with the creation of the first "Crew Speak" poster, a more simple articulation of the Values that resonates with Crew and Restaurant Managers.

Fig. 7.2: McDonald's Our Values Are Introduced in Australia to Fit Their Culture.

cochampion of Our Values. Unfortunately, after his first month as CEO, McDonald's experienced its first year-over-year decline in comparable sales in a decade. Similar negative results pounded our company month after month after that.

With that, our overt work on McDonald's Our Values fizzled away while the company scrambled to improve menu, operations, and marketing strategies in order to turn the tide. Bannan felt as though she had lost the battle, as though she had failed in fully implementing the values. I felt the same disappointment. But the truth is that McDonald's Our Values made a difference, and they still do today, though you can't measure it.

The Our Values process that Jerry Calabrese had started back in about 2006 with determined effort placed values at the foundation of the Plan to Win. For about six years, thousands if not millions of people among our system heard our messages. For some, I trust that Our Values motivated them.

With Skinner's retirement, the active integration program was gone. But the values continue within the company. The values that evolved with Ray Kroc in the early years grew internally through repeated actions and behaviors like a spider web, strengthening and deepening, sticking to the company decades after Kroc's death. Those values continue to thrive and evolve with the needs of the company. After all, values are not a program, a brochure, nor a poster. Values are living things, and they don't disappear.

Hard Knock Nuggets

Keeping Values Alive

As you think about the values that characterize your corporation, its employees, its customers, and, indeed, all of its stakeholders, consider these tips:

- **Live the values across all departments and for all stakeholders.** Values are much more than what you put on paper or a website. You should see, hear, and experience the inherent values of a company when you see others (and yourself) act and make decisions.

- **Keep values short and succinct.** We created seven values, probably three to four too many, with too many words. People are not going to remember seven values. We benchmarked Southwest Airlines, which had these simple values: Warrior Spirit; Servant's Heart; Fun-LUVing Attitude.

- **Ensure that your values are based in the history, mission, and vision of the company.** Some thought the lack of internal engagement to develop McDonald's Our Values was a roadblock. People were asking who had developed the values. They wanted to know why they should want to integrate them into their own markets. However, Skinner made it happen, skipping for the most part ongoing internal engagement and arguing that we didn't really need a kumbaya, democratic approach to develop values since they stemmed from the company's long history. I think it best that our values emanated from Founder Ray Kroc. Skinner was essentially articulating what Kroc had long before created while growing McDonald's. It's often better for values to be delivered from on high, rather than creating them from a bottom-up approach.

- **Sprinkle values in all of your words and actions.** Even though times are tough, values should remain top of mind for the leaders of a company. By regularly recognizing and rewarding those that exemplify values in action, people see that it is for real, people will go the extra mile, and people can rebound after downturns and disruptions in the business.

- **Values give us anchors, stakes in the ground.** Professor Freeman describes the benefits: "Values serve as stabilizers and shields. Values empower and inspire us. They make it so that everyone is pulling in the same direction. Values are an important driver of innovation and value creation. Values define a brand. Values help drive business strategy."[109]

8

The Battle Goes to the Board Room
A Shareholder Proposal Makes a Difference

Fig. 8.1: Surprised to Find a Path Toward More Sustainable Potatoes.

Shareholders Focus on Pesticides

As part of my training early on in my career, I traveled to Idaho to learn all about the Russet potato that makes McDonald's world-famous french fries. In the middle of the vast set of rows filled with potato vines, I asked the potato farmer how much he spent on pesticides. He grimaced and sighed and said it was by far his largest cost. I learned that about half of his costs were on pesticides. That experience seeing first-hand the magnitude of pesticides used in crop agriculture like potatoes has forever stuck with me.

159

McDonald's sold about 3.4 billion pounds of potatoes a year and served more than 9 million pounds of french fries every day at the time.[110] That's a lot of pesticides, too. According to a 2016 study by the U.S. Department of Agriculture of fertilizer usage for potatoes, the lbs/acre/ per year for nitrogen, phosphate, potash, and sulfur fertilizer rates were 233, 155, 172, and 78, respectively.[111]

The Idaho potato training trip came to me in 2009 as I read what I first thought was an outlandish shareholder proposal submitted to McDonald's: "Resolved: We request that within one year the Board [of Directors] publish a report to shareholders on policy options for McDonald's to reduce pesticide use in its supply chain, at reasonable expense and omitting proprietary information." We had no idea about the quantities of pesticides used in our supply chain. That was our suppliers' business, and usually it was several steps upstream from our suppliers.

For example, McDonald's bun suppliers bought the ingredients to make McDonald's buns. It was their suppliers' suppliers who grew the wheat and sugar. Hopefully, the farmers who grew crops knew their pesticide usage. McDonald's wasn't at all privy to this knowledge, and the task of finding this information was monumental. In addition, McDonald's supply chain extended to 119 countries, each with separate agricultural infrastructures, making it nearly impossible to know what pesticides were being used where in what quantity.

Shareholders Make Demands

I was contemplating dismissing this broad, unreasonable shareholder proposal and sending it back to our legal team, which typically would go back and forth with the U.S. Securities and Exchange Commission, whose mission is to "protect investors; maintain fair, orderly, and efficient markets,"[112] to try to get it excluded. If not excluded, McDonald's would be required to inform shareholders. Then shareholders would vote on it, all culminating at the annual shareholders' meeting. All these shareholder issues go through the Board of Directors.

From 2006 to 2015, McDonald's shareholders voted on thirty-two shareholder proposals in total, with sixteen related to CSR issues. All the issues were serious, and many of them were issues that McDonald's already was addressing, just not in the way that proponents wanted. Support was as low as 0 percent for an obesity report from the lead proponent, the Sisters of St. Francis of Philadelphia. The highest support was 28 percent for a human rights report from the American Federation of

State, County and Municipal Employees Pension Plan.[113] Table 8.1 summarizes voter support on some key shareholder proposals (see below).

The engagement process with most of the shareholder activists frustrated me. An example is illustrated with the issue of palm oil. Palm oil has been linked to deforestation and other social and environmental impacts, mostly in Indonesia and Malaysia. McDonald's used palm oil primarily in the cooking oil we sourced in Asia for our Asian business. We used small amounts in numerous baking items throughout the world. Tracing where all this came from was really hard, so we relied on GreenPalm offsets. GreenPalm is a program whereby various manufacturers and retailers purchase certificates from a certified palm oil grower to offset the usage of palm oil and palm kernel oil. The program originated with the Roundtable for Sustainable Palm Oil (RSPO) as a way to make a difference when a company like McDonald's could not trace the origins of all of its palm oil. The RSPO certified producer who places offers on the GreenPalm market receives the certificate price as a premium—additional income for working sustainably.[114]

During a conference call with proponents, I hoped to listen and learn and have a productive dialogue. I felt we were progressive on the palm oil issue. We were working with Conservation International and the World Wildlife Fund on devising actions to address our use of palm oil, which included an impending commitment to source all of our palm oil from certified sustainable sources by 2020. We shared this with the

Table 8.1: McDonald's received 16 CSR related shareholder proposals from 2006–2015, summarized in the above categories, with low level shareholder support.

McDonald's Shareholder Proposals	Voter Support (percent)
Human rights report	28
Recycling	23
Nutrition report	6
Palm oil report	6
Genetically modified organisms	4–6
Cage-free eggs	4–5
Controlled atmospheric stunning (a different way to slaughter chickens via gas)	3–4

proponents, but they picked our program apart, criticizing our use of GreenPalm certificates, claiming that they provided no guarantee that McDonald's palm oil purchases do not contribute to biodiversity loss and human rights abuses. Although they were technically correct that the certificates provided no guarantees regarding our own purchases of palm oil, the shareholder activists had no sympathy for the realities of traceability. We explained that GreenPalm certificates were an interim step for us and that we intended to make more specific commitment as we understood our sourcing more.

Unfortunately, I cannot say that any of the various shareholder proposals helped sway our company. That's because, for the most part, it seemed to me that the shareholder activists were using the forum to get media attention, not actually helping us make progress, as my palm oil example illustrates. Most of the shareholders submitting CSR proposals only had the minimum amount of shares needed to do so. SEC guidelines require $2,000 worth of shares of a company.

The best shareholder proposals are those that get discussed and agreed upon before they go to all the shareholders for a vote. I was always looking for a hook, to find where there was energy in the company to address an issue that I believed was important for us to address. This shareholder proposal was the hook I needed.

Seeking Compromise Is Good

As I reread the pesticide proposal, I recalled that farmer in Idaho who used so many pesticides on his Russet potatoes. I had had my eye on pesticides for a long time. I found it a tough nut to crack, though. Whenever I tried to discover more about pesticides upstream in the supply chain, I ran into continuous roadblocks. I was never sure whether it was because of lack of knowledge or lack of wanting to share—both of which were bad motivations. This nebulousness bothered me and made me suspect they were hiding something bad.

I felt we ought to do something about it. With this shareholder proposal, I had an opening—if only I could narrow its scope to potatoes (not all crops) and to the United States (not the world).

In my role at McDonald's, I alone couldn't decide to negotiate an agreement, so I approached our head of potato quality, Mitch Smith. Smith was McDonald's Mr Potato. He was in charge of all the quality standards for our potatoes and was extraordinarily well respected in the potato industry.

Smith was a fun, happy-go-lucky guy and a self-described "Idaho boy." He grew up in Boise, went to school to study botany and biology, and, in 1976, went to work for one of the largest, long-standing potato processing companies, Simplot, where he got on-the-ground training in the potato industry. At McDonald's, we were office neighbors at one point. I found him to be independent, blunt, honest, and self-deprecating—not unlike many of the farmers we worked with. Smith joined McDonald's in 1980. His knowledge of and passion for potatoes were amazing.

I reviewed with Smith the potato–pesticide proposal, telling him that I thought it was a good idea to focus on pesticides. He didn't immediately like the idea. "Quite frankly—and I'm being very honest—I was like, 'Well, I know the potato industry's very good at what they do, and they are sustainable, and they are looking after the land.'" Smith said. "I was kind of questioning what we needed to do this for."[115]

Despite that, Smith saw the business benefit. He saw the potential benefits to developing ways to be more efficient, use less pesticides, and reduce risk, by reducing runoff that could pollute. Smith noted that:

> The more we talked about it, the more I became aware that maybe we don't know as much as we need to know, and if we get things out there, the public will really understand that we are concerned about our suppliers and our environment and how we are in the future. Because if we have no land that grows things, we will have no products.

Our Mr Potato had found religion—in the form of sustainability passion. Given this, the two of us decided to contact the shareholder advocates.

The shareholders' lead filer was the Bard College Endowment, supported by Newground Social Investment and the AFL–CIO. As is typical of shareholder filings, investor groups rely upon a subject-matter expert to advise them. In this case, it was Richard Liroff, founder of the Investor Environmental Health Network (IEHN). Liroff was their ringleader. He was the one who primarily wrote the proposal, and he advised the shareholders on strategy.

I was apprehensive about calling Liroff and his filers. I hadn't had any success in the past convincing a shareholder proponent to agree to something more narrow yet more useful. I didn't have high expectations. It was no surprise when the call didn't start well: adversarial in tone, probably unintentionally on both our parts.

They didn't seem to take the intentions of potato farmers too seriously. As Smith noted, "[t]hey just thought growers went out and sprayed every day and didn't worry about it, and they didn't really care how much they put on it."

Smith nicely but firmly explained that, "anything you spray on a potato field or any other crop for that matter costs a whole lot of money, and [the farmers] don't want to put anymore on that crop than they have to. And so, they're doing everything to monitor, manage, and optimize what they do."

This shifted the conversation to a more positive manner, mostly because Liroff, a veteran of the shareholder process, was a learned expert on chemicals. He also understood the corporate engagement process. He was a former staff member of the World Wildlife Fund, which uses positive forces of corporate collaboration and market-based solutions as a big part of its strategy. Working with companies like McDonald's was something he knew a lot about.

Once the conversation had us all on the same page, we discussed narrowing the giant scope of the proposal. We explained to him and the filers how it was impossible for us to do what they were asking. We suggested the proposal focus only on the United States and on only one crop: potatoes. We also explained to Liroff and his colleagues we had a fair amount of control within our potato supply chain. That was because McDonald's bought such large quantities of potatoes that our suppliers had dedicated facilities to produce our french fries and hash browns, and because our potato suppliers coordinated with their farmers to farm tracts of land dedicated to McDonald's potatoes. Finally, we explained that potatoes were not like cows, whereby we bought only a small portion of its meat, and whereby we did not have such a direct link to the growing process. We used almost all of each potato; scraps were used for hash browns.

All this caught Liroff by surprise. When he originally created the proposal, he had not considered potatoes specifically. He said that he and his fellow shareholder proponents "started out by building the business case that there are risks associated with the use of both chemicals and pesticides, and there are business opportunities in moving toward safer alternatives."[116] He further explained that he initially intended to address the broader use of pesticides and chose McDonald's because he had studied the work we did with the Interfaith Center for Corporate Responsibility (ICCR). He was encouraged by the positive results we had with them on an initiative called Project Kaleidoscope, which pertained to working conditions in China at McDonald's suppliers of toys. McDonald's and Disney had collaborated with several socially responsible investment advocates on Project Kaleidoscope to develop methods to ensure steady compliance with labor standards. Liroff said about the project that, "[i]t was obvious that

McDonald's had a predisposition to engage in these kinds of sustainability issues, so we brought forward the broad pesticide resolution."

As we zeroed in on our conversation about pesticides and potatoes, I learned that Liroff had an extensive background in potatoes. He had cowritten a study in 1999 called "Reducing Reliance on Pesticides in the Great Lakes Basin." Much of its content was about the use of pesticides in potato growing. And so our counterproposal piqued his interest. "When you suggested a pilot project on potatoes, I thought it was a fabulous idea," he said. He was especially impressed with our scale, adding that, "[w]e learned in the conversation with you that McDonald's buys 5 percent of the potatoes in the U.S."

Lucky for us, and for the good of our planet, Liroff (and, he says, the investors with whom he works) had a philosophy that "a shareholder resolution is as much an invitation to dialogue as a request for action." I wish all shareholder investors thought that and acted the same way.

Liroff and his filers agreed to continue the evaluation of focusing on potatoes. "Let's see if we can get some forward movement—a commitment to continue in communication to try and figure something out together," he said, "which we believe is important for society and we think will be beneficial to the company in the long run."

Smith knew that, before we could all agree to the proposal, he had to bring his potato suppliers to the table, along with a wider net of industry leaders. He quickly gathered the National Potato Council and the Canadian Horticultural Council, along with six independent growers for a meeting. As he recalled:

> I could tell from just the body language in the room—not so much from the organizations like the National Potato Council or the suppliers, but from the growers, [who were] looking at me like, "Okay. What are you going do to us? What are you going be asking us to do that's going to cost us money and create more work for us where we already have a lot of work to make sure we meet McDonald's standards in terms of quality going into the back door of that factory?"

But Smith was able to turn the conversation around. I believe he turned the corner with them because they knew Smith was a potato guy who admired the potato industry. They knew they could trust him. After a tough start to the conversation, Smith said, "What I'm saying is [that] we need to get better. And we need to get better at what we do and how we report it, so the consumer understands that progress is being made."

Because Smith was able to corral the upstream potato stakeholders, and because Liroff and his fellow filers agreed to focus on potatoes, we were able to agree to a potato pilot project. The shareholder proposal was withdrawn. A March 2009 Reuters news story summarized the announcement[117]:

> McDonald's Corp, the largest purchaser of potatoes in the United States, has agreed to take preliminary steps to reduce pesticide use in its domestic potato supply, shareholder groups said on Tuesday.
>
> The investors said McDonald's has agreed to survey its U.S. potato suppliers, compile a list of best practices in pesticide use reduction and recommend those best practices to global suppliers. It also will share its findings with investors and include the findings in its annual corporate social responsibility report.
>
> McDonald's, the world's largest fast-food chain, said the process would support ongoing efforts to make its supply chain sustainable.
>
> "Our U.S. potato suppliers are already working with their growers to advance sustainable pesticide practices, such as reductions and alternative methods," McDonald's said in a statement.
>
> Investor groups teamed with the Investor Environmental Health Network to engage McDonald's in talks about pesticide reduction.
>
> Dr Richard Liroff, executive director at the Investor Environmental Health Network, said that some of McDonald's largest U.S. potato suppliers include ConAgra Foods Inc. unit Lamb Weston and privately held J.R. Simplot Co.
>
> "We welcome McDonald's stepping up to the plate and look forward to supporting the company's efforts to reduce pesticide use in the future," Liroff said.
>
> "These are early steps," said Liroff, who said McDonald's must first know where its stands in terms of pesticide use in potato supplies before it can set targets for reduction.

I commend the likes of Richard Liroff, who was more interested in progress than perfection. He was practical, not pie-in-the-sky, and he focused less on himself or on getting attention for his own cause and more on actually solving the problem. Smith operated in much the same way.

During the next several years, Smith worked with the Integrated Pest Management Institute, the National Potato Council, and growers in the United States and Canada. They collaborated on developing a comprehensive reporting process to document the use of pesticides, as well as fertilizer and water, on potato crops. The initiative led to the Potato Sustainable Initiative.[118]

By 2013, Smith had worked with various partners to create a Potato Grower Pesticide Stewardship survey and model. It outlined expectations and best practices for various levels, from Basic, Steward, and Expert to the highest level, Master. The study showed that 50 percent of McDonald's suppliers achieved Master level, defined as[119]:

- Certified for sustainable, environmental, and worker practices.

- Documented some level of environmental or resource improvement.

- Participated or assisted planning of resource conservation or pesticide use education.

Smith enjoyed this work. As I had learned time and time again, most people love making a difference in the world if they are given the impetus and permission—and I was no different. My greatest joy was just this: if I could get the company to adopt a new policy, program, or project that made society better, and if I could motivate someone in a functional role to take on its mantle of leadership, then nothing gave me more satisfaction.

Another joy was the many advantages of working with an outside expert like Richard Liroff. One benefit was getting an unvarnished opinion about whether what you were doing was good. Of course, it's natural to get sucked into the idea that what you are doing is good. An independent expert like Liroff is more qualified to evaluate. Liroff summarized three benefits:

> First, you sent signals to your supply chain. You are a consumer facing company. It is your reputation on the line. You need to be more involved.
>
> The reason McDonald's was silent on pesticides was simply that you left it to your three prime potato providers. As long as they were ok, you were ok.
>
> Pulling in the tier one suppliers and all their growers fostered a conversation within your entire supply chain about this

issue. And you came up with a system for moving forward, for assessing folks, to which everyone bought in. I think that is such an important positive.

McDonald's made a decision to bring in the entire industry through the National Potato Council and publicly disclose the results. It was easy for investors and others to track results over time.

As I reflect on this huge success with potatoes, which is such an important agricultural product, I realize once again that the battle to do good requires dogged, committed people on both sides. The activist side too often fights for perfection so that nothing is ever agreed upon. The business side wants to avoid conflict and controversy. When faced with talking about things such as pesticides, the company typically fails to see an upside, only downside. Raising the issue brings to light what consumers don't know or don't want to know, such as pesticides are used to grow potatoes for MacFries. But instead of coming to a typical shareholder resolution stalemate, Liroff and his filers were practical and reasonable, and Smith believed better pesticide management made the potato industry stronger and more efficient. By working together, we were able to win the battle of the boardroom—at least in this instance.

Lessons for Engaging With Investors—and for Investors to Engage With Companies

Shortly after this successful engagement, Liroff wrote a piece in *GreenBiz* summarizing some tips for dealing with activist investors.[120] These are good lessons to learn, as they can help companies deal with activist investors and activist investors deal with companies. I highlight five of his and my five top tips, respectively:

1. **Investors can be a useful antidote to senior management group-think.** Groupthink can cause senior management to fool both themselves and their investors, to the detriment of both.
2. **Investors can be silo-busters.** Chemicals, pesticides, and other sustainability issues cut across departments and supply chains. Investors can prompt senior management to bring together product designers, marketers, and other folks who ought to be talking to one another but aren't. But it pays to be flexible rather than adversarial in such endeavors.
3. **Investors can spark development of forward-looking, beyond-compliance programs.** Like star athletes, the most successful companies anticipate and move to where the ball or puck is going to be—and get there ahead of the competition.
4. **Investors can be adjunct staff or free labor—to a point.** If a company's just starting down the sustainability path or dealing with a new issue, knowledgeable investors can identify readily available resources, such as a network of sustainability officers within the company's sector. Some of the best resources exist within the nonprofit community, and investors may well know exactly where to find them. Investors can save both staff time and consulting costs.
5. **Answer investors' letters or pick up the phone.** Investors own stock in the company. Talk to them. This is Stakeholder Relations 101.

Social responsible investment (SRI) is becoming more popular with individual and institutional investors—and shareholders. If you haven't formed a strategy to engage with them, now is the time. After all, SRI had a market size of $8.72 trillion in the United States at the beginning of 2016, representing about one-fifth of all investments under management, according to a biennial report published by the advocacy group US SIF: The Forum for Sustainable and Responsible Investment.[121]

Because of the growth of SRI investments, it behooves the company to see shareholder engagement as a positive for the business with many benefits:

1. **Negotiate:** Most shareholder proposals overreach and ask too much. That's because it's oftentimes their first volley. Don't feel that

their first proposal is set in stone. Try to meet somewhere in the middle on a reasonable proposal that can do good.

2. **Educate:** Encourage sessions with the SRI community. At worst, they will learn more about your business and the issues they are interested in.

3. **Engage your experts:** Sometimes activists in the SRI community get stiff-armed by a company, often via their investor relations department or legal department, because the company doesn't want to or isn't ready to deal with their demands and proposals. When SRI activists are pushed aside like this, the company loses an opportunity to engage with experts. Each can learn from the other.

4. **Show openness:** You might not trust the group coming to visit or calling you on the phone, so it's easy to be guarded in your communications and behavior. This also is a missed opportunity. Openness is a must if you want to have meaningful discussion. Don't be afraid to disagree, either. Be frank and forthright, especially if you have your own experts in the room.

5. **Include CSR in your road show or investors' day:** Instead of waiting for the SRI community to come to you, go to them. You can organize multistakeholder groups in cities like New York, Boston, Chicago, etc. This is an impressive move because it shows confidence and transparency. It's an overt way to show you as a company that cares about what activist investors and other shareholders think.

9

The Battle for the Amazon Rainforest
How Greenpeace Chickens Changed McDonald's

Fig. 9.1: Greenpeace Chickens Have Breakfast at McDonald's.
Source: Jiri Rezac/Greenpeace.

Eating Up the Amazon

As a kid from the asphalt alleys, concrete sidewalks, and blocks and blocks of bungalows lacing the South Side of Chicago, I never dreamed I would have a hand in saving a piece of the Amazon. But I did. And when I woke up the cold spring morning of April 16, 2006, checking my

171

BlackBerry as usual, I learned that Greenpeace activists were campaigning in chicken garb at McDonald's restaurants in England. Immediately, I knew this would encompass my day, my week, even my month. At first, I figured this would be little more than a hassle. Instead, what unfurled consumed me and ushered in a sea change for our supply chain.

That same morning, Karen van Bergen got a call from McDonald's United Kingdom communication's team. She had just started her new role as chief of staff for the president of McDonald's Europe, Denis Hennequin. She previously served as head of McDonald's Europe Corporate Affairs. Tall and commanding, and a terrific leader to boot, van Bergen was about to meet her match. She recalled that:

> I'd had a pretty good relationship with Greenpeace over the years, with sustainable forestry and fish issues. All of a sudden, I get calls from our offices in the UK and Germany, finding out Greenpeace protesters are dressed up as chickens and basically hanging out at McDonald's restaurants with big signs saying, "Every bite you take out of a Chicken McNugget is a bite out of the rainforest."[122]

> I was annoyed because we had just reached a stage with Greenpeace that I thought they would give us a heads-up before they would take action. It turned out they had given us a heads-up, but that got lost somewhere in the McDonald's system.

Greenpeace was claiming in a report that McDonald's, and many others, were "eating up the Amazon." That was the title of a report the organization published that day, linking McDonald's to soy farming in the Amazon and arguing that it was causing increasing rainforest destruction. They were using guerilla-style marketing tactics to get attention. And it was working.

Van Bergen called Greenpeace that day and talked with their European lead on the Amazon campaign. Dr Thomas Henningsen was a burly, tough-looking man who looked like a one-time rugby player. He did his PhD research on the ecology of river dolphins in the Amazon and knew quite a bit about the ecosystem and also the culture of this special place. She asked Henningsen why Greenpeace was lambasting McDonald's and why he hadn't approached her first to discuss the issue. Turns out Greenpeace had contacted van Bergen's successor in corporate affairs, but he decided to not engage with Greenpeace. "Greenpeace felt that we had dumped them, and only used them when it was suitable for us," said van Bergen.

This engendered some strong hostility among Greenpeace activists. But van Bergen was determined to turn it around. She asked to meet in neutral territory, telling them: "Listen, we're going to talk about this, and I commit to open engagement. Please send me what you have on this issue." I would join her and a couple of her colleagues at Heathrow Airport in the United Kingdom in a few days. No one on our McDonald's anticipatory issues management (AIM) team, including me, had this issue on our radar screen. I knew nothing at all about the issue. That was a key part of my job, and I was sitting there empty-handed. So I cleared my desk and my mind of everything else and decided that I would dedicate all my time to developing our global position and coordinating with our colleagues from McDonald's Brazil and Europe and aligning with NGOs such as Conservation International (CI), World Wildlife Fund (WWF), etc. McDonald's Europe couldn't act on behalf of the entire company.

Greenpeace is a campaigning NGO, meaning they use sensational antics to generate attention. The organization is not known as a solutions-based NGO. And, although I had met and liked many Greenpeace people during my career, these activists were not, as a whole, a group that I trusted for acting on scientific facts rather than emotion. The organization lacked credibility as far as the average American business executive was concerned, and so I knew that no one at our home office would believe Greenpeace's latest claims. As such, I thought that, rather than getting mad at Greenpeace, I should be rational and get the facts. In doing so, I learned that Greenpeace was claiming in the report "Eating Up the Amazon" that[123]:

- Between August 2003 and August 2004, 27,200 km² —an area [in the Amazon rainforest] the size of Belgium—was lost. Three quarters of this destruction was illegal. That equals an area 10 km long by 7.5 km wide lost every day.

- In 2004–2005, around 1.2 million hectares of soya (5 percent of the national total) was planted in the Brazilian Amazon rainforest.

- Up to 75 percent of Brazil's greenhouse gas emissions result from deforestation—with the majority coming from the clearing and burning of the Amazon rainforest. Amazingly, relative to its industrialized size, Brazil is the world's fourth largest climate polluter.

Don't Get Mad

After reading the Greenpeace report, I anxiously called my long-time friend, John Buchanan at CI, to investigate the validity of it. I needed to know his honest assessment of Greenpeace's claims.

It sure pays to have an established, trustworthy NGO friend at hand when you need help right away. The best NGO relationships are those developed and nurtured during quiet times. They are not for tackling crises or short-term problems, but for the long-term good. You get to know and trust each other's character and motives, so when a crisis does hit, like this Amazon rainforest thing, you can have faith in their input and judgment.

McDonald's first worked with CI on rainforest issues as far back as 1990. We created the first environmentally themed Happy Meal with a book called *Discover the Rainforest*. We partnered with CI to start developing a sustainability strategy on food and agriculture in 1999, starting with sustainable fish. (By 2014, all McDonald's fish was sustainably sourced and met the standards of the Marine Stewardship Council.)

Buchanan partnered with us on the fish, and from 2003–2005, he codeveloped with our bun, pork, and beef suppliers, a Supplier Environmental Scorecard to measure waste, water, and energy usage, so he was familiar with our company and supply chain. The suppliers liked and respected him. In addition, he was well travelled, especially in the Amazon region. He knew first-hand what was going on in the Amazon rainforest, and he didn't pull punches. Like so many NGO experts I have worked with, his enthusiasm for what he believed in was infectious. I hoped he would say the Greenpeace Amazon study was bogus. But I couldn't reach him. He wasn't answering his phone.

By mid-morning, Greenpeace had sent to McDonald's Europe's president a fax with all of their demands. They included a list of hardball demands, insisting McDonald's stop these practices immediately, as if we could do so all by ourselves, as if we grew the soy. These demands were as follows:

1. Stop buying soya from the Amazon rainforest.
2. Stop buying meat products from animals fed on soya raised in the Amazon rainforest.
3. Demand full chain of custody for all Brazilian soya to ensure it comes from legal sources outside the Amazon rainforest.

4. Demand a hard system of IP (identity preservation) to guarantee only non-GE (genetically engineered) soya used as animal feed.
5. Develop responsible animal feed supplies in order to eliminate the pressure on the remaining ancient forests.

Considering these demands and determining how to handle them required a delicate back-and-forth interplay within McDonald's. The lines of authority and decision-making within McDonald's are confusing, with many hands stirring the pot. I often thought a couple dozen people could say "yes," but if one said "no," decision-making slowed to a crawl. Call it bureaucracy if you're cranky. Call it decentralization if you're diplomatic. Call it empowerment if you're generous. To me, getting decisions made was the most frustrating part of my job.

What's more is that I knew my U.S.-centric senior management team would view these Greenpeace demands as senseless and counterproductive. When NGOs use sensational tactics (such as entering our restaurants in chicken garb), they spark a will to fight back or to ignore the campaign.

While Thomas Henningsen led Greenpeace's European campaign, Paulo Adario led the campaign for Greenpeace in Brazil. He said their original target was Cargill, one of the five large soy traders, but he discussed with his European colleagues that "Cargill is invisible, does not have shareholders, and there is no simple choice for the consumer."[124] He looked at a report of Cargill's clients and found McDonald's. So he decided to go after their most visible client: us. McDonald's has attributes that make a prefect target: global scale, a well-known brand, and deep connections with consumers. And Greenpeace knew this, noting that "McDonald's was much more campaignable than Cargill," said Adario. "We believed McDonald's would change, because [the company] had a previous history of good steps. We felt [McDonald's] had already established that [its] doors were open for change. Cargill would be naturally influenced by a McDonald's move."

This was the price of leadership: Who goes after Number 2?

In researching the issue that morning, I learned that a lot of soy is, indeed, exported from Brazil to the general European animal agricultural community. Soy is the main feed ingredient for raising chickens. The life of a broiler chicken is about forty-two days.*

---

* "Broiler" is the term for chickens destined for meat at grocery chains and restaurants, versus chickens used for eggs, which are called laying hens. Broilers grow up to be about six pounds, and require about thirty pounds of feed in their lifetime.

I learned that McDonald's supply chain accounted for less than 0.5 of 1 percent of all soy purchased. Many companies in the same situation would argue that they were but a small part of the problem and put their head in the sand. But that's not the McDonald's way. We would tackle the issue head-on.

Before we could act rationally, I first had to calm our internal team. I described why Greenpeace pulls such crazy marketing stunts, explaining that Greenpeace does not have McDonald's marketing budget. Performing outrageous acts is how they get the word out. I told them Greenpeace is smart and strategic. I suggested that we not take their latest assault as an insult but as a compliment. They probably think we're a responsible company and will act upon the issue.

During the course of my research, I soon learned that some of the soy intrusion into the Amazon is legal. Brazil has good environmental laws, especially their Forest Code, which allows for 20 percent commercial farming in the Amazon while preserving 80 percent. Although it's an excellent code, its enforcement is inconsistent, however. Stories abounded about land grabs and indiscriminate slashing and burning of trees to make way for soy farming and cattle ranching. So now enforcement laid in the laps of companies like McDonald's.

At McDonald's, we were fortunate that the corporation already had a position on the Amazon. In the late 1980s, we created a policy that McDonald's would not buy beef from recently deforested rainforest areas, such as the Amazon. This helped guide top management as they made a decision about the Greenpeace protests in our U.K. restaurants. Although we were just a smidgeon of the overall problem, we knew we couldn't brush it off. It was our stated policy that our beef supply system would not impact rainforests. How could we not include soy? Or any other agricultural product, for that matter?

Flavia Vigio, the head of McDonald's corporate communications in Brazil, told me that morning that this issue was complicated and political, with opposing forces in Brazil each wanting the right to develop responsible farming in the Amazon. Most were considering the economic benefits to Brazil, especially employment growth, while others were adamant about preserving the Amazon, even at the cost of stymying economic growth. Vigio was supportive of the idea of forging a solution, and she had ideas about how to do it the right way. She told me that Greenpeace was not highly perceived in Brazil per se, noting that the idea of an international NGO and companies from Europe coming into their country and telling them what to do would be problematic.

Between Vigio, van Bergen, and others, I sure was getting schooled about soy and the Amazon rainforest. Then Buchanan reached out to me. I asked him to tell me that the Greenpeace report was bogus. I didn't get the answer I'd hoped for. Buchanan told me that although some of the Greenpeace claims were exaggerated, the underlying facts they laid out were true. Soy farming was, indeed, infringing upon the Amazon. Darn. So what do you do when an activist NGO is right? I've seen too many times that companies deny the issue because of the source and/or their tactics.

With CI (and eventually WWF) agreeing with Greenpeace on the merits of the issue, I knew McDonald's couldn't simply deny the issue because of its source and the tactics used to garner attention for it. I now had to work with our European team and others to hone in on a united recommendation.

Not Doing It the Greenpeace Way

Karen van Bergen was learning exactly what I was learning: This soy issue was a real one. Although we were a small player in the grand scheme of things, she agreed that we could be part of a solution—but not by succumbing to the Greenpeace's threats and demands. She would do it with the support of Denis Hennequin, McDonald's top executive in Europe.

Between Hennequin's support and van Bergen's own fearlessness, she was ready to take up the battle for the Amazon with McDonald's corporate headquarters. My boss, Jack Daly, senior vice president of corporate affairs, was an obstacle we had to overcome. At the time, he did not see an upside to engaging with Greenpeace. He thought that engaging with Greenpeace on the issue would ruin McDonald's reputation. But van Bergen disagreed. "I've got Denis's support," she told Daly. "If you keep telling me to back off, I'm still going to go ahead with [engaging with Greenpeace]."

Van Bergen believed that tackling this issue with Greenpeace was so important that she would risk her career for it. Daly thought we were negotiating with the devil. But van Bergen was convinced she was doing the right thing. Eventually Daly relented, approving travel for me so I could meet van Bergen and the team and help be a part of the negotiations with Greenpeace.

When our team (van Bergen, Else Krueck, the director of Environmental Affairs for Europe, Keith Kenny, Europe's head of supply chain for poultry,

Francesca DeBiase, the top supplier change officer for Europe, and myself) met with Greenpeace within two weeks of the launch of their campaign and you could feel the tension. It helped that DeBiase was equally passionate about sustainability. She, too, adamantly supported a way to forge a solution. (We'll learn more about DeBiase later in the chapter.)

Van Bergen was a master at cracking the air of suspicion and distrust. She turned the tables and offered to help and recruit other retailers to create a bigger market demand. She felt others would join the good cause to create a tipping point in market demand. Whereas Greenpeace thought McDonald's could unilaterally change practices in Brazil, van Bergen was adept at describing the real situation and at explaining why we needed to create a bigger demand and leverage our supplier relationships, such as with Cargill, a big trader in Brazil and one of McDonald's largest strategic suppliers.

Convincing Greenpeace of our sincerity to team up with them was challenging. "Here was Thomas [Henningsen]: My God, he was this big, scary bully. He did not hesitate to throw everything in the mix that could force us to work with them," said van Bergen.

After our second meeting with Greenpeace, there was a sudden shift. We became buddies, working arm in arm. I believe Greenpeace began to trust our sincerity. Van Bergen said, "I mean he was very impressive. I have to say he was incredibly smart. He [Henningsen] soon realized very fast that if he did what I was asking for, we could really help him break through and have success that would be enduring and lasting."

Greenpeace offered also to put their campaign against McDonald's on hold during the time of the negotiations, while Henningsen offered and almost insisted that a McDonald's team should come with them to the Amazon and experience and see first-hand the reality of the soy business connected to forest destruction.[125]

We figured out who was best connected to contact and recruit other European retailers to join with us for the cause. This led to the formation of the Soy Working Group, which included retailers such as McDonald's, Carrefour, Nestle, Tesco, Ahold, Marks and Spencer, Waitrose, Sainsbury's, and Asda. This working group served as the voice of the consumer and as a group to help guide and implement a moratorium on the soy issues that were negatively affecting the Amazon. As Ray Kroc always said, we worked better together than if just one of us were tackling this big issue.

After forming the working group, I soon scheduled a meeting with Frank Muschetto, our chief global supply chain officer. With various facts and background in hand, I started to chart out a recommendation to him.

I knew I had to work carefully with Muschetto. I knew that many details about this issue and my recommendations would make him hesitant about getting involved. And I knew that he would argue that McDonald's was such a small cog in this giant wheel that it would make little difference one way or another if we sourced soy from somewhere else. The last thing Muschetto—or, indeed, any of us—desired was getting involved in something where all we could do was spin wheels and create a superficial PR effort.

During our conversations, I found Muschetto to be tough but fair. He had been supportive of past sustainability efforts and ideas. He was a stickler on all details, including cost impacts, which we had yet to calculate. He asked a lot of questions, his intense eyes boring in on you. He looked for weaknesses in any proposal.

In presenting our proposal to Muschetto, I figured that the most persuasive angle was to emphasize our company's previous commitments to not buy any rainforest beef. I accentuated our current commitment to use no rainforest beef and argued that the same should apply to soy. I explained that we needed to do something about this in order to be consistent with our stated values. I also informed him that McDonald's Europe, including DeBiase, the head of supply chain in Europe, wanted to work with Greenpeace on a mutually agreeable solution.

As it happened, Muschetto was totally up to speed on the issue, thanks to input from his supply chain team. He was on the same page as the European team. He agreed that we should try to do something about it. Five minutes later, I walked out of his office exhilarated. We were on our way to taking concrete actions to change soy's growing impact on the Amazon rainforest. I also was amazed that the decision was made with a snap of a finger. That was Muschetto: decisive.

Shaking Hands With Greenpeace

As we huddled with Greenpeace in the U.K., I was not confident they would work with us. My perception of Greenpeace in general was that they were interested in campaigning and theatrics, not actually in creating a solution. But Henningsen and his team surprised me by saying they were open to working together—despite their own skepticism about us.

In the circles of sustainability, it's not uncommon for the players on opposite sides to dig in their heels. No one wants to budge or compromise. I give Greenpeace great credit for their openness to change their tactics with us. I also was proud of our McDonald's team. Muschetto, van Bergen, and the team in Europe had worked hard to make this happen. And then Mike Roberts resurfaced.

As president and chief operating officer of McDonald's, Roberts was McDonald's number 2 global leader. At my request, Roberts called Greg Page, the president of Cargill. "You know this is a significant issue," Roberts told Page, "and we're very interested in it being resolved in a way that best reflects the interests of all of us. What can we do together?"

Cargill made things happen after that. Without Cargill's support to work with other big soy traders in Brazil, we likely would not have achieved the eventual soy moratorium. That's the magic of our supply chain collaboration. McDonald's believes their suppliers are true partners in the long-term success of McDonald's. In times like this, it pays off to have such lasting, trusting supplier relationships. When we ask for an investment of time, talent, and resources, we can trust that the supplier will listen, consider, and help create the future with us.

In July 2006, just a little over three months after the day the chickens showed up for breakfast in multiple U.K. McDonald's restaurants, the Brazilian Association of Vegetable Oils (ABIOVE) announced a moratorium on the expansion of soy farming in the Amazon rainforest. Today, this effective moratorium is still in place.

We took Henningsen up on his offer to show us first hand the Amazon. I travelled with the Greenpeace team to the Amazon area for nine days in February 2007, along with my colleagues, Krueck and van Bergen. We took a small Greenpeace airplane to the Amazon. Six of us squeezed in. We flew four hours to the west of the state capital, Manaus, Brazil. Once we reached the city limits, after fifteen minutes, I saw nothing for the next three hours but nature: not one building, no roads, no wires, towers, or bridges. Nothing but trees, water, nature. So primeval, pristine. Pure beauty. I soaked it in. We later flew over the farming areas and saw the opposite: large swatches of land cleared off the natural forests. You could see the battle between economic development and environmental protection.

If you were a fly on the wall, I'm not sure you would have been able to tell who was from McDonald's and who was from Greenpeace. We were one team joined by a common purpose, fellow human beings, not taking shots at each other, but working as teammates to preserve the Amazon.

Fig. 9.2: The Author Travelling the Amazon With Greenpeace.
Source: Photo courtesy of Else Krueck.

When I asked Adario what made the Amazon Soy Moratorium happen so efficiently and timely, he said it was due to the simplicity of the demand: "Simplicity was the key ingredient. Everyone could understand it," said Paulo. "We drew a line in the sand and said 'no deforestation here, backed by respecting indigenous people's rights and no slavery.'"

Too many solutions have too many moving parts that shift with the winds. NGOs are famous for seeking perfection rather than progress. But Greenpeace's flexibility and simple approach created both progress and accountability in a way that was easy and cheap. No expensive, complicated verification schemes. Instead, they used an effective existing satellite tracking system to monitor soya farming expansion. "Soy doesn't move like cattle, so it's very trackable," said Adario. He added that the solution that arose didn't also try to tackle past problems such as corruption or previous deforestation. This solution was about the future, and the moratorium was only about the future. The Amazon Soy Moratorium was "somewhat revolutionary," he said. "Or at least a long step toward feeding the growing population while eliminating deforestation and controlling climate change" and, he added, "preserving companies' need for profit."

A Wake-up Call for McDonald's and Our Suppliers

I hope NGOs reading this don't think, "All we need to do is campaign companies like McDonald's. Then they'll cave in." A campaign will only be as effective as the truth of the problem it is depicting, and the company's practical role in creating a solution. In this issue with Amazon soy, flexible parties created win-win solutions for all.

The Greenpeace soy issue was such a wake-up call that Mike Roberts and Frank Muschetto set up a special supply chain leadership meeting in the fall of 2006. The message we discussed with our top fifteen suppliers (with 80 percent of our business) was that we expected them to monitor and manage emerging issues in their extended supply chain. For instance, most of our suppliers are convertors who take in raw materials such as raw beef and convert them into a product, such as a beef patty. Previously, their only role was to be responsible for their own processing facility. Now, we asked that they play a role in issues of their own upstream suppliers. This marked a pivotal sea change.

Sustainability Gets a Permanent Seat at the Table

By the summer of 2007, Francesca DeBiase, the European head of supply chain, was promoted to global vice president of strategic supply chain. I couldn't wait to see how we could take sustainability to a new, strategic, integrated level. Her decade of European experience suggested that she did not have the typical American reticence about social concerns within the business context.

DeBiase was not confronting a blank slate. The underpinnings of McDonald's caring about its products beyond price, quality, and service emerged in the early 2000s, before sustainability was a known concept and discipline. Ken Koziol had laid the pipeline in this area, putting the fourth dimension of sustainability on the map for McDonald's supply chain (see Chapter 6). But as the soy issue in the Amazon showed, we still were not where we needed to be: We still were reacting to events around us instead of defining our own strategy and priorities.

I met with Francesca DeBiase first thing upon her arrival in Oak Brook in July 2007. She was imposing—tall and zoned in with a full focus, listening to every word I said as if it were my last.

DeBiase was deeply affected by her ten years in Europe and, in particular, the Greenpeace Amazon experience. "I thought sustainability was critical for us beginning with the Greenpeace 2006 report, 'Eating up the Amazon'," she said. "We were alerted to it. We wrapped it up quickly. We took it very seriously, but we were reacting to it, right? We weren't taking a proactive approach."[126] Her thoughts reminded me so much of Koziol's.

DeBiase was excited about the possibility of embedding sustainability into McDonald's global supply chain in a more concrete way. She said, "The success of what we did with Greenpeace and the complicated soy issues in the Amazon showed me that we can change a market by working together with our suppliers." That experience brought laser focus on two priorities that DeBiase wanted to achieve on sustainability:

> One is that we need to embed sustainability into the business. And second, that the people who work on sustainability need to have a strong seat at the table when making decisions. For supply chain, that means that it should be no different from the sourcing person making sourcing decisions, the person who focuses on quality assurance. You need to have the same strength of the seat at the table.

DeBiase's priorities were spot-on. I was ready to do everything I could do to make her vision a reality. When working with Koziol, I enjoyed being proactive and developing programs and policies we believed in, not forced upon us. On the other hand, I struggled with the situation with the Coalition of Immokalee Workers (CIW). For every step forward, we still approached so many issues in old-school ways. Why did one issue take so long to solve (CIW) while another went relatively briskly (Greenpeace Amazon Soy)? Because we still were not being strategic enough. Sustainability had not become a core value of our business, and it didn't have a seat at the table. But we soon found someone to take up that role.

Just four months into her new global position, DeBiase discussed the need to support sustainability in a bigger way with the Supply Chain Leadership Board (SLB), which was comprised of the top officers from all the major areas of the world. DeBiase received an endorsement from the SLB, which allowed us to hire someone to deliver upon this vision, to pull it all together, and take the seat at the table. She recalled that:

> We had a SLB meeting in October (2007) and I presented to the supply chain leaders that we need to own it, and take the lead

in creating a long-term strategy for sustainable supply chain. I proposed that we work together and collaborate to come up with what the mission and goals should be.

To meet the demands of embedding sustainability into the day-to-day behavior of our supply chain, I hired Jessica Yagan, who previously was an intern for my department. She had degrees from Stanford and Harvard and had just finished her final year at Harvard's School of Public Policy. "I was determined to work on how link profit and social good inside of a corporation," she recalled. "Ever since college, I've been focused on how to better use capitalism toward creating social and environmental outcomes we want in the world."[127]

Now occupying a seat at the table, DeBiase agreed that it was best to have Yagan shadow the supply chain department, go to their meetings, and function as a part of their team. So began the chance for her to make her dream of working for a company to find the intersection between profit and social good. As she worked, she learned that[128]:

- In the United States alone, people eat more than 1 billion pounds of beef at McDonald's in a year, which equals 5.5 million head of cattle.

- McDonald's sells more than 1 billion cups of coffee each year around the world, including 500 million cups a day in the United States alone.

- McDonald's is the nation's largest purchaser of beef, pork, and potatoes. It is the second largest purchaser of chicken.

- McDonald's serves about 9 million pounds of fries globally per day.

- Each year, McDonald's buys 3.4 billion pounds of potatoes.

- McDonald's bought 54 million pounds of fresh apples a year at the time.

As part of her work, Yagan worked with DeBaise to form the Sustainable Supply Steering Committee (SSSC), with representatives around the world. She also worked to integrate within the supply chain department as a whole. It took time to gain the trust of the rest of the team and fully understand the business. By understanding the business goals of her supply chain colleagues, she was able to help them see how sustainability could help them. "I was able to demonstrate over the first several months that I was there to help them achieve their business goals," she said, "To make supply chain more resilient, to make prices less volatile." Indeed, within five months of accepting the assignment, Yagan had collaborated with the SSSC members, working together to finalize a proposal to present at the SSSC meeting. She presented the first draft around Valentine's Day, 2008.

She presented the first draft of the vision and principles, which were supported by the team. Eventually these were tweaked and published in McDonald's 2009 sustainability report, "The Values We Bring to the Table."

The McDonald's Sustainable Supply Chain (2008)

McDonald's vision for sustainable supply is a supply chain that profitably yields high-quality, safe products without supply interruption while leveraging our leadership position to improve the ethical, environmental, and economic impacts of doing business for both McDonald's system and the world at large.

Yagan also worked with the SSSC to develop principles to guide their work[129]:

- Leverage our size to make a positive, meaningful impact on land management practices.

- Partner with suppliers to find the best solutions.

- Seek the best scientific advice to guide our work.

- Focus our efforts on the areas where we can achieve the greatest impacts.

- Identify ways to validate and measure our progress.

- Support credible, multistakeholder efforts to promote sustainable land management.

- Balance trade-offs between land conservation and regional economic development needs.

Taking another page from my learnings from working with the Environmental Defense Fund on the waste issue and with Temple Grandin and the animal welfare issue (see Chapter 2), I helped win approval to open the door to McDonald's supply chain for WWF. The SSSC agreed to allow WWF to study our supply chain in order to help us prioritize global, sustainable sourcing initiatives based on impacts and the influence of key ingredients for our food. In 2010, WWF was given access to the full scope of information, including volumes and geographic sources regarding four types of ingredients purchased for our products: beef, chicken, coffee, and oils, such as palm and canola. In addition, WWF interviewed experts within our supply chain to help us analyze, from a sustainability perspective, which ingredients McDonald's should prioritize.

Findings from WWF's Supply Risk Analysis helped create McDonald's Sustainable Land Management Commitment (SLMC), a commitment to ensure that, over time, the agricultural raw materials for our food and packaging originate from sustainably managed land. This would evolve into goals incorporated into the 2020 CSR & Sustainability Framework (see Chapter 12). The SLMC paved the road to the future for the sustainable sourcing of beef, fiber-based packaging, fish, coffee, palm oil, and poultry. These priorities put us at the forefront of addressing important global challenges such as biodiversity loss and deforestation. During this process, we learned that integrating a sustainability mindset into the supply chain is the ultimate sign of a sustainable organization. Yagan noted that:

> People always ask me what got accomplished when I was at McDonald's (Jessica left McDonald's in 2014), and I think the stories about what I did with sustainable fish, coffee or beef might be more exciting for people. But honestly, I think the thing that made the biggest difference on an ongoing basis is that integration process. I just firmly believe that sustainability isn't going to happen if it sits outside the normal incentive process.

> Any organization is still made up of a bunch of individual people, right? One of my first observations about the people who worked in McDonald's supply chain was that many of them personally cared about sustainability issues but weren't working on them because they didn't believe it was supposed to be part of their job - that sustainability was not a business issue and that they should not think about it at work. When they could see the direct connection between human rights or environmental progress and business outcomes, it not only gave them permission to act, it unleashed more enthusiasm for and pride in their jobs.

Hard Knock Nuggets

How to Mainstream Sustainability

In my early days, sometimes I was wary to call a spade a spade when dealing with strong attacks from outside activist NGO groups, out of not upsetting them, or escalating conflict. By 2006, though, I had some experience, and I was ready to partner with van Bergen to work in a direct, honest way with Greenpeace, to tell them what they are right about and what they got all wrong. NGOs tend to ask for the world. But too often they don't know much about the practical world. We as business leaders need to give them the unvarnished truth.

Van Bergen summarized her view of working with NGOs, noting that so many companies view NGOs first as the enemy. She sees it very differently:

> The lesson I have learned, not only with Greenpeace—I've dealt with a lot of NGOs—if you are serious about the issue and you have a serious NGO—and I consider Greenpeace a very serious NGO—you know where they come from, and you try to understand each other, you almost always can find a common ground. And if you can't find common ground, you say, "No, we don't agree, and with great respect we're going to go our own way." But in 99 percent of the cases, you will find something that's a win for them and win for you.

Our experience with Greenpeace was quite an achievement. As a result we were able to eventually mainstream sustainability within McDonald's supply chain. Some lessons learned are as follows:

- **Give sustainability a seat at the table.** Sustainability absolutely needs to have a seat at the table. It should be there in the form of an employee whose key duties include sustainability as an important part of his or her job. Sustainability should be one filter for all decision-making, just like cost and quality are. It should be on every agenda.

- **Use a scorecard to monitor sustainability.** Until suppliers (or other functions) take sustainability to the level of mainstreaming by measuring, reporting, and being held accountable, the efforts cannot be fully integrated.

- **Work to achieve a shared vision.** Once McDonald's agreed to its sustainable supply chain vision, it accelerated alignment and a common understanding of expectations among the company, its suppliers, and NGOs.

- **Open the doors.** It is a repetitive theme in my journey that working with outside experts and giving them the keys to your business and people works wonders. They give you the insight and credibility to solidify a sustainability agenda. Remember that, no matter how well intended and smart employees people are, a company cannot on its own declare what is best for all of society. Partners are absolutely necessary in making change and in keeping sustainability on track.

10

The Battle to Make a Pig's Life Better
How Much Room Does a Sow Need?

Fig. 10.1: Mother Pigs (Sows) in Gestation Stalls.
Source: Jo-Anne McArthur/Essere Animali.

A Blue-Chip Meeting About a Blue-Chip Issue

In early May 2012, I organized a blue-chip meeting. Years ago, in a training exercise, we were given an actual blue chip as a way to call out a distinct top priority. There aren't many moments in your career when you know that now is a momentous time. This time, though, I knew it was a big deal, so I prepared even more than usual. The purpose of this meeting was to talk about what McDonald's should do about gestation

189

stalls—i.e., a confining housing system for individual sows (mother pigs). This was very much a blue-chip meeting because if we decided to phase out of gestation stalls, it would be big news that would impact a sizable portion of the pork industry, which was reluctant to change, and it would challenge McDonald's to make a difference on a product far upstream in its supply chain.

We entered the small conference room tucked in the corner of the global supply chain department. Jeff Hogue, whom I had hired just a week earlier to be my right-hand man, and I were the last to arrive. Already in the room were the CEO, Jim Skinner; the president, Don Thompson; the chief supply chain officer, José Armario; and the vice president of strategic sourcing, Francesca DeBiase—all of them chitchatting away.

Armario and DeBiase began the meeting by pulling out a sow gestation stall picture and passing it around. They explained the housing system for sows and said they couldn't support this practice. They explained that there were plausible alternatives, and they recommended we make a decision to commit to a timeline to phase out with our suppliers.

Thompson leaned in, really engaged, and asked many questions: How difficult would it be? What were the barriers? How much would it cost? "We owe it to ourselves to listen to all sides of the story," Thompson said. "So whether I agree with the Humane Society of the United States (HSUS) or not—or whether I agree with the pork producers or not—the point is, listen to all sides. What really makes sense? What are the realities of the situation?"[130]

This could be a first for McDonald's: Never before had we committed to a date certain supply chain change that involved something we didn't have some sort of control over. The closest example was going to larger cages for laying hens in 2001 (see Chapter 3). In that instance, all twenty-eight regional supplies refused to continue supplying eggs to McDonald's. It was difficult to fathom: Usually what the customer asks is what the customer gets. As one of the biggest customers of eggs, we were surprised that the issue became so contentious. McDonald's had to work hard and long with Cargill to create a dedicated supply chain just for McDonald's eggs. McDonald's was forced to leave our current supply arrangement for eggs and start anew.

The egg issue had taken quite some time to resolve, and we became more than a little familiar with all the ins and outs of the issue. In much the same way, the gestation stall issue was not new to us when we gathered at this blue-chip meeting to discuss it. In fact, the issue had a long backstory.

The Search for Alternatives Begins

Back in 2001, our independent, scientific Animal Welfare Council (AWC) advised us to find alternatives to gestation stalls. They believed that stalls were not the right thing to do, mostly because of the restrictive space to live. The individual sow could only stand or lie down, and could not walk around. They lived on a concrete floor with steel bars surrounding them. Each sow spent most of their lives in a stall, except when giving birth; only then were they moved to a farrowing area with more room.

Dr Temple Grandin, a founding member of McDonald's AWC, was a consistent proponent of phasing out of gestation stalls. She said "Gestation crates for pigs are a real problem," she said. "Basically, you're asking a sow to live in an airline seat. I think it's something that needs to be phased out."[131]

Of all the things I have seen during my many tours of animal agriculture facilities, not that much surprised or bewildered me. But gestation stalls did. In 2000, with Grandin as my guide, I toured my first sow facility, astonished as I observed a few thousand sows all lined up in rows, each confined to what seemed like a little prison.

Paul Shapiro, my contact for many years at the HSUS, described in *Mother Jones* the life of a sow:

Yet despite pigs' many lovable qualities, of all the billions of beasts confined in our meat factories, the most miserable may be the 5.9 million sows that churn out the piglets that grow into chops, bacon, and ham.

Throughout their four-month pregnancies, many of these sows live in cages just large enough to contain their bodies. As the sows grow bigger, the tight confinement means they can lie face down but can't flop over onto their sides. The floors under these "gestation crates" are slotted so that urine and feces slip through into vast cesspits. Immobilized above their own waste, the sows are exposed to high levels of ammonia, which causes respiratory problems. Just before they deliver, they're moved to farrowing crates, in which they have just enough space to nurse.

Once the piglets are weaned, it's back to the gestation crate for the breeding sow, which averages two and a half pregnancies per year. After three or four years, the sow is slaughtered for meat.[132]

Although I was nowhere close to sharing the sentiments of the animal rights community, the sight of these confined sows put me off. It didn't seem right. Of course, I knew enough to steer away from anthropomorphism. Yet I thought these sows looked sad and lonely. Then I slapped myself back to my rational self, reconciling myself to the idea that these are animals for meat production. Of course, "ethics" is in the eye of the beholder. The pork producers were very comfortable with the ethics and health of these animals. Our AWC wasn't. Neither was much of McDonald's supply chain team.

At that time in 2000–2001, one of our major suppliers of pork extensively used the practice of tethering of sows instead of using crates. This appeared to me as even worse than the confined stalls. My heart sank when I saw thousands of sows bound with a rope or chain around their necks, attached to a wall. Executives, managers, and veterinarians for these facilities cited the good health of the animals to explain away any negative aspects of this practice. The common mantra I heard was that only a healthy animal can be a productive animal.

As I saw it, managers who argued that tethering was perfectly comfortable for the sows were overly married to productivity. They also were detached from how a consumer would view such tethering. Our team had no data about consumer sentiment on this particular topic, but I felt it was a barbarian way to handle any pigs. I assisted our supply chain management to get rid of the tethers ASAP, a task we accomplished within the next year.

In 2002, as result of McDonald's AWC recommendation, we asked our pork suppliers to find alternatives to the gestation stalls, and instead switch to group housing. For the next several years, we had some success with direct suppliers that handled sows. Cargill and Smithfield, for example, both made good progress. However, our voluntary "ask" did not move the marketplace as much as we'd hoped for. In fact, ten years after our request, gestation stalls remained the dominant method of housing; about 85 percent of all sows in the industry were confined this way.

I knew that just asking for change on a voluntary basis would have its limitations. But we believed we could not force or mandate change. We had no authority or power to do so because sows were way upstream from any McDonald's direct purchasing process. As with other products, McDonald's purchases from suppliers that are simply converters, who in this case buy pork and turn it into sausage patties and links. The sows come from McDonald's converting suppliers' suppliers' supplier.

In the meantime, HSUS was leading an effort to get rid of gestation stalls through legislation, corporate engagement (and pressure), and campaigns directed toward consumers. The cause was easy to explain and easily aroused emotions. All the Humane Society had to do was show a picture of a sow stuck in a gestation stall: It told the story, tugged at the heart, and won the argument without saying a word.

By late 2011, HSUS and our main contact there, Paul Shapiro, started to pressure McDonald's to announce a phase out of gestation stalls. This put us in a bind: As far as the pork producers were concerned, Shapiro and HSUS were trying to kill their industry, not improve it. Producers viewed HSUS as advocates for vegetarianism and animal rights.* Yet I could see why the pork industry was not a fan of HSUS. It seemed to them that the society was trying to thwart their very livelihood. For example, on the HSUS's website is the following statement[133]:

> *On Farm Animals and Eating With Conscience*
>
> Considering the foregoing abuses of animals, degradation of the environment, and detriment to human health, The HSUS promotes eating with conscience and embracing the Three Rs—reducing the consumption of meat and other animal-based foods; refining the diet by eating products only from animals who have been raised, transported, and slaughtered in a system of humane, sustainable agriculture that does not abuse the animals; and replacing meat and other animal-based foods in the diet with plant-based foods.

But it was not HSUS pressure alone that motivated us at McDonald's to consider doing more to end the use of gestation stalls. By 2010, our team had long been disappointed in the lack of progress with our voluntary ask a decade earlier. I was working with our supply chain to reassess what we should do. While most whom I worked with wanted to phase it out, we honestly did not know how we could control the supply chain to ensure a commitment if we made the demand to stop using gestation stalls.

The Decades-Long Conundrum Faces a Deadline

HSUS was threatening to bring up the gestation stall issue at McDonald's impending May 2012 shareholder meeting. This threat created the opportunity for us to discuss this issue once again.

---

* As PETA defines it, "Animal rights means that animals are not ours to use for food, clothing, entertainment, or experimentation." Animal welfare is more limited, denoting keeping animals free from neglect, abuse, and other cruelty.

Thompson set the tone. "If there are things that are not in line with the values of McDonald's," he began, "then we should be a force in driving positive change."

Hogue's eyes opened wide in wonderment as he was a witness to his new company leadership style, recalling Thompson saying, "I don't like this. I don't feel that we should support this [the use of gestation stalls]. Fundamentally, this is not something that I want to see in my supply chain."[134]

The conversation turned to cost, which would be substantial. One of our internal estimates of the suppliers' cost to transition to new housing systems was as high as $25 million a year. We believed we could minimize this cost to us and to the industry conversion by making 2022 (a decade hence) the deadline for the phaseout. We thought this would be enough time to allow for normal transitioning, retiring assets, and investing in capital expenditures. We also discussed whether we had enough pull with our direct suppliers to actually have the ability to work with them to make this commitment. We ultimately determined that we had confidence that our direct suppliers could work with their upstream suppliers to follow through on the conversion. And, finally, we discussed whether to carry out this initiative globally.

Supply chain studied it hard, and although we wanted to make this change globally, we saw so many roadblocks to achieving success around the world. According to McDonald's supply chain analysis, for example, China accounted for 46 percent of total world production for pork; the European Union accounted for 24 percent; and the United States accounted for 10 percent. If we ordered the conversion in China, McDonald's would somehow have to find and trace the millions of sows all around China, with 65 percent of farms having ten or fewer animals. That would be a formidable if not impossible endeavor, so we decided to not include a global commitment, instead focusing solely on the United States.

I explained that the pork industry leadership and its national trade group, the National Pork Producers Council (NPPC), would react negatively and mount some serious opposition. I, along with others from our public affairs and U.S. supply chain departments, had recently visited NPPC headquarters in Iowa to discuss our impending decision. In no uncertain terms, NPPC leaders bluntly told us we were wrong in every way. They were convinced that gestation stalls kept the animals safe and healthy.

After a full discussion during our meeting at McDonald's, Thompson agreed with the recommendation from Armario and DeBiase. McDonald's

USA would commit to phasing out use of gestation stalls by 2022. Thompson also recommended that we issue a joint announcement from HSUS and McDonald's. He wanted to get the public's attention.

The Plan for Ending Gestation Stall Use

On May 31, 2012, we publicly announced the end of gestation stalls by 2022, a move for which Dr Temple Grandin expressed public support. "This change is complex and will require additional resources," she said. "The ten-year timeline that McDonald's has outlined is necessary to research and identify better housing alternatives and ensure proper training of employees. This is really good forward thinking, and I commend McDonald's for doing it."[135]

The industry reaction, however, couldn't have been further away from Grandin's. Indeed, it was hypercritical of McDonald's. In public comments, NPPC leadership professionally objected. In private conversations, the pork industry was mad to the max. They believed McDonald's was not following good science. Rather, McDonald's was kowtowing to the HSUS.

As reported by *Agri-Pulse*, Everett Forkner, president of the National Pork Board, expressed disappointment with the decision and said it could put significant pressure on smaller farmers who use gestation stalls to care for their animals:

> For a producer who has built a new barn in the past few years, McDonald's announced timeline could force them to make significant investments. So to make the conversion, my fellow producers are going to have to go to a banker with a plan that is likely to increase costs and reduce productivity—not a plan that is likely to inspire great confidence in a banker or investor.[136]

Despite this pushback, the McDonald's–HSUS announcement lent impetus that led to a tipping point. We were hopeful that our announcement would pull others along with us, not least of which because we knew we alone could not mandate a change to the hog industry. While McDonald's buys a lot of pork, it adds up to about 1 percent[137] of the 23.2 billion pounds used annually in the United States.[138] But, just as we had hoped, the McDonald's announcement did, indeed, create an avalanche of similar commitments from scores of others, including Burger King, Wendy's, Safeway, and Costco. By the end of

2012, the majority of food retailers, grocers, restaurants, and food service chains in the United States made similar commitments. I knew McDonald's had the power to create a movement, but we created a stampede. That stampede was witnessed by Jeff Hogue, who had barely a month of work at McDonald's under his belt. He noted that:

> It was one of the most amazing parts of my career because I [was] just starting out, not really knowing what direction this sustainability program could go at McDonald's. Here I [was] getting a first-hand glimpse of what leadership [was] thinking about and how they see the issues.
>
> When McDonald's makes a decision to go in one direction, it pretty much changes the world.

With Hogue's splash exposure to McDonald's senior management, culture, and values that make up McDonald's, he was jazzed up to help me develop what would be a first for McDonald's, and a real breakthrough: McDonald's 2020 Sustainability Framework (see Chapter 12). But before we could get there, we had to tackle something much bigger and even more transformational: sustainable beef. I knew that our announcement about gestation stalls, given how unilateral it was, would make our work on beef, which required extensive collaboration, much more difficult.

The Secret Sauce of Sustainable Influencing

There are so many aspects of sustainability leadership. It's an art with many interpretations. Along my journey leading change and trying to influence others, as well as with working with others to lead change, I've learned some important lessons. Here are my top seven insights on influencing sustainable change:

- **Ask.** We had a sign displayed every-way in my first place I worked for McDonald's that resonates with me even today. In big, blue, bold letters was written ASK. ASK. ASK. It is amazing how you can get people to think differently and change course by asking—not by demanding, pushing, or mandating.

- **Be Here Now.** On my desk for the past twenty years has been perched a daily reminder: "Be Here Now." Whether you are with a staff member or an external stakeholder, give them 100 percent of your undivided attention. Don't think about the White Sox, Neil Young, the next episode of *Atlanta*, or your next meeting.

- **Think From the Outside In.** Too many people think from inside out. I say the opposite. Influencing begins with thinking from the outside in. When visiting with someone I wanted to influence, I would read up on what they do as much as I could so I could get into their mind. I would shape my questions and input to serve their needs and priorities.

- **Acknowledge Your Shadow.** As a leader, everything you do, everything you say, and every way in which you conduct yourself casts a shadow far and wide. This is a privilege, not a burden. Be aware of the subtle ways in which you model your behavior to your followers.

- **Communicate Endlessly.** McDonald's masterful turnaround CEO in the early 2000s was Jim Cantalupo, who was brought out of retirement to reignite the business. When I asked him what the biggest surprise of being CEO was, he said: "99 percent of the job is communicating." You can't spend enough time figuring out effective ways to communicate to and excite your staff, partners, customers, and other stakeholders.

- **Be the Best Expert.** You should be the most knowledgeable person in your field of expertise. I always tried to spend 15 percent of my time keeping up with corporate social responsibility (CSR) trends and reading about and listening to other experts so I could be the subject-matter expert on CSR at McDonald's.

- **Always Deliver on Your Promises.** How often do people say they will follow up on something but then fail to do so? How often do colleagues fail to communicate with each other? Trust and integrity open the door to influencing someone else. You build trust and integrity by delivering on your promises—and by quickly admitting it when you can't.

11

The Battle for Better Beef
The Quest for Sustainable Beef

Fig. 11.1: This McCow graphic was used by GreenBiz for its
exclusive story about McDonald's commitment to purchase
sustainable beef by 2016.
Source: Courtesy of GreenBiz.

The Ecologist, the Corporatist, and the Beef Lobbyist

Jason Clay was raised on a small farm in Missouri, studied anthropology,
and headed off, young and idealistic, to Sudan to help displaced refugees
and famine victims. After calculating how many body bags would be
needed, he realized, "This is God's work, but it's not my work. It's not the
work I set out to do."[139]

In 1988, Clay attended a Grateful Dead concert to benefit the rainforest and the people that live there. "I met a guy, his name was Ben [of Ben and Jerry]. He asked me, 'What can I do to save the rainforest?'

Clay asked Ben, "Who are you and what do you do?"

"I'm Ben and I make ice cream," said Ben.

So Clay said, "Well, you've got to make a rainforest ice cream and you've got to use nuts from the rainforest to show that forests are worth more as forests than they are as pasture."

Though Rainforest Crunch and the 200 others products Clay helped launch reaped $100 million in sales, Clay saw it as a failure. It wasn't solving the problem of deforestation. "We were attacking the wrong driver. We needed to be working on beef and lumber. We needed to be working on soy. Things that were not being worked on."

These experiences finally led Clay to devise a new way of leading change for agriculture. He joined the World Wildlife Fund (WWF) in 1993 and started to work on focusing the market power of big companies on the commodities that most impact the planet. Clay led roundtables with leaders from the entire value chain to address sustainability issues regarding soy, sugarcane, palm oil, cotton, and a dozen more commodities. So effective were these roundtables that Clay, along with WWF, worked out a four-step formula for them:

- Get a critical mass of buying power.

- Include stakeholders from farm to fork.

- Create voluntary measures for improvement based on outcomes.

- Allow for innovation via outcome-based performance.

Clay was fast making a name for himself in the sustainability of food and agriculture. I first met him at a sustainable food conference, where I found him to be Kissinger-like as he addressed his audience. He presented his business case with deep knowledge and conviction. His combined knowledge of agriculture and sustainability was brilliant—so brilliant that I wanted him to meet our new global head of strategic supply chain, Francesca DeBiase, who wanted to integrate sustainability into supply chain and make changes that could positively change markets (see Chapter 10). I thought we should take on beef.

I had been advocating for sustainable beef starting with hiring whiz kids from UC–Berkeley Haas School of Management in 2006 for a four-month research project. We provided them with an open door to examine our beef system in order to make recommendations that would be shared in our next public corporate social responsibility (CSR) report.

I was convinced that if people saw the same beef system, from farm to fork, that I saw in my own travels, their impressions would be much more positive than their beginning mindset. Modern agriculture is a mystery to most of us because only about 1 percent of the U.S. population is associated with crop and animal agriculture. In contrast, since the birth of the United States and throughout the nineteenth century, more than 50 percent of the population was involved. This was similar throughout most of the developed world. The global food system since the turn of the twentieth century evolved from rural farming to more industrialized farming because bigger systems were needed to handle a global population of more than 7.6 billion in 2018 versus just 2 billion when the Declaration of Independence was signed in 1776.

The Berkeley MBA students indeed were complimentary of what they saw in McDonald's beef system, but they called out something that rang true to me. As they stated in our CSR report:

> But for McDonald's to consider its operations truly sustainable, it should begin to look beyond fixing incremental problems within its current system and, instead, consider transforming the [beef]system itself. Because of its global reach and international scale, McDonald's is ideally situated to lead the U.S. beef industry to explore more sustainable practices.

This commentary made me wonder whether McDonald's could transform the beef industry—and, indeed, whether we should. As it stood already, our track record of sustainable transformation was respectable. We had taken on waste, packaging, and recycling in collaboration with the Environmental Defense Fund (EDF; see Chapter 1), which impacted most of the global food service industry. The same can be said of our work with Dr Temple Grandin on integrating animal welfare standards with meat suppliers (see Chapter 2). The Amazon Soy Moratorium had just been completed, and it had a huge, industry-wide impact of stopping damaging practices across the Amazon (see Chapter 9). If we could do just one more big thing, I believed we ought to take on beef: It sat at the core of McDonald's menu, and it represented important societal issues on many fronts.

For example, The United Nations Food and Agricultural Organization detailed, in 2006, numerous negative impacts of beef production. As the organization noted in its controversial report, "Livestock's Long Shadow:"[140]

Livestock's Long Shadow

by the Food and Agriculture Organization of the United Nations

2006

Livestock's contribution to environmental problems is on a massive scale, and its potential contribution to their solution is equally large. The impact is so significant that it needs to be addressed with urgency.

Land degradation:
The livestock sector is by far the single largest anthropogenic user of land. The total area occupied by grazing is equivalent to 26 percent of the ice-free terrestrial surface of the planet

Expansion of livestock production is a key factor in deforestation, especially in Latin America, where the greatest amount of deforestation is occurring: 70 percent of previously forested land in the Amazon is occupied by pastures.

The livestock sector is a major player, responsible for 18 percent of greenhouse gas emissions measured in CO_2 equivalent. This is a higher share than transport.

The livestock sector is a key player in increasing water use, accounting for over 8 percent of global human water use, mostly for the irrigation of feed crops. It is probably the largest sectoral source of water pollution, contributing to eutrophication, "dead" zones in coastal areas, degradation of coral reefs, human health problems, emergence of antibiotic resistance, and many [other issues.]

Livestock now account for about 20 percent of the total terrestrial animal biomass, and the 30 percent of the earth's land surface that they now pre-empt was once habitat for wildlife. Indeed, the livestock sector may well be the leading player in the reduction of biodiversity, since it is the major driver of deforestation, as well as one of the leading drivers of land degradation, pollution, climate change, overfishing, sedimentation of coastal areas, and facilitation of invasions by alien species.

This report was not pretty, and we had to take it seriously. After all, it was written by what the average person would consider a nonbiased, objective body: the United Nations.

Many beef organizations, including the National Beef and Cattlemen's Association, fiercely rebutted many of the facts and conclusions noted in the report. For example, they pointed out that beef's contribution to greenhouse gasses was overstated. In the United States, it was 3 percent—not 18 percent.[141]

Whatever the truth is, the reality is that beef has long made significant social and environmental impacts, and it is the core product of McDonald's. If McDonald's was going to be a sustainable company, beef was the issue I thought we should tackle next. I needed to find an expert such as EDF was for waste. I need a Temple Grandin–like NGO leader to advise McDonald's on sustainable food, agriculture, and beef.

Jason Clay was the expert who I thought could do this. So I quickly invited Clay to visit DeBiase and me during her second week on the job. It was a hot August 2007 day when Clay arrived at our resplendent campus, which was in full bloom. Clay and DeBiase soon realized that they had very different backgrounds. Clay's career had been built in farming and food, while DeBiase's career path had been in finance. Although different, their career paths did cross at key intersections, particularly since DeBiase had had a big hand in the success of the Amazon Soy Moratorium.

The meeting with Clay and DeBiase fueled our shared interest in the sustainability of beef. As DeBiase noted:

> The purpose of the meeting was to discuss how [WWF] works with global supply chains and potential areas where we could work together. One of the areas that [Clay] talked about was beef. And when he shared the story around the fact that beef had a significant environmental impact on the world, and that there wasn't a roundtable for beef yet, and roundtables had been successful in other areas, then, in my mind, this was an area where we could work together.

Jason made the concept of sustainable beef possible through two powerful arguments. First he showed a picture of two pieces of land with the same location, soil, water, and other conditions. One was desolate and unproductive. The other lush, carrying four times the amount of cattle. Then, he hesitated before saying, in a quiet deep tone, "The only difference is management."

The second persuasive argument Clay made resonated with the McDonald's supply chain team because it was all about best management practices (BMPs)—or "better management practices," as Clay called it. Clay told us that 15 percent of producers with best practices could be scaled, as illustrated in the Performance Curve graph (see Fig. 11.2). If only we could get greater adoption of the best practices. Clay further noted the following:

- Today's BMP is tomorrow's norm.

- There are no BMPs, only better ones—and better is far better than worse.

- BMPs are the means to an end, not the end.

- The focus should be on results. Let producers find the best way to achieve them—and don't be proscriptive.

This meeting was proving positive and successful. Clay and DeBiase agreed that the next step should be to have WWF experts return to McDonald's to talk to our global beef teams about the potential in starting a roundtable. It was beginning to feel like history was, perhaps, in the making.

Accelerating Better Practice Adoption

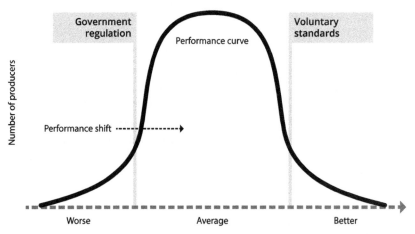

Fig. 11.2: World Wildlife Fund/Jason Clay's Performance Curve.

In order to make the roundtable as effective as possible, Clay knew that he would need a leader from the beef production side to participate so that, together, we could initiate a movement toward sustainable beef. He decided to approach the biggest beef producer in the world: JBS. Clay figured he would need his best statesmanship to win over JBS. They scheduled a meeting in early 2010. It wouldn't be an easy discussion: To Cameron Bruett and the rest of the JBS leadership team, Clay and WWF and the like were the enemy. "When I sat down with WWF, I probably felt like any other farmer or rancher would," said Bruett. "Who gave these guys the badge to police our centuries-old industry, which has been feeding people around the world all this time? Why are they coming in and saying we're destroying the planet?"[142]

Just like Clay and DeBiase had their differences, Clay and Bruett also came from different places. Whereas Clay tells a story as he talks and can ramble in interesting ways, Cameron is staccato and rattles off his opinions as if on speed. Bruett majored in animal science at the renowned Tuskegee University, founded in Alabama by Dr Booker T. Washington. Bruett and the JBS team were wary of Clay as he began to spell out his vision for sustainable beef. Clay talked about collaboration and targets and sustainable intensification of science-based agriculture. He expressed deep knowledge of cattle raising and beef production, and he explained that he understood that JBS needed to make money.

By the end of the discussion, Bruett was a convert. "We saw WWF and Jason as an entity that wanted to partner with the people who were in the industry to identify solutions," he said. The roundtable helped change the stereotype Bruett and JBS had of NGOs—that of one-sided, single-minded attack dogs. Bruett found that:

> WWF truly wanted to make positive changes on the ground. It wasn't a fundraising activity for them. You certainly can shame and embarrass companies into taking action, but it's never as powerful as when of their own volition and free will they choose to make those decisions because it's in the best interest of everyone.

The strength of WWF is that the organization understands both business and the environment. Clay served as a charismatic leader to deliver the message. As a result, he was able to bring to the table seemingly disparate stakeholders and get them to work together. Bruett agreed that Clay's efforts meant a great deal:

> I give Jason a lot of credit because he recognized that he was dealing with businesses that needed to be profitable in order to thrive and to make return to their shareholders, but he also had a passion for protecting the environment, which many of us companies in fact share that passion.

Changing the Sentiment of Us Versus Them

While WWF was building closer ties and gaining trust with McDonald's and JBS, the relationship between McDonald's and much of the beef industry upstream of their direct suppliers was mostly dormant.

One of the key reasons for this, and as we have noted in previous chapters, is that McDonald's was not close to upstream suppliers. As with most retailers, we were detached from raising animals and dealt only with the suppliers that made our hamburger patties. Indeed, McDonald's prided itself on the spirit of collaboration with their suppliers, who are part of the three-legged stool: company staff, owner–operators, and suppliers. Each part is equal and interdependent, and all have in common the mutual goal of McDonald's success. However, McDonald's considered our suppliers to be not upstream suppliers but direct suppliers, such as Otto & Sons, a huge beef patty processor/convertor. Otto & Sons bought raw ground beef from the packer and processed it into hamburgers to sell to McDonald's.

The beef industry is fragmented,[143] with multiple layers of suppliers upstream from McDonald's and Otto & Sons:

- the purebred breeder
- the commercial producer
- the stocker or backgrounding operations
- the cattle feeder
- the beef packer
- the convertor
- the retailer

Again, these facets of McDonald's supply chain operate individually and interdependently. Each does its own job, and there's not much cooperation among the various parts of the value chain. This made addressing the bigger sustainability impacts, which are three or four steps upstream at the rancher and feedlot level, a real challenge.

Another reason for the stress between McDonald's and some in the animal agricultural industry in particular stemmed from McDonald's reaction to new societal demands for safer, healthier food and well-treated, healthy animals. Activists were learning that their most effective weapons were to attack brands and provide radical transparency. Animal activists, for example, found ways to go undercover at a meat plant, videotape the abuses, and then "name and shame" in some kind of sensational public disclosure. McDonald's was on the receiving end of some of these antics, including a Mercy for Animals video that exposed problems that forced McDonald's to pull business from that supplier. In 2011, the Associated Press reported the incident[144]:

> McDonald's Corp. said Friday it has dropped a Minnesota-based egg supplier after an animal rights group released an undercover video of operations at the egg producer's farms in three states.

> The video by Mercy for Animals shows what the group calls animal cruelty at five Sparboe Farms facilities in Iowa, Minnesota and Colorado. Its images include a worker swinging a bird around by its feet, hens packed into cramped cages, male chicks being tossed into plastic bags to suffocate and workers cutting off the tips of chicks' beaks.

> "The behavior on tape is disturbing and completely unacceptable. McDonald's wants to assure our customers that we demand humane treatment of animals by our suppliers," Bob Langert, McDonald's vice president for sustainability, said in a statement.

As a result of such sensational activist campaigns, the public learns about various abuses and then customers hold retailers like McDonald's accountable for their entire supply chain, even though McDonald's only actively manages the last step on the supply chain. There's the big disconnect: Customers logically view McDonald's as having knowledge and control of the Big Mac all the way from farm to fork. But the truth is that we know how to grill burgers, make fries, and clean the bathrooms—not how to use antibiotics or raise animals. Similarly, animal producers believe they are doing things right, but they often don't have the knowledge or skills to inform the public about their good stewardship. These disconnects lead to stalemates at best and friction at worst, among food retailers, animal producers, and activists.

Finally, another reason for the tenuous relationship among McDonald's, WWF, JBS, and the rest of the beef industry stemmed from McDonald's perceived track record over the past decade of stepping up, getting too involved with farmers, and acting like government regulators. As far as the beef industry was concerned, we were the bad guys for:

- mandating larger cages for laying hens after we caved to PETA;

- ending the use of gestation stalls for pork after we caved to the Humane Society of the United States; and

- developing McDonald's initial policy of limiting growth promoting antibiotics in meat (particularly on chickens) after we caved to the Humane Society of the United States.

Many in the beef industry believed that McDonald's was kowtowing to the activists. They argued that McDonald's didn't have the right to set agricultural policy for them. The told us that McDonald's should stick to serving food and managing our restaurants, and that we should let farmers and producers do what they do best, which included being good stewards of land and animals.

Despite having to take actions to address sustainability issues on our own, we were, in fact, on the side of modern animal agriculture. We understood their needs, and we needed them as true partners to keep serving safe, affordable, high-quality food. This ongoing conflict among McDonald's, our suppliers, and activist organizations was not healthy at all. We should be partners, not enemies.

Unfortunately, that wasn't necessarily the prevailing sentiment. Distrust abounded. Bruett, for example, shared his perception of McDonald's at that time:

> The original approach from McDonald's was "We're frustrated. We want movement. You guys—the packers, producers, and feeders—aren't making the right commitments and steps. And you guys need to do this, because this is what our consumers want and you're not being responsive

to our customers." It was a very antagonistic approach. It was a push relationship rather than a pull. It was pretty aggressive.

DeBiase was aware of this history of antagonism, and so she knew there would have to be a dramatic shift if the beef roundtable were to be successful. She also knew that McDonald's purchasing power was limited. McDonald's is one of the biggest buyers of beef, yet McDonald's purchases just 2 percent of all marketplace beef. That's certainly a significant figure, but it doesn't give McDonald's snap-your-fingers power with the beef value chain.

With all these challenges in mind, DeBiase engaged her right-hand person to lead the engagement with the beef industry. Gary Johnson, who had crafted McDonald's sustainable fish program (see Chapter 6) and led McDonald's beef procurement strategy, jumped right into the fray. He applied three guiding principles to turning around McDonald's relationship with the beef industry: transparency, understanding, and collaboration.

When it came to transparency, Johnson's mantra was "No hidden agenda." Johnson knew that transparency depended in large part on trust and credibility. "If I was not credible," he said, "they would read right through that, and it's not part of my DNA to begin with. So I had to be very transparent."[145]

He also knew he couldn't move the needle unless there was a common understanding of what sustainable beef meant. "There were thousands of definitions of what sustainable beef was," he said. "I have my definition. They have their definition. I can't talk to anyone unless there is shared definition."

His third principle was the big one: collaboration. "This is not about forcing a sustainable beef definition," Johnson said. "This is not McDonald's definition. This is everybody in the beef chain's definition."

Johnson had many ties to the beef industry, and he worked his network to create the synergy and support needed for a successful value chain sustainable beef roundtable. "Ranchers, farmers, are kind of the salt of the earth," he said. "They don't want anybody to force 'sustainability' on them. They feel they have enough regulation on them from local and national government. Once they found out this was going to be a collaborative effort, things really happened for the good."

A Sustainable Beef Powwow

Sure enough, the lack of trust began to dissipate as Johnson employed his three key principles. The founding sponsors representing the whole value supply chain (i.e., McDonald's, WWF, and JBS, along with recruited companies of Cargill, Walmart, and Intervet/Schering-Plough Animal Health) decided to host a global conference to create consensus on a common definition of sustainable beef and, hopefully, to gain support to develop a sustainable beef roundtable. Getting other partners like Walmart, Intervet, and Cargill on board was a giant leap forward. It meant we were gathering critical mass as the first global conference for sustainable beef convened in Denver in the fall of 2010.

Three years had passed since Clay and DeBiase had had this big idea of a beef roundtable. This was a conference, not a roundtable, so matters were going slowly. That said, the conference was a resounding success. More than three hundred stakeholders gathered for a three-day conference that achieved increased clarity and deepened alignment around the key issues that influence the sustainability of the beef production system, both positive and negative.

I gave a keynote speech. I thought long and hard about how to reach and motivate these important stakeholders and how to help shed some of the animosity that the producers had pent up. I emphasized trust and our consumers. Just as the beef industry believed that people like me were detached and uninformed about cattle rearing and processing, I thought the cattlemen were detached from consumer trends. "Building trust with our consumers is huge" I said, adding that:

> Part of earning consumers' trust is showing that the products McDonald's buys, like beef, are produced in a responsible way. Consumers expect a socially responsible supply chain. McDonald's success requires serving food in a convenient, safe, fun, and very responsible way.

> Sustainability, in general, has been incorrectly defined by too many stakeholders. The food industry is under attack and is being negatively portrayed by too many elitists and radicals. What the heck? The guy that heads up the U.N. effort on climate change called on people to eat less beef.

> Animal welfare abuses and food safety threats are being defined by this ugly depiction on modern agriculture as "factory farming." The real story is that the beef industry is made up of excellent men and women and processors that take pride in what they are doing and manage their businesses responsibly.

Today there is window of opportunity to come together and demonstrate that we all can be very proactive and strategic in our approach and tell our story even more.[146]

Indeed, we were able to come together and find ways to be proactive and strategic in our approach to sustainable beef. By any measure, the conference was a success. WWF described the results of this first-ever conference on creating a more sustainable beef industry[147]:

"This was an unprecedented event and a great first step in our journey to achieve a more sustainable beef industry," said Jason Clay, Senior Vice President of Markets at WWF. "On a planet with finite resources, global beef stakeholders understand the business, social and environmental value of doing more with less. Through this multi-stakeholder process, we will build on existing practices and drive continuous improvement throughout the global beef system."

As an important source of protein for many of the world's population, global demand for beef is growing. With global populations expected to peak at more than nine billion by 2050, industry and NGO partners have a shared interest to improve beef production in some of the most environmentally sensitive regions of the world.

The conference produced robust feedback centered on the "triple bottom line"—to be environmentally, socially, and economically sustainable. At the conclusion, the conference hosts challenged the participants to incorporate this feedback to develop on-the-ground programs that enhance sustainable beef, driven by new relationships developed in Denver.

"This is a powerful first step in bringing all the key stakeholders of the beef sector together for a transparent dialogue and to identify the real potential of the beef industry to be more sustainable," said Gary Johnson, Senior Director, McDonald's Worldwide Supply Chain.

"By incorporating sustainability into Walmart's own operations, we have seen first-hand the opportunities it creates to increase efficiency and reduce costs," said Pete Eckes,

Walmart's senior director of business development for meat. "By making the sustainability practices of producers and suppliers a factor in deciding which beef we buy for our 8500 global locations, Walmart and Sam's Club can provide the access to customers that is needed to make this effort a success."

Putting Meat Behind the Global Roundtable for Sustainable Beef

After the Denver conference in 2010, DeBiase saw that the slow development of the sustainable beef "movement was not close to the more rapid acceleration we all expected." The Global Roundtable for Sustainable Beef (GRSB) was finally and formally organized as a nonprofit group nearly two years later, in February 2012. Its founding members were AllFlex, Cargill, Elanco, Grupo de Trabalho da Pecuaria Sustentavel, JBS, McDonald's, Merck Animal Health, National Wildlife Federation, Rainforest Alliance, Roundtable for Sustainable Beef Australia, Solidaridad, The Nature Conservancy, Walmart, and WWF.

Based on the snail's pace we were making, Johnson decided to hire a full-time director to prod and poke the GRSB toward tangible actions. He tapped Michele Banik-Rake, a thirty-year veteran in McDonald's supply chain. She had spent the past three years within McDonald's U.K. supply chain department. Johnson asked Banik-Rake to help lead the committee on defining beef sustainability. Johnson sensed how highly motivated and capable she was to get this done.

Sustainability was top of mind for Banik-Rake when she arrived at the U.K. offices. In fact, she was at first skeptical of why they made recent sustainable food changes, such as serving organic milk and cage-free eggs. "I'm thinking, 'Wow. Spending an extra £3 million to go to free range eggs. What was the return that the consumers would care about that kind of thing?'" she said. "The organic milk, it just seemed overboard to me when I first arrived."[148]

Just like DeBiase, as Banik-Rake was exposed to more, she jumped on the sustainability bandwagon "One of the things I was asked to do was develop a platform on which the U.K. could focus its efforts around food sustainability. This became 'Farm Forward,' and a multiyear sourcing and communications plan was built on it. Those three years really formed and changed my thinking around sustainability, a real epiphany."

Banik-Rake's style was direct. She couldn't stand inaction and lack of decision-making. Her open, blunt manner reminded me of one of the core problems I see with many in the workforce: They don't bring their whole selves to work. As Jim Skinner used to ask of such people, "Are you all in?"

Banik-Rake was all in, and she quickly assessed McDonald's efforts to develop sustainable beef through the GRSB as "very slow. It was just sort of stagnating."

Johnson, being on the inside of GRSB, saw first-hand how slow they were. So Johnson asked for a meeting at McDonald's with Bruett and laid out the cards, telling Bruett that this was a "go or no go" situation. Johnson told Bruett that McDonald's would not continue unless there was strong leadership within the GRSB. Some constituents were asking Johnson to be the GRSB president, but Johnson did not see that as being a good move because it would look like McDonald's defining beef sustainability, when in fact it should be the beef industry doing so. Johnson was adamant. He said, "I called this meeting with Cameron and was willing to walk away from the GRSB unless the beef industry (JBS in this case) took hold of it."

At the meeting, Banik-Rake asked Bruett whether he had a plan to move the initiative forward. Bruett did have a plan. He brought to their meeting a thirteen-part plan detailing what he thought needed to happen with the roundtable. The crux of Bruett's plan was to put beef producers front and center. He wanted the beef producers to lead the effort rather than acquiesce to what retailers wanted. He was on the same page as Johnson. Bruett described his target audience:

> It's the guy who has twenty mother cows in Georgia some-
> where, who's doing this kind of as a hobby. To go to his ranch
> to tell him he needs to track his nutrient management in order
> to sell to Walmart or McDonald's, I mean he's just going to
> look at you and say, "Get the hell off my property." Then if
> you come in with some big panda bear [WWF] or some NGO
> he's going to say, "I'm going to shoot you if you don't get off
> my property."

Bruett's plan and infectious positive attitude pleased Johnson and Banik-Rake, and after that meeting, McDonald's recommitted to the GRSB.

Bruett also was pleased. He saw a new attitude from McDonald's that he liked. No longer was McDonald's (or other retailers) the overt aggressor. Instead, they were happy to work in the background. Bruett recalled that:

> McDonald's really transitioned from to "Here's the McDonald's way, here's what we want. Fill out this checklist in order to do business with us." So when that shift happened from McDonald's they really became more trusted in the producer community and more seen as an ally with the packers. McDonald's finally understood and accepted that and said, "Okay, we need to be seen as a partner all the way down the chain."

Bruett credited this shift in large part to Gary Johnson, saying that "Gary was talented and nuanced in dealing with conflict." Indeed, Johnson was known to think long and hard about the political forces and motivations of all the stakeholders. He brought balance and a more steady pace as he worked back channels to explain the whys and hows and to get understanding and support for sustainable beef. Banik-Rake also appreciated this:

> When it came down to needing an executive committee (GRSB) vote or key decision on something, that's where Gary honestly shined. He'd make the phone call. Gary knew how to strike the right tone to get everyone on board.

Banik-Rake and Bruett were ready to get down to brass tacks and actually start tackling the development and criteria of sustainable beef principles. Banik-Rake decided to arrange a three-day meeting in Chicago. McDonald's hosted twenty-five GRSB members in January 2013. They made a lot of tangible progress.

Bruett was key to creating support for the GRSB and defining the principles and criteria. He was awesome. For the next year to eighteen months, Brett attended every kind of meeting you can imagine.

Less than two years after Banik-Rake was hired to ride herd for McDonald's in its part of the GRSB, and two years after Bruett took over the reigns of the GRSB, the GRSB announced a set of global principles and criteria at their November 2014 global conference in Brazil. The GRSB defined sustainable beef as a socially responsible, environmentally sound, and economically viable product that prioritizes the following:

- planet (relevant principles: natural resources, efficiency and innovation, and people and the community);

- people (relevant principles: people and the community and food);

- animals (relevant principles: animal health and welfare, efficiency and innovation); and

- progress (relevant principles: natural resources, people and the community, animal health and welfare, food, efficiency, and innovation)

Holding this meeting, agreeing on a single definition of sustainable beef, and creating this set of principles and criteria was a watershed moment—for McDonald's as well as for other retailers, beef producers and NGOs like WWF. Bruett said that:

> The passage of a global definition for sustainable beef is truly a momentous achievement, not only for GRSB members, but also for the entire global beef value chain. This definition provides a common platform and consistent approach to discuss the economic, social and environmental issues we face irrespective of the region of the world one might be located.[149]

Convincing the C-Suite

In the meantime, in 2013, while GRSB was still closing in on how to define sustainable beef, McDonald's was developing its first C-suite-driven strategy, which would become McDonald's 2020 Sustainability Framework. (We'll learn more about this in Chapter 12.)

The team that DeBiase and I headed up to develop the framework was united in the belief that making a commitment to purchase sustainable beef was central to our work. We had the support of supply chain, of course, with DeBiase as colead. However, the framework, which included a bold commitment to purchase sustainable beef, needed approval from the top officers of our company.

The C-suite group was cautious about entering this unchartered ground. They were wary of setting nonfinancial goals and nervous about not meeting those goals. We were asking them to endorse an audacious goal: to start purchasing sustainable beef in the next couple of years even though we still had no definition of what sustainable beef was. As Gary

Johnson described, "We were kind of pushing rope until top management heard about it for the first time in the NGO event."

CEO Don Thompson told me he wanted to set up a half-day session about sustainability for the First Look meeting he was organizing for April 2013. First Look convened the top forty global leaders of our company during a two-day meeting to discuss strategy for the upcoming one to three years. Thompson had started to put CSR and sustainability on the agenda for all the top management meetings. He was driving the strategy to get our brand out in front, change our image, and show consumers that McDonald's had Good Food, Good People, and was a Good Neighbor.

For the first time ever, sustainability was not only on the First Look agenda, but Thompson had carved out a half day to discuss it. He gave me general direction to educate the group about the main goal of our CSR efforts. This was new to most attendees, who were not conversant about sustainability. I viewed this half-day session as the ultimate opportunity to turn the tide for our top people. I wanted them to see, hear, and feel that CSR and sustainability was a bona fide way to grow our business profitably and to build our brand health in an impactful way.

At first, I thought of bringing in various leaders from my extended McDonald's team to present data and strategies to spark a dialogue. Then I thought that listening to insiders is not always as jolting as bringing in outsiders. That prompted me to remember a recent meeting with Coca-Cola's top management organized by their outstanding chief sustainability officer, Bea Perez. Perez had invited others and me from big brands and NGOs, such as Walmart, Disney, and WWF to Coca-Cola's meeting. She wanted her management team to hear directly from their customers what sustainability meant to each of our organizations. It was a terrific session, with great questions and interaction with the Coke executives. So I borrowed the idea from Coca-Cola and decided to present sustainability from an outsider's perspectives.

NGO leaders comprised the first panel: Greenpeace, WWF, and the Alliance for a Healthier Generation. The second panel was comprised of chief sustainability officers of Unilever, Coca-Cola, and Walmart, and the CEO of Business for Social Responsibility, Aron Cramer, who oversaw relationships with a couple hundred corporate members. These people, and their companies, were the top-tier leaders on integrating sustainability into business. I wanted our top management to hear from great businesses that sustainability is good for business, not just a do-good side effort.

Top on my list for the half-day session was to move our management team on the notion of sustainable beef and have them see it as a good business strategy to consider it. I teed up our independent moderator, Jason Saul of Mission Measurement, who asked the preeminent external panelists "What one big sustainability strategy would you put in place if you were CEO for a day at McDonald's?

Among those panelists was Suzanne Apple, senior vice president of private sector engagement for WWF. She had a way of taking on tough, constructive situations as if she was coming into your family room to have a heart-to-heart conversation. I could tell she was connecting when the top forty McDonald's executives' heads and elbows all clicked forward, eyes zooming in on what Apple had to say.

> "I would say you've got to start with beef because beef is McDonald's, and McDonald's is beef," she said as she eyed McDonald's CEO and others. Apple and others on the panel talked about how beef is core to McDonald's business and central to many of the sustainable agricultural issues of our times. Apple finished with a clarion challenge. "If you are going to be a sustainability leader, you can't do anything until you take on sustainable beef."[150]

Others on the panel chimed in with similar thoughts. Aron Cramer, for example, reflecting on his first-hand experience in the room, said, "It was unanimous that all participants felt the company should focus on the subject that was so central to McDonald's business and also the achievement of a sustainable world, given the impact of beef on climate and water."[151]

Cramer observed McDonald's leadership, including Thompson, responding with open minds. He recalled that, "Having been in many similar meetings, I remember thinking that most CEOs and leaders would respond with a sense of defensiveness to a suggestion like this, and in this case, that was not evident." Despite Cramer's fears that his insights would be rejected, Thompson thought the session with business sustainability leaders and NGO experts raised some key points[152]:

> They thought that, in many cases, we were further along that we may have given ourselves credit for. They also thought that we could do more. We expect more from McDonald's. We expect you to be a leader. We expect you to move people, and constituencies, and supply chain in a way that will help us advance the mission and the goal.

This was very positive statement. They weren't attacking us. They were just saying that, "You know what? We think you could do more. We're disappointed when you don't do more. And we don't fully understand why you wouldn't do more."

The First Look meeting room was buzzing. It was a seminal moment for my company, a tipping point with senior management, who now understood our team's vision for a sustainable McDonald's. What's more is that they could see exciting possibilities for working with sustainable beef—and beef is what we were known for. This day marked McDonald's sustainability epiphany. It marked a sea change whereby top McDonald's executives converted to a different view of CSR. They now truly saw it as the way to grow our business by making a positive difference in the world. This also was a turning point for beef sustainability: Sustainable beef was no longer a wacky idea irrelevant to McDonald's business. Instead, sustainable beef was now considered to be core to our business growth and brand health.

Thompson became even more convinced about the feasibility of sustainable beef when he visited Ireland later that year:

> I remember visiting John [Power, a cattle farmer included in McDonald's U.K. Flagship Farm program] and his family, and talking about what he was doing. And how the water that was being utilized was filtered through these reed banks, and much more.
>
> I just thought the way John talked about it, it gave me a lot of hope. When we left, we knew we could bring this to the rest of the world. We could make a real dent in the carbon footprint by doing this. That's what led me to say, "We can do this at McDonald's." It is a big goal, but that's what we need to do.

Kick-Starting a Movement

All this led to the goal we proposed to our management team by the end of 2013. We asked them to accept and approve the most ambitious goal outlined in our 2020 Sustainability Framework: to start buying a portion of our beef from verified sustainable sources by 2016.

This was barely three years away, and we still had no stakeholder definition of sustainable beef (the GRSB completed this in late 2014, as noted above). Given this, we knew we could not set a date certain goal to buy 100 percent sustainable beef, as we had done with fish, packaging, palm oil, and coffee. Even so, we knew we had to put a marker out there. I've seen too many guidelines, principles, and voluntary commitments disappear in the havoc of running the day-to-day business. So I pushed for a tangible commitment. It was the only way to demonstrate the sincerity and authenticity of our sustainability work. The goal prompted a lot of debate with management and our suppliers. But, by late Fall 2013, we won approval for this big kahuna goal. We would begin to purchase sustainable beef by 2016 (and in 2016, we set further goals for 2020).

All this led me to propose that McDonald's make a solo, huge, public announcement about our sustainable beef commitment five months ahead of the public release of our new 2020 Sustainability Framework, slotted for May 2014. I had several good reasons for this: We needed to make a clarion call to the beef industry in order to jumpstart the actual procurement of sustainable beef. They needed to know that we were no longer doing this in theory, but in reality. I hoped McDonald's commitment would snowball into others in food service making similar commitments. It also would show the beef industry that the GRSB work on principles and criteria was not an esoteric policy exercise taking place in an ivory tower but it was a real goal that would lead to actual procurement changes. In addition, I believed that a public announcement would lock in McDonald's commitment. Once you go public, how can you backtrack?

I proposed we offer an exclusive story to Joel Makower of the GreenBiz Group. I had known Makower since the early 1990s. His unbiased journalism is unmatched, plus he had done many in-depth stories, not fluff. Makower's interest was not necessarily the what, but the why and how of what companies do.

McDonald's needed a why and how story. And that story had to target not the general public, but the beef industry. Since we knew that the beef industry was suspicious of sustainability and skeptical of McDonald's motivations, we needed a full-blown, deep dive into the complex factors involved in our drive for sustainable beef. We wanted to show how we were collaborating, not mandating. We wanted to explain how this was an effort to sell more beef, which would be good for McDonald's and good for the entire beef industry.

I proposed to our media team that we have an open-door strategy with Makower. We would bring him in for a day and a half and provide access to all the key players in our supply chain department, including DeBiase, Johnson, and Banik-Rake, as well as our suppliers and partners, such as WWF, GRSB, and Cameron Bruett of JBS.

I was instantly shot down. Our communications lead wanted to narrow the topics and contacts we allowed Makower, suggesting that we be open while carefully selecting who Makower could talk with. I disagreed. I countered that we couldn't do this story with a false openness. We had nothing to hide, I argued, so we should give Makower 360-degree access. I reminded him that sustainable beef is a complex story that needed full coverage.

He wouldn't budge. I was forced to go over his head. I met with Heidi Barker, vice president of communications, to explain the idea and then proposed the strategy and how the article would be good for McDonald's and for moving the beef industry closer to us. Barker agreed, and soon we set up Makower with our contacts and an invitation to visit our campus in November 2013.

About two months later, on January 7, 2014, we would make the public announcement detailing our commitment to sustainable beef. In my vision, it would be the biggest, most transformational nonfinancial announcement in McDonald's history.

Makower opened the long-form, three-part, twenty-thousand-word feature story this way[153]:

Two Steps Forward

Exclusive: Inside McDonald's Quest for Sustainable Beef

By Joel Makower

Tuesday, January 7, 2014

Part 1 of a three-part series running this week. Part 2: How a Big Mac becomes sustainable. Part 3: Can the beef industry collaborate its way to sustainability?

Today, McDonald's announces that it will begin purchasing verified sustainable beef in 2016, the first step on a quest to purchase sustainable beef for all of its burgers worldwide.

Behind McDonald's lofty ambitions is a complex story that has been unfolding over the past several years. It involves engaging the global beef industry, from ranchers and feedlots to restaurants and supermarkets, as well as environmental groups, academics and the McDonald's senior executive team.

I watched the story unfold for much of 2013 and recently interviewed nearly a dozen McDonald's executives, one of the company's largest beef suppliers and its principal NGO partner on this initiative, along with other industry experts. The story is remarkable not just because of its scope and scale, but also as a case study on what it takes to nudge a large and entrenched industry toward sustainability in today's global marketplace.

Where it mattered the most—i.e., how the beef industry interpreted our effort—the story achieved its purpose. Bruett worried at first. "My initial reaction was, 'Well, what has McDonald's been buying up until then?'" he said. "I was nervous that the signal sent was that the other beef wasn't sustainable. Okay, you're serving sustainable beef now. What have you been serving the past sixty years?"

Once Bruett absorbed the whole story, though, he relaxed. "I think the marketing of it was done responsibly," he said.

So if I look a the evolution of [sustainable meat] marketing, where it's got to be something hyphen-free (antibiotic-, gluten-, cage-, hormone-free) in order to attract a customer, McDonald's didn't really take that approach with the sustainable burger.

It wasn't a "This is free from antibiotics, this is free from hormones, this is the cattle that have been heavily petted." It was more based on this definition we created at GRSB that was balanced, that addressed all these critical issues.

McDonald's showed concern to environmental NGOs, sure, but also concern to the producers and their profitability and their ability to expand their operation and pass it on to the next generation. Everyone had a shared responsibility in bringing that sustainable beef.

Makower's story elated our McDonald's team. So did the positive reaction from the beef industry. The communications strategy helped the beef industry understand our motives. The secret of the story's success was that is was unplugged. And I cannot tell you how important it is to use this unrehearsed, unscripted approach to any sustainability communication effort.

The minute a big brand such as McDonald's retrenches to safe corporate speak and there's any sign of hiding something, the effort becomes moot and self-destructive. If it is doing something meaningful, sincere, and good, a company needs to stand tall and be completely open and transparent. Humbleness should mark the approach, not simplicity or hyperbole.

Bruett's initial worry turned into the opposite feeling. "I thought the announcement story did tremendous benefits for sustainable beef because it didn't turn off the producers," he said. "It didn't turn off the packers. Because it was balanced, science-based, practical, and it's not telling a myth to the consumer that once you peel back the onion you can't justify."

We did it. No one campaigned against us for this. We had no activist pressure for a sustainable burger. The tide had turned. We were proactive and strategic and dictated what we wanted, not what the activists wanted. Finally.*

What It Takes to Lead Sustainability

I observed many terrific leaders in my sustainability career. I was a sponge learning from the Yastows, Grandins, Koziols, DeBiases, and so many others profiled in this book. What do they have in common?

---

* Update note: In 2017, McDonald's issued a Global Sustainable Beef Report. It includes an update on purchasing sustainable beef in Canada. It also includes new goals for 2020.

What short list can I pass on to those leading change today and tomorrow?

Sustainable leadership is about:

Courage: Accept and relish the fact that leadership in sustainability means changing something that will meet resistance and that you need strength to face the grief that is to come. For example, Francesca DeBiase, Jose Armario, Don Thompson making the tough decision to phase out of gestation stalls (Chapter 10), knowing the acrimony of the pork industry was to follow.

Conviction: Leading a sustainability change is not for the weak-kneed. Conviction, really having a firmly held belief, is required as the contagious springboard to bring others along. For example, Gary Johnson insisting that the fish suppliers work with Conservation International despite their pushback (Chapter 6).

Cleverness: By this, I mean the positive quality of being clever, ingenious, and innovative. Sustainability solutions most often need a new way and approach. For example, Shelby Yastrow's creative thinking to work with unusual partners, like the EDF and Dr Temple Grandin (Chapters 1 and 2).

Contrariness: Since sustainability means a change from the status quo, being a contrarian is a positive attribute. As Woodrow Wilson once said, "If you want to make enemies, try to change something." For example, Karen van Bergen leading the Amazon Soy Moratorium effort. Since McDonald's part in the problem truly was small, the conventional approach would have been to stay clear of any engagement.

It's ironic that while it takes a lot of courage, conviction, cleverness, and contrariness to battle to make sustainable change, a really good leader knows how to do so and still attract others to the mission or cause because they know how to collaborate.

Collaboration: Even though a sustainability leader has conviction and more, they need to possess the strength to listen and be open to change and adaptation. For example, Jan Fields leading the Happy Meal change (Chapter 5). She believed in listening so much that she conducted a national listening tour, too.

Cheerfulness: Despite the serious nature of sustainability issues, good cheer goes a long way. Having an overt optimism is the best magnet to build support. For example, Joe Beckwith, who while leading downright serious safety issues for McDonald's, always had a smile, a joke, and a sense of humor.

Charisma: This does not necessarily mean a magnetic personality because it's not a personality-driven approach that I am referring to, rather, it is the ability to attract attention and admiration; to gain trust. To me, this adds up to the art of influencing others. For example, Jason Clay of the WWF. He did all this and more to influence McDonald's supply chain leaders to realize that sustainable beef is possible.

12

The Battle to Lead Both Business and Society
The Profits of Sustainability

GROWING OUR BUSINESS <u>BY</u> MAKING A
POSITIVE DIFFERENCE IN SOCIETY

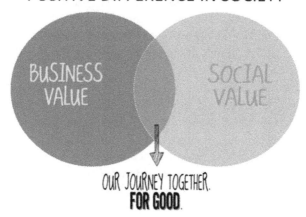

Fig. 12.1: The Shared Value Model I Used as the Primary Rationale for McDonald's 2020 Sustainability Framework.

Battling Risk Averseness

In April 2013, the time had finally come to present a draft to our C-suite of our company's 2020 Sustainability Framework. Two years had passed since Don Thompson asked me to colead (with Francesca DeBiase and Jerry Sus, Senior Director from our Innovation Center) the development of a bold sustainability plan.

It was admittedly slow going to form teams, get feedback, develop drafts, and vet the framework with internal stakeholders from various

225

areas of the world. We took a big leap forward when Thompson took over as CEO in August 2012, after Skinner's retirement. Thompson's first memo as CEO to the McDonald's system was on August 12, 2012. He ignited all of us on the corporate social responsibility (CSR) team (and many others) by stating in a memo that was the catalyst needed to move our Sustainability Framework out of its slumber:

> At McDonald's our Brand and business are inextricably linked, and making a positive difference in society will contribute to our overall success. Few companies are in such a position. We have an incredible iconic Brand we can leverage to enrich the world and in turn accelerate our growth. That is what we will do in a more focused and ambitious way than ever before.

Thompson also made CSR & Sustainability a new department in the company, combining Ronald McDonald House Charities (RMHC), Diversity, Community Affairs, and Sustainability. He created a new senior vice president role, reporting to him, and promoted J.C. Gonzalez-Mendez. For the first time in McDonald's history, the broad role of CSR had a seat in the C-Suite.

Thompson put a respective business leader in charge of CSR & Sustainability when he tapped Gonzalez-Mendez. He wanted to send a signal to our internal system that this function is akin to leading the United States, Europe, Asia, and Latin America groups. Thompson was determined to improve our brand perception as a part of his legacy. Gonzalez-Mendez was recently president of the Latin America group. Before that, he was U.S. supply chain chief supply chain officer. He had extensive business chops.

I believe the most perfect leader for CSR in any company comes from the core business, as did Gonzalez-Mendez. That doesn't mean there isn't a big role for specialists like me. In fact, I got in the saddle with Gonzalez-Mendez and was as enthusiastic as ever to bring CSR & Sustainability to the mainstream within McDonald's.

This change coincided with the penultimate time of my career. Twenty-five years earlier, I had accepted a temporary environmental role that led to addressing the very first, hot societal issue McDonald's faced: waste. The years that followed, chronicled in this book, were shaped primarily in the way McDonald's responded to events around us. We scrambled, tried hard to be responsible, and took some actions. As we did this, our brand had been sullied; our reputation smeared. We all felt we were a much more responsible company than most people perceived us to be. But we were now fast approaching the mountain top, ready to plant our stake in the high ground, claiming what we stood for and owning how McDonald's was going to define and shape its own destiny as a responsible, sustainability-minded company.

With this new thrust, Thompson charged us with developing a sustainability plan that would evolve from this From/To evolution:

- From a sustainability journey that was motivated by the right thing to do
  … to sustainability as central to growing our business and brand.

- From disjointed good acts and deeds
  … to alignment and agreement across our McDonald's system.

- From a potpourri of global activities
  … to a focused vision and global framework.

- From getting little credit
  … to sharing our story and getting credit.

I presented the entire 2020 Sustainability Framework at the First Look meeting in April 2013—on the same day we brought sustainable beef to the forefront (see Chapter 11). In the circular room, our top forty-two leaders listened as I presented our aspirations and goals. It started well. I described our plan, starting with a simple way to express our overarching vision: "Grow Our Business and Make a Difference in the World." I got some pushback, but that pushback made it better. Several officers suggested we change the wording to "Grow Our Business By Making a Positive Difference in the World." Adding "by" was brilliant, because it directly stated the connection between doing good deeds and doing what's good for business. "Positive" was a smart change, too, because so many of our critics claimed we were a negative factor for society.

We then went through the goals we proposed for the pillars of food, sourcing, and planet.

That's when the discussion turned more cautious. Many attendees asked what level of confidence we had that we would attain the 2020 goals. For example, our aspiration for the sourcing pillar was that "all of our food and packaging come from verified sustainable sources." The specific 2020 goals included 100 percent sustainable fish, palm oil, coffee, and packaging. Could we really do this everywhere, in all 119 countries where McDonald's had restaurants, all of which had different infrastructures and challenges? Risk aversion started to dominate the discussion as everyone wondered what would happen if we fell short of our goals.

Failing was a legitimate concern, especially for those goals that depended upon franchisee participation. For example, one of our draft goals was to improve our energy efficiency 20 percent per restaurant by 2020. Considering that our global energy bill was approximately $2 billion, the business rationale was solid: Improving energy efficiency would save us $40 million. The goal also hit the sweet spot for good societal impact, given that our use of energy was the number one way we could directly reduce greenhouse gas emissions (GHGs). (The biggest source of GHG emissions was in the supply chain, due to impacts from livestock, but these were outside our direct control.)

The dialogue at the meeting questioned this commitment since 85 percent (at that time) of our global operations were owned and operated by independent franchisees. We could not mandate that they do this. Instead, we would have to convince about five thousand owner–operators that this was a good idea.

Another concern that dampened the bold goal setting was the trans-fatty acid (TFA) debacle (briefly described in Chapter 5) colored much of the cautious attitude expressed in the First Look meeting. McDonald's U.S. business had announced in September 2002 a commitment to phase out TFA cooking oil because of growing health concerns. We were sincere in setting an aggressive six-month goal to complete the conversion. We received praise for doing so. This was all part of our anticipatory issues management process. Unfortunately, the conversion process took much longer than planned and wasn't 100 percent complete until May 2008. The supply chain implications were more intricate than we had antici-pated. For example, our primary supplier of the new oil needed to plant new canola fields in Canada. In the meantime, as we missed our stated deadline, a class action lawsuit was filed by a public interest group against McDonald's for not taking the appropriate steps to inform the public of the delay. McDonald's ended up settling the case with Bran-sTransFat.com, agreeing to the following[154]:

- Donate $7 million to the American Heart Association, to be used for public education regarding trans fats. McDonald's was also required to spend up to $1.5 million on publishing notices to ensure that the public knows the status of its trans fat initiative.

- Encourage substitution of partially hydrogenated oils by the food industry.

- Hold conferences on health issues associated with trans fat and the substitution of partially hydrogenated oils.

The results of this lawsuit flabbergasted me. Why were we being sued for trying to do good? Our effort and motivations were sincere, yet we were punished for it. The legacy of the TFA problem loomed large as we dug deeper into the Sustainability 2020 framework.

Several attendees suggested we tone down the plan, making it less bold and more achievable. I began to realize I had lost my pitch for the ambitious goals—at least in this session. Rather than trying to recover my footing during the few minutes remaining, I knew I needed to stop and regroup.

The level of risk aversion surprised me to a certain extent, largely because I thought we had gotten clear direction from Thompson to be bold. I learned later, however, that Thompson thought about the goals in a different, more practical light. "I wanted achievable goals," he said, "because if you're going to fuel a movement that will be sustainable in the corporate culture, people need to feel good about the fact that, 'You know what? We can do this.'"[155]

Thompson was concerned that if the company didn't meet these aspirational goals, people, especially our internal staff, owner–operators, and suppliers might get disenchanted with the effort. He was walking a tightrope. "I wanted us to have some really bold and bodacious goals," he said. "But I also wanted them to be goals that we could really hit. And we could tell our constituencies and consumers, 'Hey, this is what we did. And we did this together.'"

My partner in developing the sustainability framework, Francesca DeBiase, observed the same play-it-safe approach with the internal team working on goals for the supply chain. "They were looking at goals the way we at McDonald's normally looked at our financial goals," she said. "Even though we were setting goals for 2020, they wanted to know they could beat that in three years."[156]

Francesca summarized the formula for credible goal setting for sustainability:

- Set really ambitious goals. And even when you don't know how you're going to achieve them, you certainly are going to do whatever you can to achieve them.

- You're going to invest where you need to invest.

- You're going to bring the best suppliers along.

- You're going to come up with the best innovation to get there.

- You might not know how to get it, so that makes people very uncomfortable. (It made the beef, poultry, and pork boards very uncomfortable.)

- If we don't achieve our goals, we'll be very transparent about why and what we did.

- But that's the only way you make significant change.

Unfortunately, she also noted that, "This concept was foreign to most people internally." DeBiase, who led one of McDonald's gigantic supply chains (indeed, one of the largest in all of business), charged ahead against this ingrained risk-averse cultural mindset and pressed for stretch goals.

I needed to get the C-suite executives in the same place as DeBiase. But how? I had a choice to make. Leadership had asked me to make the framework easier to achieve. Should I dumb it down? Or should I stick with the bold goals and come back to senior management to explain why they were best for our company?

My next opportunity to pitch the framework came two weeks later. I addressed the core leaders of our executive team, about sixteen of them, who headed up all major functions and business units. I resolved, on behalf of our team, to not give in, to not make our plan a plain, generic, safe one. External stakeholders would eventually see the framework as flimsy and that McDonald's wasn't committed to serious sustainable transformation. Internal stakeholders would see that we were gaming the system.

I thought long and hard about how best to moderate a discussion about the two conflicting priorities. On one hand, senior management wanted us to be a leader on CSR. On the other hand, they wanted minimum risk. How could I convey the Catch-22 we were in because we could not do both? I decided to present several types of research to show how other companies viewed these issues. I began with a self-created Leadership Spectrum model (see Fig. 12.2). The idea was to force a discussion about the trade-offs between (1) assuming low risks and staying out of trouble versus (2) bold leadership and the opportunity to make a significant impact on society and our business.

I worked with a credible third-party NGO, Business for Social Responsibility, to place other big, branded companies in this matrix. I thought that by comparing us to other Fortune 500 companies, I could show how McDonald's was an out-of-step laggard. For example, Unilever was a universally acclaimed leader in sustainability, taking on bold goals and assuming high risk. Unilever had created a set of more than a

Fig. 12.2: Leadership Spectrum and Smart Risk Taking.

hundred goals. One of them was to help a billion people improve their health and well-being by 2020. Another big goal was to reduce their environmental footprint by half. They talked openly about how they did not yet know how they would achieve these goals. Other companies, such as Coca-Cola, Walmart, Starbucks, and Proctor & Gamble (P&G) also were placed on the chart.

How far on the horizontal line did McDonald's want to lead on food, sourcing, and the planet? How much (smart) risk were we willing to assume in the vertical axis? This tool worked great. I felt the wall of risk resistance dissipate.

The second tool I employed was a quick study my team had conducted. We researched the top Fortune 50 brands to analyze if they had set sustainability goals, and, if so, how many. Only six companies had no goals. Most companies had set four to six ambitious goals. Setting stretch goals was the norm. Without directly saying so, we showed that McDonald's was an anomaly.

Next, I shared how major companies had set goals, not achieved them, and still flourished. Our management team was concerned that if we did not meet our goals, we would get in trouble with the public, with NGOs, and with lawsuits. It would be TFA-free déjà vu all over again.

I referenced several companies, from Starbucks to P&G, and illustrated public examples of each not achieving their stated goals. Each company had external communications explaining why they failed to meet their sustainability goals. Each explained how they had adjusted their goals. I demonstrated that each continued to receive support from the NGO community because they were being open and transparent, trying hard, stretching themselves, and making progress, even though they still were falling short. I explained how external stakeholders want this combination of truly going after something meaningful and difficult, giving it a concerted effort, and being honest about problems, pitfalls, and progress.

For example, in 2012, Starbucks had set an aggressive goal to 5 percent of its coffee served in reusable cups by 2015. In 2015 they had reached only 1.8 percent.[157] The opinion I expressed to the management team was that although they had some critics, the overall sentiment from their stakeholders was a thumbs-up for trying, making some progress, and being forthright with the challenges.

These examples provided practical reassurance that CSR goal setting was different than compliance with laws and regulations where violations are subject to fines and even imprisonment.

Finally, I showed a study (see Fig. 12.3) from GlobeScan[158] about expectations from companies on social and environmental leadership. What I emphasized from the report was that leadership was a combination of both what you do and how you do it. I felt that our management (and most corporate management across the board) believed that the only way to prove leadership on CSR and sustainability was to work on the *what*: tangible actions and specific progress. *What*, indeed, is critical, but when reviewing the list in Fig. 12.3, you can see several categories that are more about the *how*. For instance, the list includes values,

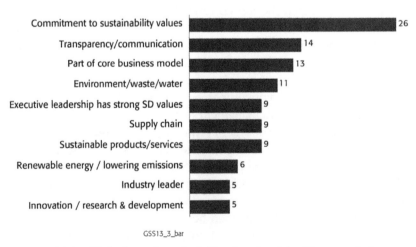

Reason a Company Is Considered a Sustainability Leader
% of Total Mentions, All Respondents, 2013

Commitment to sustainability values	26
Transparency/communication	14
Part of core business model	13
Environment/waste/water	11
Executive leadership has strong SD values	9
Supply chain	9
Sustainable products/services	9
Renewable energy / lowering emissions	6
Industry leader	5
Innovation / research & development	5

GSS13_3_bar

Fig. 12.3: GlobeScan Sustainability Leadership Characteristics.

transparency, and integration into the core business, industry leadership, and innovation. Yes, stakeholders expect companies to get stuff done, but they also have an equal desire to know why you are doing it, whether you are being honest and open, how are you engaging with stakeholders to listen and learn, and whether you are reporting problems as well as progress.

The Leadership Spectrum and sustainability benchmarking I described to the group hit them like a jolt of adrenaline and pivoted the discussion. They became supportive of the bold goals. Our team still had to fill in a few holes in the plan, but I was thrilled and confident that we were on a path to finalize a sustainability road map for the future that would make a positive difference for society.

Developing Shared Value Goals

As I went through this process, I realized that nothing had made a greater impact on my thinking on how to influence McDonald's leaders than the "Shared Value" concept presented by Michael Porter and Mark Kramer, well-known business management gurus, published in *Harvard Business Review*'s January/February issue of 2011. Their article, "Creating Shared Value: How to Reinvent Capitalism—and Unleash a Wave of Innovation and Growth,"[159] revealed to me the most convincing way to position CSR in any company, including McDonald's. Shared Value reframes CSR and sustainability from being something peripheral and largely focused on doing good, such as philanthropy, to being a core business function that provides another avenue of growth by connecting business value and societal value.

The Shared Value model was the home run approach we needed to solidify McDonald's sustainability plan. The mindset at McDonald's needed to change. We had long viewed CSR only as doing good. By doing so, we were limiting CSR to a do-gooder approach without financial benefit. There's nothing wrong with this, and the idea of doing the right thing can create terrific programs. But, in order to get business leaders locked in to CSR, I needed to show them that CSR is a proven business strategy that helps business grow and prosper. That was not the common wisdom among McDonald's executives. Up to this time during my tenure at McDonald's, I had heard plenty of comments that essentially said, "CSR is not going to sell us any more Big Macs." But now I had the business strategy to change the discussion. I quickly adapted Shared Value as McDonald's fundamental way to rethink CSR. Every chance I had, in every meeting and presentation, I used the McDonald's Shared Value framework (Fig. 12.1).

This framework helped me explain that, when an internal stakeholder might challenge whether a certain goal we were considering was really something we would do, I would respond by saying our approach is to work on only the most important things in our business that impact society. We would do so to bring value not only to society but also to help our own growth through sales, cost reduction, brand enhancement, and other business benefits. With McDonald's Shared Value in hand, I worked with my direct team and dozens of others on our extended CSR team to develop our sustainability plan.

My team worked tirelessly. Jeff Hogue, who joined McDonald's in May 2012 as senior director, was my right-hand man. He wanted to be more engaged with a consumer-facing big brand. He hit the jackpot with McDonald's. I delegated a big job to Hogue as my point man for the sustainability framework. He took it on like he was the Energizer Bunny, a nickname my team and I often called him in admiration.

The Sourcing Pillar

We all believed food was at the core of our sustainability efforts. How we sourced our food in a sustainable way was our most important pillar due its reach, ripple effects, and transformative power. As such, the supply chain team led by Francesca DeBiase developed a bold aspiration to buy all of our food and packaging from verified sustainable sources. As detailed in Chapters 9 and 10, McDonald's set goals to buy sustainable beef by 2016 and to buy 100 percent sustainable fish, coffee, palm oil, and packaging by 2020.

The Planet Pillar

I built the leadership structure for our sustainability plan so that a top officer of the company led each pillar. For the Planet Pillar, since it dealt with restaurant operations, I visited my long-term friend and colleague, Ken Koziol, who was senior vice president and global chief operations officer. Thanks to our previous work together, he needed no introduction to sustainability.

I assured Koziol that my crack team, comprised of Jeff Hogue and Jenny McColloch, would help him and his operation's team determine the best sustainability goals for the restaurants. Ken agreed. Hogue and McColloch were soon working with Koziol and his lieutenants to develop energy and recycling goals that would benefit the planet.

Energy was both easy and difficult. The easy part came in making the financial case. McDonald's spent $2 billion annually on its global energy bill. Because of the sheer number of McDonald's outlets and offices, it is one of the biggest users of electricity in most markets. Also, a food service operation such as McDonald's is energy-intensive per square foot. A McDonald's restaurant has a lot of cooking frying tools, HVAC systems, lighting, and refrigeration/freezing appliances, all running concurrently in a small footprint. Today, the energy needed for 36,000 restaurants worldwide is equivalent to the needs for 2.5 million residences.

We already had plenty of energy-saving technologies in place to achieve 20 percent–plus energy reduction levels for new restaurants. How much we could deploy in remodels and retrofits, however, was a more difficult proposition, particularly considering budget and practical limitations.

The difficult part with this goal was getting access to the capital to make these investments. Though the financial payback was on average three to five years, energy investments competed against many other priorities for the company's capital that had better returns or addressed other business opportunities. By addressing energy use, a restaurant could save $6,000–$10,000 annually. Utilities comprise the third largest cost for a restaurant, with food/paper and people running about 30 percent each and Utilities at about 5 percent.

The other challenge we had was whether to include the franchisees in this goal. The cold, hard facts were that owner–operators were independent businesspeople. We could not force them to accept this goal, so we articulated the goal for company restaurants only: to increase energy efficiency by 20 percent by 2020. By being more energy efficient, McDonald's was addressing one of society's biggest issues (i.e., climate change) and reducing our carbon footprint.

Climate Change

The entire team working on the planet and sourcing goals wanted McDonald's to take a progressive position on climate change. After a decade of rebutted efforts to forge a proactive policy on climate change, I was determined to make this part of our 2020 Sustainability Framework.

Hogue developed drafts of our position, working with our internal government relation's team and with the World Wildlife Fund (WWF), our key external advisor. My direction to him was to frame the goal in the least politically neutral language possible. I didn't want the discussion to fall into a political debate with people taking sides.

When Hogue finished a draft that we were happy with, I found to my surprise that we didn't go far enough with it. José Armario, our top supply chain officer, said we could be more bold and set GHG emission reduction goals that were not in the plan. After all these years of hearing only internal resistance, his prodding was encouraging.

I wasn't so sure, however, that we could get top management alignment to come together around another big goal. Sometimes big progress is going from nowhere to a midpoint. That's where my head was. I so much wanted a positive climate change policy that I thought the first step was to go midway. I figured we could do more later.

It took Hogue a few dozen drafts and numerous internal legal and governmental affairs hurdles to get to the final version. WWF helped us create the final version, rating it as "middle of the pack" for big brands, but as a leadership position for the quick service restaurant industry.

Winning approval for this remains one of my favorite achievements at McDonald's. Considering the long-term resistance we had faced, the first and last paragraphs of our position statement were especially gratifying:

> McDonald's Corporation, together with its subsidiaries (the Company) understands that climate change presents a global challenge with broad and far-reaching implications for generations to come. We acknowledge the findings of the 5th Assessment Report of the Intergovernmental Panel for Climate Change (IPCC)—"that human influence on the climate system is clear" and "limiting climate change will require substantial and sustained reductions of greenhouse gas emissions."

> ... At McDonald's, we view climate change as an important business and societal issue to monitor and address. As a responsible company and leading global brand, we will leverage our size and position to reduce the impact of our business on climate change.

It's moments like this that make the grinding it out worth it. I'm glad that Armario gave me a nudge to go bolder. As a member of that top management team, his advocacy helped us get it approved.

Recycling: Harder Than It Looks

Setting a goal for recycling was unlike setting goals for energy reduction. We already had technological solutions in place for energy efficiency. But there wasn't much technology available to handle McDonald's funky food and packaging waste. Recycling McDonald's trash, with all the syrup, ketchup, and other food remains made our waste stinky and unwanted by recyclers.

In addition, even though our packaging was mostly paper-based (more than 80 percent), much of it had plastic or wax laminates and other nonorganic features to keep the food hot or the drinks cold. For example, most people think the paper hot cup is "paper," but it has about a 10 percent plastic laminate. Recyclers want pure paper, like newspapers.

As of 2014, McDonald's global average recycling rate was an average of 35 percent for on-premises waste. Two components made up most of this 35 percent. McDonald's Europe was already recycling more than 50 percent of its on-premises waste, with plans to achieve 70 percent by 2020. Most of McDonald's in Asia had very low rates.

The biggest chunk of our recyclable material came from all the corrugated shipping containers used by our suppliers for each restaurant's food and paper products. The other big portion was used cooking oil, which was picked up by processors that transformed it into biodiesel fuel.

You'd think economics would be a great driver to increase recycling, but McDonald's waste bill already was relatively low. Often I would ask an interested stakeholder how much money he or she thought an average McDonald's restaurant spends on trash. I would commonly get answers as high as $1 billion a year. The truth is that it cost just $200 million to dispose the more than 2 billion pounds of trash McDonald's in the United States produced every year. On average, a single McDonald's restaurant spent about $10,000 a year on trash. Compared to the $75,000 energy bill for a single restaurant, waste was a minor cost.

Our team opted for a goal of 50 percent on-premises recycling by 2020. It may be the biggest stretch goal we have because the technology to increase recycling is not off the shelf today and because getting consumers involved may be necessary (going against what we and others have learned, which is that most consumers do not want to be bothered to separate waste from recycling after eating out).

The Food Pillar

Addressing nutritional concerns was a decade-old dilemma for McDonald's. I detailed the steady onslaught of escalating concerns and attacks on McDonald's food as a source of obesity, especially with kids, in Chapter 5.

I have lot of passion for health, my own health included. To me, the obesity problem is one of the most serious issues of our times. The question is: What is McDonald's role in solving this problem? The whole concept of "healthy food" is perplexing because healthy eating is a lifestyle of making good food choices for yourself and your lifestyle. A healthy lifestyle is comprised of many factors, including food intake, physical activity, hereditary characteristics, and emotional components.

I saw nothing wrong with our core products. Why can't we serve good tasty food for people on the go? Who should be the one to tell me I cannot eat a Big Mac? Maybe I'm playing several sets of tennis tonight and need the calories. With that in mind, I argued that McDonald's has a responsibility to provide some balance by offering a range of menu items with a variety of portion sizes and nutritional options.

We had internal debates about how to put less salt, sugar, calories, and fat (what we internally nicknamed "sin ingredients") into our food while still providing great taste. I compared it to packaging, where we still use disposable packaging, but we continually strive to make it smaller, lighter, and better for the environment.

The business case for more balanced choices and more nutritional improvements was that we wanted customers to feel good about visiting McDonald's more often. McDonald's average customer visited us two or three times a month. By adding better nutritional choices, we thought we could increase frequency beyond that.

In our 2020 Sustainability Framework, we committed to doubling our sales of fruit and vegetables and agreeing to set a goal for further sin ingredients reductions in the near future.

The People Pillar

We decided not to set a specific people goal because McDonald's was a franchising company, with 90 percent of the restaurants (and the people within them) controlled by about five thousand independent owner–operators. We literally could not tell them what to do with their people. For this reason, I didn't get too involved in our company's various people issues.

But since I spent a lot of time in public, explaining CSR to various audiences, many asked about and challenged what they saw as McDonald's low-wage problem. I defended it then, and I still do.

McDonald's business model is set up for part-time workers, and the work is entry level, not requiring high skills or education. I believe McDonald's provides a first-class place for a first job. Employees learn discipline, hard work, collaboration, teamwork, and much more.

The chance that an unskilled or first-time worker can climb the ladder at McDonald's is real. Thousands have been promoted and earned generous salaries to support their family as supervisors, managers, and even owner–operators.

Cody Teets, a former McDonald's vice president of franchising, wrote a 2012 book called *Golden Opportunity: Remarkable Careers that Began at McDonald's*. In it, she shares many stories how people, some famous, got their first jobs at McDonald's and how the lessons they learned there helped them build a career within McDonald's and outside McDonald's. I believe one of the best aspects of McDonald's role in society is exactly as Cody describes. We give people great opportunity to learn and grow. Her book highlights some great examples:

> Jay Leno credits a McDonald's owner-operator for encouraging him to enter a company talent show that proved to be the spark for his career as a comedian.

> Andrew Card, former White House Chief of Staff, worked his way through college at McDonald's, honing the leadership skills that he credits with preparing him for him many roles in government.

> Astronaut Leroy Chiao worked in a McDonald's in California where he learned the skill of interacting with many different people doing many different jobs to accomplish a common goal, much like the NASA missions, which he would later fly.

The Community Pillar

J.C. Gonzalez-Mendez, the officer sponsor for the Community Pillar, thought that setting a goal for the Community Pillar would be a piece of cake. "I thought that Community was going to be an easy fix," he said, "because I thought, 'We'll do Ronald McDonald House Charities on steroids.'"[160]

RMHC started in Philadelphia. Fred Hill, a player for the Philadelphia Eagles, had a daughter who was suffering from leukemia, which prompted the football team to raise in excess of $100,000 to support the hospital. This was met with much gratitude from Dr Audrey Evans, an oncologist at the Children's Hospital of Philadelphia, and her team, but also with a request for another $32,000 to fund a house in which the families of the children in the hospital could get proper rest, away from the ward.

In turn, this request was met by Ed Rensi, an area manager for McDonald's (and future company president). The company was using the Eagles' players as part of an advertising campaign and offered to donate the proceeds from the sales of shamrock shakes to the cause. In return, Rensi asked that the house be known as the Ronald McDonald House. And so it was, on October 15, 1974, that the first Ronald McDonald House opened its doors. In the intervening years, RMHC has spread across the world.[161]

I worked within RMHC in various roles for several years, including a couple when I was in charge of giving out national grants. I have seen the good work RMHC does. Within McDonald's, it is not just a PR effort to support RMHC. It is a real passion for so many people around the world.

RMHC has always been an independent 501(3)c nonprofit, with strict firewalls between RMHC and McDonald's. McDonald's provides staff to run the global charity, but this staff is dedicated to the charity and intentionally quarantined away from the McDonald's restaurant business. Gonzalez-Mendez sums up the big dilemma, noting that everybody except McDonald's believes that McDonald's owns RMHC. Despite the perception that RMHC is a McDonald's charity, it is not so, and the nonprofit has many other donors. As a result of what some considered to be blurred lines, "[i]t was difficult to set a McDonald's goal for RMHC," said Gonzalez-Mendez. "That firewall as so big, so tall, that it was impenetrable."

The situation got even worse in late October 2013, when Gonzalez-Mendez read the headline: "McDonald's Slammed Over Ronald McDonald House Giving." The story summarized a report by the NGO called Corporate Accountability called, "Clowning Around With Charity: How McDonald's Exploits Philanthropy and Targets Children." One of the main claims of the report was that McDonald's was chintzy for what it gives to charity, the implication being that the global company wasn't contributing enough money.[162]

According to a *Forbes* story about this same issue:

> In 2011, McDonald's donated $34 million in cash and in-kind donations (including hamburgers and fries, and volunteer hours donated by employees) to RMHC and other charities. That is only .08 percent of their $5.5 billion net income, says the report, far less than what is donated by similar companies like Yum! Brands (Taco Bell and KFC) or Coca-Cola. And in 2012 McDonald's customers gave more than $50 million at donation boxes, making giving from customers 1.5 times as much as that from the company itself.[163]

How should one measure the success of a philanthropic effort? If you were to measure by pure direct financial contributions, McDonald's had been a below-average giver in its philanthropic efforts. If you measure the actual social impact, then McDonald's support of RMHC stands tall. As Gonzalez-Mendez notes:

> I don't think there is a charity that has done as much good as Ronald McDonald House Charities, and 89 cents of every dollar goes back to its programs. Last year (2016), I think RMHC served 7 million children through the 360 Houses and 200 Ronald Rooms. They have 347,000 volunteers. They provide the best medicine for children and families, which is togetherness.

Other companies establish philanthropic foundations and give away money to good causes, writing check after check. This is a good thing, too. To me, though, McDonald's is a role model for philanthropic impact by helping to support with extreme focus the one charity of choice it is dedicated to. I believe the heart of McDonald's people, including its suppliers and owner–operators, added up to much more than what money can measure.

The other, more insulting claim of the "Clowning Around" report was that McDonald's was using the charity to bolster its brand. The report asserted that, by linking Ronald McDonald, in particular, to the charity, "McDonald's gains an emotionally-loaded marketing vehicle while shielding itself from critics."[164]

McDonald's fired back. In a statement provided to ABC News, Bridget Coffing, senior vice president of McDonald's corporate relations, said that:

> This report is shameful and misleading. We hesitate to even dignify it with a comment, but that would be a disservice to

the McDonald's employees, franchisees, suppliers, and customers who have partnered tirelessly to support the tremendous work of Ronald McDonald House Charities (RMHC).
This is a thinly veiled attack on our brand at the expense of
the millions of families and organizations who have benefitted
from RMHC. McDonald's categorically rejects this self-serving
and biased document and stands proud of the significant
financial support and volunteer hours we have and will
continue to provide to RMHC and other charities
worldwide.[165]

I fully agree with Coffing. I am all for keeping RMHC pure and clean,
and keeping it as one of the very best charities in the United States. When
it comes to doing good, I believe the highest good a company can do
should relate resources to its core business. In McDonald's case, serving
safe, affordable, high-quality, responsible, and sustainable food. For
McDonald's, that means developing sustainable food, reducing climate
change, and recycling more.

I was not discouraged by not setting a specific global community goal.
In addition, giving back to the community is the antithesis of a global
approach. Every community needs something different.

Sustainability Introduced at Worldwide Convention

We completed McDonald's 2020 Sustainability Framework by early
2014 (see Fig. 12.4). I credit Jeff Hogue for getting us to the finish line. He
said he generated one hundred thirty-seven versions of the framework
in the two years he spent developing it. Considering how long it
took, and considering how many hundreds of internal and external
stakeholders we reached out to, and considering all the changes that
resulted, one might think our process was overly bureaucratic. As
Hogue said:

> There was a lot of frustration. But all this outreach is the only
> way it's going to work. If you have to go the extra mile to get
> people to a place where they take ownership, and they take it
> forward and they create change, like McDonald's has and does
> and will do, it's worth it.[166]

Fig. 12.4: McDonald's 2020 CSR & Sustainability Framework.

Thompson wanted to introduce the new sustainability priority to the McDonald's system at its biannual worldwide convention. He wanted Carter Roberts, CEO of the WWF (US) to help do so. Thompson and Roberts had met a couple times and seemed in sync with each other. So on May 1, 2014, in Orlando, the same hot place where twelve years ago Ken Koziol first talked about sustainability to a silent supplier audience, Roberts was one of the first speakers introduced the opening day of this huge McDonald's gathering. In front of him were 15,000 McDonald's leaders, suppliers, and owner–operators.

I sat upfront, close to the stage, super excited. This was a first. Sustainability on the main stage! I thought of all the years it took to get here. For me, it was like finishing a marathon race along a zigzag path. We're at the finish line now, with a proactive sustainability strategy leading us along a new path and journey.

Roberts had a folksy way. He opened his speech by saying, "Thank you Don for having me, and congratulations on the ambitious sustainability goals and framework you announced this week. Those goals and framework matter. A lot."[167]

I thought about how we all traveled an arduous journey to create "Our Journey Together for Good." And I thought about how this whole McDonald's sustainability journey started with Carter Robert's future wife, Jackie Prince (Roberts), who helped lead the Environmental Defense Fund partnership with McDonald's in 1990/91 (Chapter 1).

Carter Roberts continued his speech:

> You hold in your hands… the ability to reduce the destruction of the world's oceans and forests … by getting your sourcing of food and energy right.
>
> We at WWF are gratified to be your partner in moving this forward.
>
> I'm not saying it will be easy.
>
> But I urge you to see it through because in the end, your customers will reward you for taking steps to protect the planet that is their home.

Roberts then shared a very personal story, about the health of his daughter, and how they found comfort far from home at the door of the Ronald McDonald House in Minneapolis. Roberts stopped talking, choked up, very emotional. He introduced his daughter, now 12 years old and healthy, and his wife, Jackie, to the McDonald's assembly. Fifteen thousand people were choked up too, and all stood up to applaud them.

Roberts humbly bowed his head in thanks to the audience. He finished his speech:

> "So on behalf of my family,
>
> And on behalf of WWF,
>
> I wanted to say thank you.
>
>
> For not only helping to protect the world – our home –
>
> by seeing through your commitment to sustainability
>
> but also for providing me,
>
> my wife Jackie
>
> and our daughter,
>
> a much-needed home
>
> in our time of need.
>
> Bless you."

The Future of Good Business Means Embedding Sustainability

My McDonald's journey ended on March 1, 2015. I decided to retire once the new Sustainability Framework was in place. Leave on a high note. I felt my own McDonald's journey reached a peak.

Francesca DeBiase assumed executive oversight upon my retirement and also became the chief global supply chain officer, too. McDonald's continues to accelerate and evolve its sustainability efforts, announcing new progress on cage-free eggs, making recycling available to all restaurants by 2025, setting additional goals for sustainable beef, focusing on health and kids for Happy Meals, and taking an even more aggressive approach on climate change. Sustainability by definition is a journey. Issues change. Society shifts. Expectations fluctuate. Frameworks like the one I helped develop need to evolve and change.*

For today's leaders and for emerging leaders, McDonald's sustainability journey should serve as an inspiration that change for the better is always possible and as a reminder that business leadership means having both financial and nonfinancial acumen. It means integrating the idea of Shared Value as a core fundamental of growing your business. The corporate success model of the future is about balancing profits and purpose, about doing well and doing good. They are not in opposition. They are the very definition of running a good business.

The battle to do good is still evolving, but it's becoming less a battle and more of a fundamental facet of business success. The battle becomes an opportunity when business leaders become open to stakeholder engagement and are no longer afraid to deal with tough societal issues that overlap with their business.

If you develop your company's own proactive, strategic sustainability framework, you don't have to go through the battles, internally or externally, described in this book and experienced by many other companies. The number of companies that have embedded CSR/Sustainability/Shared Value frameworks into their core business, where it is C-Suite driven and consistently on their top management agenda, is

---

* In early 2018, McDonald's announced its Scale for Good framework. Steve Easterbrook, President and CEO said: "We are proud to build on our strong commitment to the communities where we operate. With these bold actions, McDonald's is embracing our leadership responsibility and demonstrating the incredible opportunities we can create for our customers, our people and our stakeholders when we harness our Scale for Good around the world."

still relatively small. It's difficult to estimate. Certainly most Fortune 500 companies produce CSR reports and have CSR staffs, but that doesn't mean the initiative is fully embedded. Most smaller to midsize public and private companies are not as advanced on these issues. But they should be. Indeed, now is the time to act. Now is the time to develop your organization's sustainability strategy so you can win the battle between doing well and doing good—and do both.

A Sustainability Framework Template

CSR and sustainability issues can either paralyze your company or propel it. It is much better to take a proactive stance on such matters than to succumb to attacks from activists, consumers, and other stakeholders. That means that developing a CSR/sustainability strategy for your organization is crucial. The framework I developed, with collaboration from The Context Network, for McDonald's provides an excellent template for your own work in this area (see Fig. 12.5).

As you can see, this framework consists of five key elements: vision, principles, engagement, goals, and accountability. Let's look at each of these:

- **Vision: Setting a Vision That Inspires**
  - Set a vision of the future that can inspire and motivate your people, suppliers, customers, and key external stakeholders.

  - Relate the vision to a purpose that is beyond company profits.

  - Don't make the vision a business objective; it needs to be a business and societal aspiration.

Fig. 12.5: Framework for Sustainability Strategy Development.
Source: Developed in Collaboration With The Context Group.

- **Values: Laying the Foundation**
  - Make your company's values a fundamental part of your sustainability framework. Values define your company's culture and ways to conduct business. Sustainability ideas are most likely a part of many of your existing values.

  - Don't park sustainability in a box, making it peripheral to the business. In good times and bad, values always are a steadying force.

- **Pillars: Establishing Focus**
  - Establish three to five overarching priorities. Appoint an executive sponsor as a functional leader (i.e., an officer of supply chain, marketing, or operations) to lead each pillar.

  - Create an aspiration for each pillar, some long-term dream goal, like what McDonald's supply chain did: "We will buy all food and packaging from verified sustainable sources." It puts everyone involved on the same page and direction.

  - Don't recreate the wheel. This is not rocket science. Most companies have similar pillars, but their actions are unique to their own business product. For instance, many companies have pillars related to people, community, diversity/inclusion, sourcing, and the environment.

- **Goals: Developing Smart Goals to Spur Action**
  - Set a few goals for each pillar that are specific, measureable, actionable, relevant, and time bound (SMART).

  - Develop stretch goals. Without stretch goals, you're not going to get the innovation you need.

  - Work with stakeholders to determine a materiality matrix. Really it is a shared value matrix, laying out what is most important to society and most important to business success.

  - Don't set too many goals, and don't try to be all things to all people. You can get more done by targeting less.

- **Accountability: Creating Accountability Makes Sustainability Real**
  - Instill internal governance for clear responsibility.

  - Develop measurement and ongoing reporting (internally at a minimum).

  - Create a scorecard detailing the business results and societal benefits.

  - Integrate accountability goals into individual and department performance evaluations.

  - Engage your financial department; credible internal controls for data and metrics are a must.

- **Engagement: Sharing Progress and Engaging With Stakeholders**
  - Stay in touch with key stakeholders, letting them know when issues change and new issues pop up.

  - Communicate your progress—and lack of progress—on a regular basis. Both are necessary for credibility.

  - Apply these three characteristics in all your work:
    - Humbleness

    - Honesty

    - Openness

  - Engage with stakeholders in good times and bad. When you miss the mark and make a mistake, don't waffle. Be direct and acknowledge it.

Endnotes

1. Personal interview with Don Thompson with transcript, June 28, 2017.
2. E.L. Plambeck and L. Denend, "The greening of Wal-Mart", *Stanford Social Innovation Review* (Spring 2008). Available at: https://ssir.org/articles/entry/the_greening_of_wal_mart.
3. M. Friedman, "The social responsibility of business is to increase its profit", *The New York Times Magazine* (1970, 13 September). Available at: https://www.colorado.edu/studentgroups/libertarians/issues/friedman-soc-resp-business.html.
4. A. Pasternack, "The most watched load of garbage in the memory of man", *Motherboard* (2013, 13 May). Available at: https://motherboard.vice.com/en_us/article/nzzppg/the-mobro-4000.
5. L. Gibbs, blog "McDonald's Decades Later Eliminates Foam Everywhere, Center for Health, Environment & Justice". Available at: http://chej.org/2018/01/11/mcdonalds-decades-later-eliminates-foam-everywhere/.
6. Office of Solid Waste, U.S. Environmental Protection Agency, "The Solid Waste Dilemma: An Agenda for Action/Final Report of the Municipal Solid Waste Task." Force, Office of Solid Waste, United States Environmental Protection Agency, 1989.
7. Personal interview with Ed Rensi with transcript, December 28, 2016.
8. B. Handwerk, "Whatever happened to the ozone hole?", *National Geographic News* (2010, 7 May). Available at: https://news.nationalgeographic.com/news/2010/05/100505-science-environment-ozone-hole-25-years/.
9. Personal interview with Mike Roberts with transcript, January 6, 2017.
10. Two sources for Shelby Yastrow: Personal interview with transcript, September 30, 2016; Yastrow's unpublished notes entitled Shelby Stories, October 8, 2016.
11. Personal interview with Fred Krupp with transcript, June 24, 2017.
12. F.D. Krupp, "New Environmentalism factors in economic needs", *Wall Street Journal* (1986, 20 November). Available at: https://www.wsj.com/articles/SB117269353475022375.
13. William "Bill" Gifford, "McDonald's: the greening of the golden arches", *Rolling Stone* (1991, 22 August).

14. Personal interview with Jackie Prince (Roberts) with transcript, August 15, 2017.

15. Personal interview with Ellen Silbergeld with transcript, October 20, 2016.

16. M. Parrish, "McDonald's to do away with foam packages", *The Los Angeles Times* (1990, 02 November). Available at: http://articles.latimes.com/1990-11-02/news/mn-3787_1_foam-packages.

17. J. Holusha, "Packaging and public image: McDonald's fills a big order", *The New York Times* (1990, 2 November). Available at: http://www.nytimes.com/1990/11/02/business/packaging-and-public-image-mcdonald-s-fills-a-big-order.html?pagewanted=all.

18. C.S. Clark, "Fast food shake-up", *CQ Researcher* (1991, 8 November). Available at: http://library.cqpress.com/cqresearcher/document.php?id=cqresrre1991110802.

19. M. Parrish, "McDonald's to do away with foam packages", *The Los Angeles Times* (1990, 02 November).

20. E.N. Berg, "McDonald's plans to reduce it's garbage", *The New York Times* (1991, 17 April). Available at: http://www.nytimes.com/1991/04/17/business/mcdonald-s-planning-to-reduce-its-garbage.html.

21. G. Bush, President of the U.S., "Remarks on presentation of the president's environment and conservation challenge awards", (1991, 31 October). Available at: http://www.presidency.ucsb.edu/ws/index.php?pid=20169.

22. EDF, "McDonald's and Environmental Defense Fund Mark 10th Anniversary of Landmark Alliance". Available at: https://www.edf.org/news/mcdonalds-environmental-defense-fund-mark-10th-anniversary-landmark-alliance.

23. Guardian staff, "McDonald's two win partial appeal victory", *The Guardian* (1999, 31 March).

24. N. Klein, from "*No Logo*", chapter, "The Arches: The Fight for Choice", 1999. Available at: http://www.mcspotlight.org/media/books/mclibel_excerpt.html.

25. Patricia Wynn Davies, "What a judge said about McDonald's: They take advantage of animals, children and their workforce", UK *Independent* (1997, 19 June).

26. Personal interview with Peter Singer with transcript, April 5, 2014.

27. Personal interview with Shelby Yastrow, September 30, 2016.

28. Personal interview with Temple Grandin with transcript, March 8, 2014.

29. Personal interview with Janet Riley with transcript, March 12, 2014.

30. Personal interview with Gary Platt with transcript, March 8, 2014.

31. Personal interview with Paul Simmons with transcript, March 8, 2014.

32. Personal interview with Erika Voogd with transcript, March 5, 2014.

33. http://www.cpr.org/news/story/temple-grandin-why-slaughter-houses-have-gotten-so-good.

34. From PETA's Website, Seeking Permission to Use. Available at: https://www.peta.org/blog/question-mccruelty/.

35. PETA Website. Available at: https://www.peta.org/issues/animals-used-for-food/factory-farming/chickens/egg-industry/.

36. "McDonald's targeted with 'Unhappy Meals'", *USA Today* (2000, 20 June).

37. Personal interview with transcript with Bruce Feinberg, June 17, 2014.

38. Personal interview with transcript with Dr. Jeff Armstrong , April 14, 2014.

39. Personal interview with transcript with Dr. Joy Mench, April 14, 2014.

40. United Poultry Concerns Website. Available at: http://www.upc-online.org

41. M. Kaufman, "McDonald's taking steps to improve care of hens", *The Washington Post* (2000, 23 August). Available at: https://www.washingtonpost.com/archive/politics/2000/08/23/mcdonalds-tells-farmers-to-treat-chickens-better/e03b291a-d563-4321-b14e-57ec73338952/?utm_term=.cc2d6a1a3fdd.

42. M. Kaufman, "McDonald's taking steps to improve care of hens", *The Washington Post* (2000, 23 August) and Jennifer Ordonez, "McDonald's hen-care guidelines lead egg producers to warn of higher prices", *The Wall Street Journal* (2000, 24 August).

43. This article is an excellent read about McDonald's decision to commit to cage free eggs: Kowitt, *Fortune,* "Inside McDonald's Bold Decision to Go Cage Free", August 18, 2016.

44. Personal interview with Walt Riker, January 10, 2018.

45. "McDonald's targeted with 'Unhappy Meals'", *USA Today* (2000, 20 June).

46. T. Rowe, "PETA takes on McDonald's", *The Lakeland (Fl) Ledger* (2000, 15 June).

47. J. Hood, "Dogged determination helps PETA in the PR jungle", *PR Week* (2001, 26 February) Available at: https://www.prweek.com/article/1238120/analysis-client-profile-dogged-determination-helps-peta-pr-jungle-20-years-peta-fought-against-cruel-treatment-animals-julia-hood-reports-how.

48. M. Spector, "The extremist", *The New Yorker* (2003, 14 April). Available at: https://www.newyorker.com/magazine/2003/04/14/the-extremist

49. Paul Simmons personal interview with transcript, March 8, 2014.

50. Temple Grandin personal interview with transcript, March 8, 2014.

51. Center for Disease Control and Prevention, "Phthalates Factsheet". Available at: https://www.cdc.gov/biomonitoring/Phthalates_FactSheet.html.

52. Brian Bienkowski, "United Nations Panel Call Hormone Disrupters a 'Global Threat,'" *Scientific American* (2013, 19 February). Available at: https://www.scientificamerican.com/article/united-nations-panel-calls-hormone-dispruptors-global-threat/.

53. Personal interview with Mike Donahue with transcript, April 4, 2017.

54. D.D. Anderson, Ph.D., "Key concepts in anticipatory issues management", *Corporate Environmental Strategy*, 5, no. 1 (Autumn 1997): 6–17.

55. From McSpotlight Website. Available at: http://www.mcspotlight.org/case/pretrial/defence/environment.html.

56. M. Marriott, "Koch faults McDonald's packaging", *The New York Times* (1987, 30 December). Available at: http://www.nytimes.com/1987/12/30/nyregion/koch-faults-mcdonald-s-packaging.html.

57. W. Saxon, "Phil Sokolof, 82, a Crusader Against Cholesterol, Is Dead", *The New York Times* (2004, 17 April). Available at: http://www.nytimes.com/2004/04/17/us/phil-sokolof-82-a-crusader-against-cholesterol-is-dead.html.

58. Personal interview with Joe Beckwith, January 12, 2018.

59. Consumer Product Safety Commission Website, "CPSC, McDonald's Corp. Announce Agreement for Firm to Pay $4 Million Damage Settlement", (1999, 29 June). Available at: https://www.cpsc.gov/content/cpsc-mcdonalds-corp-announce-agreement-for-firm-to-pay-4-million-damage-settlement.

60. Adapted from Dr. Deborah Anderson with permission.

61. C.E. Mayer, "Mattel seeking alternative to plastic", *The Washington Post* (1999, 10 December). Available at: http://articles.latimes.com/1999/dec/09/business/fi-42151.

62. M. Warner, "Would you like a gas guzzler with that?", *The New York Times* (2006, 10 August). Available at: http://www.nytimes.com/2006/08/10/business/media/10adco.html.

63. Environmental Working Group Website, "McDonald's responds to hummer protest". Available at: https://www.ewg.org/enviroblog/2006/09/mcdonaldâ€™s-responds-hummer-protest#.WoQwAzaYbdk.

64. *Fortune's* "Most powerful women", (2010, 30 September). Available at: http://archive.fortune.com/galleries/2010/fortune/1009/gallery.most_powerful_women.fortune/25.html.

65. Personal interview with Jan Fields with transcript, January 25, 2017.

66. Unfortunately, Mike Donahue left the company in 2006 and the structure and momentum for the AIM process broke up.

67. B. Tuttle, "Why we're eating fewer happy meals", *Time* (2012, 23 April). Available at: http://business.time.com/2012/04/23/why-were-eating-fewer-happy-meals/.

68. http://www.foxnews.com/story/2002/09/21/fat-teens-sue-mcdonald.html.

69. https://www.surgeongeneral.gov/news/testimony/obesity07162003.html.

70. https://www.nytimes.com/2005/02/12/business/mcdonalds-settles-trans-fats-lawsuits.html

71. http://www.nationalacademies.org/hmd/~/media/Files/Report%20
Files/2005/Food-Marketing-to-Children-and-Youth-Threat-or-
Opportunity/KFMOverviewfinal2906.pdf.

72. https://letsmove.obamawhitehouse.archives.gov/white-house-task-
force-childhood-obesity-report-president.

73. "McDonald's hamburger hell", *Bloomberg Businessweek* (2003, 3 March).
Available at: https://www.bloomberg.com/news/articles/2003-03-02/
mcdonalds-hamburger-hell.

74. Personal interview with Steve Levigne, February 2, 2017.

75. Personal interview with Neil Golden, February 16, 2017.

76. R. Jaslow, "McDonald's bows to happy meal critics, cutting fries and
adding fruit", *CBS News* (2011, 27 July). Available at: http://
www.cbsnews.com/news/mcdonalds-bows-to-happy-meal-critics-
cutting-fries-and-adding-fruit/.

77. D. Jackson, "Michelle Obama Praises McDonald's", *USA Today* (2011, 26
July). Available at: http://content.usatoday.com/communities/the-
oval/post/2011/07/michelle-obama-praises-mcdonalds/
1#.WQ3MVTaud0t.

78. R. Jaslow, "McDonald's bows to happy meal critics, cutting fries and
adding fruit", *CBS News* (2011, 27 July). Available at: http://
www.cbsnews.com/news/mcdonalds-bows-to-happy-meal-critics-
cutting-fries-and-adding-fruit/.

79. Email correspondence with Neil Golden, May 8, 2018.

80. http://www.who.int/mediacentre/factsheets/fs385/en/.

81. Clinton Foundation Website, "McDonald's and Alliance for a Healthier
Generation Announce Progress on Commitment to Promote Balanced
Food and Beverage Choices", (2005, 25 June). Available at: https://
www.clintonfoundation.org/press-releases/mcdonalds-and-alliance-
healthier-generation-announce-progress-commitment-promote.

82. P. Sellers, "Why McDonald's U.S. boss Jan Fields is moving on", *Fortune*
(2012, 16 November). Available at: http://fortune.com/2012/11/16/
why-mcdonalds-u-s-boss-jan-fields-is-moving-on/.

83. Personal interview Don Thompson with transcript, June 28, 2017.

84. https://www.blackrock.com/corporate/investor-relations/larry-fink-
ceo-letter

85. Blackrock Website, "Larry Fink's Annual Letter to CEOs: A Sense of
Purpose". Available at: https://www.blackrock.com/corporate/en-no/
investor-relations/larry-fink-ceo-letter.

86. Personal interview with Ken Koziol with transcript, March 2, 2017.

87. D. Gilmore, "What took so long for Bangladesh and Pakistani apparel
supply chain issues to rise to the surface?" *Supply Chain Digest* (2013, 18
June). Available at: http://www.scdigest.com/assets/Experts/13-06-
18.php?cid=7160.

88. Personal interview with Mats Lederhausen with transcript, June 28, 2017.

89. B. Sawickim "See how many McDonald's restaurants are located in your state", *Rare* (2016, 5 September). Available at: http://rare.us/rare-life/food-and-drink/see-how-many-mcdonalds-restaurants-are-located-in-your-state/.

90. Personal interview with George Basile with transcript, February 27, 2017.

91. Personal interview with Gary Johnson with transcript, January 10 and 12, 2018.

92. Personal interview with Jim Cannon with transcript, January 7, 2017.

93. Email correspondence with Jon Safely, January 10, 2017.

94. Marine Stewardship Council Website, "McDonald's USA first national restaurant chain to serve MSC certified sustainable fish at all U.S. locations", (2013, 24 January). Available at: https://www.msc.org/newsroom/news/mcdonalds-usa-first-restaurant-chain-to-serve-msc-certified-sustainable-fish-nationwide.

95. R. Lindsay, "Robert F. Kennedy Jr. Statement on Smithfield's Pig Factories", *Behind Highbrow* (2009, 7 May). Available at: https://robertlindsay.wordpress.com/2009/05/07/robert-f-kennedy-jr-statement-on-smithfields-pig-factories/.

96. Personal interview with John Hayes with transcript, April 4, 2017.

97. US Justice Department, "Smithfield Foods Fined $12.6 Million, Largest Clean Water Act Fine Ever", (1997, 8 August). Available at: https://www.justice.gov/archive/opa/pr/1997/August97/331enr.htm.

98. T. Conklin, "An animal welfare history lesson on the five freedoms", *Michigan State University Extension* (2014, 25 February). Available at: http://msue.anr.msu.edu/news/an_animal_welfare_history_lesson_on_the_five_freedoms.

99. Personal interview with Dennis Treacy with transcript, April 13, 2015.

100. B. Nisson, "Critical Analysis of the report, Economic Impact: Tomatoes in Florida", Research Institute on Social and Economic Policy (RISEP), Florida International University (2006, 30 April). Available at: http://ciw-online.org/blog/2006/04/nissen_report/.

101. Coalition of Immokalee Workers Website, "CIW Responds to McDonald's Announcement of New Standards", (January). Available at: http://ciw-online.org/blog/2006/01/ciw-responds-to-mcdonalds-announcement-of-new-standards/

102. Personal interview with Greg Asbed with transcript, August 26, 2016.

103. Email correspondence, Greg Asbed, June 11, 2018.

104. Coalition of Immokalee Workers Website, "McDonald's USA and its produce suppliers to work with the coalition of immokalee workers", (2007, 9 April). Available at: http://ciw-online.org/blog/2007/04/ciw_mcdonalds_release/.

105. Personal interview with Jerry Calabrese with transcript, August 8, 2016.

106. Personal interview with Jim Skinner with transcript, August 10, 2016.

107. E. Weinreb, "How Walmart associates put the 'U' and 'I' into sustainability", (2013, 9 January). Available at: https://www.greenbiz.com/blog/2013/01/09/walmart-associates-u-i-sustainability.

108. Personal interview with Kathleen Bannan with transcript, January 17, 2017.

109. Extracted from Ed Freeman's powerpoint presentation of Oct. 4, 2007 to McDonald's entitled "Linking Values to Business"; personal interview with transcript with Ed Freeman, July 29, 2016.

110. https://www.inc.com/peter-economy/mcdonalds-just-made-a-stunning-announcement-that-will-completely-change-future-of-fast-food.html.

111. https://www.nass.usda.gov/Surveys/Guide_to_NASS_Surveys/Chemical_Use/2016_Corn_Potatoes/ChemUseHighlights_FallPotato_2016.

112. https://www.sec.gov/about.shtml.

113. http://www.proxymonitor.org/Results.aspx.

114. http://greenpalm.org/about-greenpalm/how-does-greenpalm-work.

115. Personal interview with Mitch Smith with transcript, February 26, 2018.

116. Personal interview with Richard Liroff with transcript, July 18, 2016.

117. https://www.reuters.com/article/us-mcdonalds-pesticides/mcdonalds-to-take-steps-to-cut-potato-pesticides-idUSTRE52U6AN20090331.

118. Website: http://potatosustainabilityinitiative.org.

119. http://corporate.mcdonalds.com/content/dam/AboutMcDonalds/2.0/pdfs/2012_2013_csr_report.pdf

120. https://www.greenbiz.com/blog/2010/10/14/10-lessons-investor-engagement.

121. https://www.wsj.com/articles/how-much-do-you-know-about-ethical-investing-1499349815.

122. Personal interview with Karen van Bergen with transcript, October 21, 2016.

123. Greenpeace Website, "Eating up the Amazon". Available at: http://www.greenpeace.org/usa/wp-content/uploads/legacy/Global/usa/report/2010/2/eating-up-the-amazon.pdf.

124. Personal interview with Paulo Adario with transcript, July 4, 2016.

125. Email correspondence with Dr. Thomas Henningsen, May 31, 2018.

126. Personal interview with Francesca DeBiase with transcript, April 5, 2017 and February 17, 2016.

127. Personal interview with Jessica Yagan with transcript, February 10, 2017.

128. K. Lehnardt, "96 Interesting facts about McDonald's food", *Fact Retriever* (2016, 19 August). Available at: https://www.factretriever.com/mcdonalds-food-facts.

129. AboutMcDonald's Website. Available at: http://corporate.mcdonalds. com/content/dam/AboutMcDonalds/2.0/pdfs/2012_2013_csr_report. pdf.

130. Personal interview with Don Thompson with transcript, June 28, 2017.

131. Humane Society of the U.S. Website, "Scientists and Experts on Gestation Crates and Sow Welfare" (October 2012). Available at: http:// www.humanesociety.org/assets/pdfs/farm/HSUS-Synopsis-of-Expert-Opinions-on-Gestation-Crates-and-Sow-Welfare.pdf.

132. T. Philpott, "You won't believe what pork producers do to pregnant pigs", *Mother Jones* (July/August 2013 issue). Available at: http:// www.motherjones.com/environment/2013/06/pregnant-sows-gestation-crates-abuse.

133. Humane Society of the U.S. Website, "Statement on Farm Animals and Eating with Conscience". Available at: http://www.humanesociety.org/about/policy_statements/statement_farm_animals_eating.html?credit=web_id94248401.

134. Personal interview with Jeff Hogue with transcript, October 19, 2017.

135. "McDonald's USA Outlines 10-Year Plan For Ending Gestation Stall Use", *Southern Farm Network* (2012, 1 June). Available at: http://sfntoday.com/ mcdonalds-announces-end-to-gestation-stall-use-nppc-reaction/.

136. S. Wyant, "McDonald's plans phase out of pork produced in gestation stalls", *Agri-Pulse* (2012, 4 June). Available at: https://www.agri-pulse.com/articles/1853-mcdonald-s-plans-phase-out-of-pork-produced-in-gestation-stalls?iframe=1.

137. S. Strom, "McDonald's set to phase out suppliers' use of sow crates", *The New York Times* (2012, 13 February). Available at: http://www.nytimes. com/2012/02/14/business/mcdonalds-vows-to-help-end-use-of-sow-crates.html.

138. M. Brunker and M.C. White, "The big bucks of bacon: American meat by the number", *NBC News* (2015, 26 October). Available at: https:// www.nbcnews.com/business/economy/look-u-s-meat-industry-numbers-n451571.

139. Personal interview with Jason Clay with transcript, May 31, 2017.

140. Food and Agriculture Organization of the United Nations, "Livestock's Long Shadow", 2006. Available at: http://www.fao.org/docrep/010/ a0701e/a0701e00.HTM.

141. American Cattlemen, "Cattle Carbon Footprint" (2010, 6 June). Available at: http://www.americancattlemen.com/articles/cattle-carbon-footprint.

142. Personal interview with Cameron Bruett with transcript, June 1, 2017.

143. Tim Smith, "6 basic segments of beef cattle industry – all you need to know before raising beef cattle", *Matheson Farms* (2011, 22 February). Available at: http://www.mathesonfarms.com/posts-and-comments/ 6-basic-segments-of-beef-cattle-industry-all-you-need-to-know-before-raising-beef-cattle/.

144. T. Phillips, "McDonald's and target drop egg supplier", *Global Animal Website*. Available at: https://www.globalanimal.org/2011/11/22/mcdonalds-and-target-drop-egg-supplier/59434/.

145. Personal interview with Gary Johnson with transcript, January 10, 2018.

146. A. Condra, "Rounding up better ways to raise world beef", *Food Safety News* (2012, 14 March). Available at: http://www.foodsafetynews.com/2012/03/rounding-up-better-ways-to-raise-beef/#.WThryjaufUo.

147. World Wildlife Fund Website, "WWF and Beef Industry Leaders Advance Sustainable Beef Production Through Multi-Stakeholder Engagement" (2010, 4 November). Available at: https://www.worldwildlife.org/press-releases/wwf-and-beef-industry-leaders-advance-sustainable-beef-production-through-multi-stakeholder-engagement.

148. Personal interview with Michelle Banik-Rake with transcript, May 10, 2017.

149. Global Roundtable for Sustainable Beef Website, "GRSB Releases Global Principles and Criteria for Sustainable Beef". Available at: http://www.grsbeef.org/Resources/Documents/News%20Releases/GRSB%20Releases%20Global%20Principles%20and%20Criteria%20for%20Sustainable%20Beef%20(WIth%20Links).pdf.

150. Personal interview with Suzanne Apple with transcript, February 8, 2016.

151. Email communication with Aron Cramer, June 19, 2017.

152. Personal interview with Don Thompson, June 28, 2017.

153. J. Makower, "Exclusive: Inside McDonald's quest for sustainable beef", *GreenBiz* (2017, 7 January). Available at: https://www.greenbiz.com/blog/2014/01/07/inside-mcdonalds-quest-sustainable-beef.

154. Ban Trans Fats Website, "The McDonald's settlement". Available at: http://www.bantransfats.com/mcdonalds.html.

155. Personal interview with Don Thompson with transcript, June 28, 2017.

156. Personal interview with Francesca DeBiase with transcript, April 5, 2017 and February 17, 2016.

157. See 2014 Starbucks Global Responsibility Report, pages 8–9.

158. Adapted from GlobeScan research with permission.

159. M.E. Porter and M.R. Kramer, "Creating shared value", *Harvard Business Review* (January/February 2011).

160. Personal interview with J.C. Gonzalez-Mendez with transcript, June 6, 2017.

161. McDonald's United Kingdom Website, "The history of RMHC". Available at: http://www.rmhc.org.uk/who-we-are/history-of-rmhc/.

162. C. Zara, "McDonald's Corp (MCD) Exploits Ronald McDonald House Despite Giving Scant Financial Support, Report Alleges", *International Business Times* (2013, 29 October). Available at: http://www.ibtimes.com/mcdonalds-corp-mcd-exploits-ronald-mcdonald-house-despite-giving-scant-financial-support-report.

163. B. Hoffman, "Report finds McDonald's skimps on charity donations", *Forbes* (2013, 30 October). Available at: https://www.forbes.com/sites/bethhoffman/2013/10/30/report-finds-mcdonalds-skimps-on-charity-donations/#7ae49b7228b3.

164. Corporate Accountability Website, "Clowning around with charity: How McDonald's exploits philanthropy and targets children". Available at: https://www.corporateaccountability.org/resources/clowning-around-with-charity-how-mcdonalds-exploits-philanthropy-and-targets-children/.

165. S. Kim, "McDonald's accused of being cheap toward its charitable arm", *ABC News* (2013, 31 October). Available at: http://abcnews.go.com/Business/mcdonalds-accused-stiffing-ronald-mcdonald-house-charities/story?id=20720859.

166. Personal interview with Jeff Hogue with transcript, May 22, 2017.

167. Email correspondence, Carter Roberts, June 18, 2018.

Index